I0521709

THE METAPHYSICS OF

STRANGER THINGS

This publication in *not* endorsed by **NETFLIX** or by the producers of *Stranger Things*, nor any writers or actors affiliated with the same.

THANK YOU FOR SUPPORTING
INDEPENDENT PUBLISHING

A SYSTEMOLOGY SOCIETY PREMIERE COLLECTOR'S EDITION

THE METAPHYSICS OF

STRANGER THINGS

011

TELEKINESIS, TELEPATHY & SYSTEMOLOGY

(AN UNOFFICIAL FIELD GUIDE)

BY JOSHUA FREE

THE JOSHUA FREE IMPRINT
JFI PUBLICATIONS

© 2023, JOSHUA FREE

ISBN : 979-8-9871249-0-1 (hardcover)
ISBN : 979-8-9871249-1-8 (paperback)

All Rights Reserved. No part of this publication may be reproduced in any form or by any means, electronic or mechanical, including photocopying, recording, or any electronic system, without permission from the publisher. This book is a "religious artifact" and is not intended to substitute medical diagnosis, treatment or other professional health advice.

This publication in *not* endorsed or authorized by **NETFLIX** or by producers of the hit online TV show *Stranger Things*, nor any writers or actors affiliated with the same.

For entertainment and journalistic purposes only. No claims are made concerning personal results or effectiveness of any techniques or abilities described herein, nor representation of the Mardukite Academy or **Founding Church of Mardukite Zuism.**

The majority of this work is based on independent experimental research by the **Systemology Society** and does not reflect creative efforts, plot-points or contain significant spoilers for the TV show. (We're just really big fans. Please don't sue us.)

A MARDUKITE SYSTEMOLOGY PUBLICATION
Mardukite Research Library Catalog No. "Liber-011"
Systemology Grade VI/VII Class-6 Explorative Edition
Developed for Mardukite Academy & Systemology Society,
the Founding Church of Mardukite Zuism
and unofficially for fans of the epic Stranger Things series.

cum superiorum privilegio veniaque

FIRST EDITION
November 2022

Published from
Joshua Free Imprint – JFI Publications
Mardukite Borsippa HQ, San Luis Valley, Colorado

IN A WORLD FULL OF TENS BE AN
ELEVEN

Lines separating philosophy, psychology, mysticism and spirituality all blend together in the metaphysical soup that is served up by Joshua Free in this unique approach to exploring spiritual techniques for developing the kind of mind-power we all dream about.

Discover the metaphysical truth about the *Universe* (and maybe even *yourself*) as we explore what lies beneath the epic saga, *Stranger Things*. You're invited to a world where fantasy, science fiction, and horror unite and games like *"Dungeons and Dragons"* become reality.

The *Stranger Things* creators and actors have helped transport viewers to new philosophical vistas and emotional curves like nothing has before. Cinematic heights of achievement are turned *Upside Down* for all times to come after this unique illumination of the dark spaces between the spaces all around us—something that we can never forget.

But where exactly do these depths lead?
What inspired the iconic themes that make the show legendary?
How real are these astral gateways and psionic abilities?
Can anyone be like *Eleven*?

Now is your chance to find out.

The secrets of *Life,* the *Universe* and *Everything* hidden right within the folds of pop-culture!

Uncover a world of secret "mind control" projects, just like at *Hawkins National Laboratory.* Decades of psychedelic experiments among other developmental programs for psychic powers, remote viewing, and telekinesis (psychokinesis, PK) are revealed.

This edition also includes over twenty confidential files from Mardukite Research Org. (Systemology Society) specially declassified for this esoteric journey into THE METAPHYSICS OF STRANGER THINGS. Get an inside look at the operations of a real-life underground organization pursuing the truth about rehabilitating spiritual abilities for an actual "metahuman" evolution on the planet.

And, if you dare, even experiment with these techniques yourself!

In a world full of "tens"—be an *Eleven!*

Advance Reviews for
THE METAPHYSICS OF STRANGER THINGS:

"Now I *believe* in the unbelievable..."
—REED PENN, *author, systemologist*

"One of the *strangest* books I've ever read..."
—JAMES THOMAS, *promoter, systemologist*

"It's like a koala-bear crapped a *rainbow* in my brain!"
—ROWEN GARDNER, *author, mystic*

"If you've mastered telekinesis and you know it, raise *my* hand!"
—ADDIE STONE, *editor, mystic*

∞

EDITOR'S NOTE

"The Self does not actualize Awareness
past a point not understood."
—*Tablets of Destiny*

While preparing this book for publication, the editors
have made every effort to present this material in a straightfor-
ward manner—using clear, easy to read and understand language.

Clear understanding of this material is critical to
apply philosophies of *Mardukite Zuism* and
NexGen Systemology spiritual technology to Life.
Wherever a word that is defined in the glossary
first appears in the text, it will be **bold**.

The *Seeker* should be especially certain not to simply
"read through" this book without attaining proper "knowledge" and understanding. Even when the information continues to be "interesting"—if at any point you find yourself feeling
lost or confused while reading, trace your steps back. Return to
the point of misunderstanding and go through it again.

It is expected that a *Seeker* will work through this material multiple times to achieve optimum results.

And *now* responsibility for this power and its actualization is
passed on to you, the *Seeker*.

Take nothing within this book on faith.
Apply the information directly to your life.

Decide for yourself.

∞

INFINITY OF NOTHINGNESS

"When you stare into the Abyss long enough,
the Abyss stares back at you."
~ Friedrich Nietzsche.

DEDICATION

To Millie Bobby Brown
and the Duffer Brothers

TABLET OF CONTENTS

BE A PART OF THE SOLUTION.

SPAY OR NEUTER YOUR DEMODOG.

(CONTACT LOCAL SHELTERS FOR ADOPTION.)

[A PUBLIC SERVICE ANNOUNCEMENT FROM THE SYSTEMOLOGY SOCIETY]

:: TURNING SYSTEMOLOGY UPSIDE-DOWN ::
— An Introduction by the Author —

The scope of this book—and the expanse of work it represents—is a canvas that stretches across perhaps the widest territory of human experience, thought and comprehension imaginable. This statement is meant quite literally, and while it may seem like a *pitch* to throw in here as an opening, it is likely not to be properly appreciated or understood until the *Seeker*/reader reaches the end. **Responsibility** for communicating this presentation also lends to the present author a difficulty in finding the most appropriate starting point. It seems the best approach would be just to jump right into it directly—and start, as they say, at the beginning... when "*Projekt-011*" first made itself manifest at the Office HQ of the Systemology Society...

...but first!—undoubtedly there are many newcomers to our unique brand of intellectual and spiritual pursuit (as a result of this book) that may not fully understand what we are talking about right from page one. And we know that an **individual** tends to lose interest in a subject when coming across too many aspects they don't understand—and often this can be triggered simply by going past a misunderstood word. For easy reference and study, words that are defined in the glossary of this book are **bold** when they first appear in the text. Therefore, it is important that we take a few moments here—at the beginning—to provide some proper context or background to the book you are now reading and very briefly explain *what* the Systemology Society *even is.* [And if you are completely new to this flavor of metaphysics, you might check out "*Mardukite Zuism: A Brief Introduction*" in the appendix of this book, before reading on.]

—*The Systemology Society* assembles and publishes materials to assist *Seekers* in applying specialized '*systematic*' techniques (primarily along the lines of 'selectively directed **attention**' and 'creative thought') that may lend to increasing '**Actualized Awareness**' beyond the "normal" **standard-issue "Human Condition"**—which is to say, reaching for "**metahuman**" and even higher "spiritual" states of Knowingness and Beingness. A *Seeker* may be assisted directly by a

Pilot, and even receive training from the *Mardukite Academy* "Flight School" to be a *Pilot* themselves and **help** others.

—*The Mardukite Academy of Systemology* (formerly *Mardukite Research Organization*) studies these techniques (including their historical background and theory). It provides resources and **esoteric** research capabilities for *The Systemology Society* and disseminates further education of the technology and philosophy.

—Within the scope of a once-underground religio-spiritual faction called *Mardukite Zuism*, there are *Ministers* and *Spiritual Advisers* that learn and practice effective application of these same *systemological* techniques and teachings in everyday life.

Origins for my unique brand of Systemology extend back to ideas personally formulated back in the 1990's, while still operating and writing for the underground occult scene as a teenager, using the pseudonym "*Merlyn Stone.*" My academic interest at the time could be generalized as psychology, but more along the lines of the "New Thought Movement" and its parallels with "New Age" traditions of "magick" and traditional occultism. My teenage ambitions sought to validate "magickal" pursuits with psychology and "New Thought." This immediately led to a personal behind-the-scenes formulation of an "original thesis" to support a higher **understanding** that seemed to be missing from existent material **sciences** and metaphysical philosophies. Thus, the whole field of my Systemology started to come into being. But, slowly. A decade would be spent on it quietly in spare-time before even releasing the first short discourses to the underground in 2011. These are now collected within the text: "*Systemology: The Original Thesis of Mardukite New Thought.*"

Even as an extension of the Mardukite Organization, the early years of Systemology were mostly quiet and unnoticed and several attempts were made at bridging the two. It was not until 2019, after nearly another decade of behind-the-scenes and secretive development that the first official and professional presentation of Mardukite Systemology took place. In October 2019, "*Liber-One*" (an official Mardukite Esoteric Library Catalogue designation) was released by JFI Publications—now in print as "*The Tablets of Destiny Revelation.*" Two months later, the "*Liber-2B*" follow-up appeared: "*Crystal Clear (A Handbook for Seekers).*" All of these materials—"*Syst-*

emology: The Original Thesis," "*The Tablets of Destiny Revelation*" and "*Crystal Clear*" appear in the complete Grade-III Mardukite Systemology anthology: "*The Systemology Handbook.*"

This last statement of course begs the question of 'what are the *Grades*'? And this is something that has only been established by the Systemology Society relatively recently. Prior to this, only the "Mardukite Chamberlains" (*Grade-II*) and the "Merlyn School of Magick & Druidry" (*Grade-I*) existed. Calling attention to the **gradients** at that time hardly seemed necessary—there were only two of them. However, the structure of an occult organization outlined during the "Merlyn Stone" years in the late 1990's directly called for an as yet undeveloped *Grade-III* or "**Master Grade**" that would act as a vehicle to higher paths or routes to "**Ascension**"—an *Ascension* that could essentially free an individual from their entrapment in the Physical Universe (or "*Beta-Existence*" as it is referred to in Systemology vocabulary). In 2019, "Mardukite Systemology" became that *Grade-III*, which had been anticipated for two decades, completing the work necessary for a 'Master Level' of instruction and synonymous 'Master Grade' **threshold**. Everything beyond beyond *Grade-III* composes the "Wizard Grades" or "Wizard Levels."

Systemology carries an aura of being highly 'obscure' and overtly 'esoteric', although its intention is to *systematize* and *demystify* those same **levels** and **facets** of **knowledge**. True: it *is* a **paradigm** and *does* have its own vocabulary—but it is a *meta*-paradigm and does not exclude itself from the entire body of knowledge and range of *Awareness* capable to humanity. Therefore, it is not *exclusionary*—tipping our hat to *Charles Fort*—it **treats** the 'whole' as a *meta*-system and each of the related parts as its own system interrelated to other systems. It is also concerned with freeing the Human Spirit (actual *Self* or "I-AM") from artificially composed limitations and standard-issue **considerations** of the Human Condition. This, in itself, has always been dangerous business; and yet we continue to look further and press upon whatever boundaries are found at each turn of the upward spiral on our ascent. Each higher *Grade* presents new goals and objectives for exploration within the field of Systemology. As such there are many parallels (the less sadistic and malevolent ones, anyway) between experimental research of the Systemology Society and the work of Hawkins National Laboratory on the *Stranger Things* series.

Although I had heard of the show during the first couple seasons, I really knew very little about it other than it somehow involved the 1980's. As my long-standing readership and fan-*Seekers* are aware, maintaining the new face and evolution of Mardukite and Systemology work while standing on unstable and unconventional territory in my own life has occupied the entirety of my attention since 2016. The first phases of work ran between 2006 and 2015, but a behind-the-scenes focus shift began to really take form in 2016 and of which is responsible for the present state of development at the Mardukite Academy, Systemology Society, Founding Church of Mardukite Zuism, and all of the volumes published for our Esoteric Research Library—including ten titles for the Systemology "Grades."

By 2020, the "Mardukite HQ" and "Mardukite Field Office" had, at one time or another, already occupied over a dozen states in the U.S. since its **inception** in 2008, as I moved about from place to place—sometimes with a partner or in the company of others, but often in solitude, working remotely **via** the internet. A new phase of work and personal life manifested as reality after I permanently relocated "Borsippa HQ" to San Luis Valley (Colorado) in Summer 2020. I say "permanently" because it continues to operate there today with no anticipation of change. The first half of GRADE-IV (mainly the discourses comprising "*Metahuman Destinations*") I developed while still residing in Denver, yet the remainder of (what we consider a "cycle") this developmental experimental research would take place in San Luis Valley up until Spring 2022 with the publication of "*Way of the Wizard*" (LIBER-3E) and the complete GRADE-IV anthology "*The Metahuman Systemology Handbook.*" The Grade took two full years to complete.

Midway through the work on GRADE-IV in Winter 2020-Spring 2021, I began consolidating several years of personal notes and combining current experimental research to release a project titled: "*Imaginomicon: Approaching Gateways to Higher Universes*" (LIBER-3D). As the first real manual for "Wizard Level-0," the "*Imaginomicon*" introduced the new Systemology concept of "*ZU-Vision,*" which is to say "Spirit Vision" from the perspective of the true *Self*, or *Alpha-Spirit*, independent of the physical body ("**genetic vehicle**") and **exterior** to this Physical Universe ("*Beta-Existence*"). Sometime in 2020, the description and experiments regarding this prompted someone in the Systemology Society to say something about "that girl on *Stranger Things.*" I shook and shrugged, not really having any context for the statement, but pressed onward with the work as *"Projekt-011."*

During the course of developing *"Imaginomicon"* (*LIBER-3D*, completed on Beltane 2021 and published June 21 that year), the subject of *Stranger Things* came up no less than half a dozen times. With the work being done on *"Imaginomicon,"* and a brief break before starting up the project that would later become *"Way of the Wizard: Utilitarian Systemology (A New Metahuman Ethic)"* (*LIBER-3E*), I decided to look into a full description of *Stranger Things* and immediately ordered up season one on DVD that month. After binge-watching season one in little more than a day, I ordered seasons two and three. I realized I was a late-comer to this subcultural niche, but I was never one for trends anyway. Originally, I played the DVD in the 'background' while working on various book releases for *JFI Publications*. Yet, right from the beginning, with a mere utterance of *"The demogorgon is tired of your silly human bickering!"*—it had my full attention. By the time of *"Mornings are for coffee and contemplation,"* I knew I was watching this series through to the end.

Within hours of my first viewing, I was already obsessed with *"Eleven"* (011) more than anything else I can recall from adulthood in this lifetime. This in itself left me feeling strange, given my usual cool and detached handling of medias and those **participating** in their creation—of which I've had run-ins with more than a few. But this present project and its introduction is not about "name-dropping"—and I've found that most are hesitant to ever openly acknowledge me due to the **encompassing** nature of my work. As I learned socially in high school: being well-known and being well-liked (or even accepted) are two completely different things.

More to the point, *Stranger Things* keyed-in on an area of focus we were playing with under the guise of *"Phase-Ten"* (the name some knew it by within the *Council of Nabu* for the *Mardukite Org*) in 2017 at the original San Luis Valley "Mardukite Babylon Site" prior to settling more permanently at the "Borsippa HQ" location (eleven miles away) in 2020. Protocols for advanced "NexGen Systemology" work were systematically developed for experimenting with many things (such as *"ZU-Vision"*), but among these was what the surface world-at-large generally refers to as *"Remote Viewing"* and *"Telekinesis."* Strangely, we even code-named this pursuit *"Projekt Stargate"* before realizing similar efforts existed already among the "Intelligence Community" and ironically called the *"Stargate Project."* Of course, when mentioned candidly, many of those not initiated into our folds half-a-decade ago still thought the reference pertained to some type of interstellar "teleportation artifact" such as seen in the movie of the same name. So, even the Mardukites and Systemology use "code-names" for unpublished projects and misdirection concerning publicity over ongoing research and/or development. This is just the way of things—and in our case carries no insidious agenda other than the continuance and preservation of the work.

As an early exploration of upper-grade *'Wizard-Level'* Systemology work, this 2023 edition of *LIBER-011* or THE METAPHYSICS OF STRANGER THINGS is highly speculative; but it is firmly grounded, particularly within the "Mardukite Systemology" (otherwise *'NexGen Systemology'* or *'Metahuman Systemology'*) paradigm. It follows from a logical progression of esoteric journeys walked by several individuals independently—concurrent or consecutive—across **time** and **space**.

It is important for the present author to note (particularly for Systemologists) that the material in this book is not necessarily a *'Route'* toward anything—and it does not, in itself, represent any specific *'Step'* on the *Pathway*. It reflects something that may or may not even be directly encountered on one's *Ascension*, nor is it a requirement for progression; although it does reflect a new type of "unlimited" or "infinity" *processing* in the same flavor as what is introduced in the presentation of "*Imaginomicon*" (*LIBER-3D*) for GRADE-IV, although this is much more speculative—which is why it is being presented out of sequence with the normal gradient progression of material. It reflects a potential 'by-product' of the *Pathway* on one hand and a general formula for changing **considerations** and reality **agreements** with the Physical Universe (*Beta-Existence*). For these reasons, perhaps, it is a valuable investigation into rehabilitation of spiritual abilities—though as you will see, particularly in "Part One" of this book, the matter is generally handled with far less "***Self-Honest***" **intentions**.

For the present author, this journey spans more than a quarter-of-a-century—in the current **incarnation** or lifetime, at least—collecting and consolidating related and relevant experimental research materials. Of course, this includes the *'Arcane Tablets'* (mentioned in previous volumes) from—yes—thousands of years ago in obscurity, but also more recent esoteric efforts and modern discoveries (or, that is to say, underground *'New Thought'* interpretations) too.

Extending our look on the **backtrack** of Human history on Earth—even a mere 150-years of *esoterica* in public light—we find the 'Theosophical Society', 'Hermetic Order of the Golden Dawn', various German 'occult lodges', rising American 'New Thought' movements of the early and mid-1900's, and ever since, an exponentially increasing interest (public and private) in 'magick', 'mysticism', 'new consciousness' and 'psychic-like potential' in today's literal and metaphoric "New Age."

What do these things—and, no doubt, countless other relevant examples that could be easily added to this list—have in common?

They all relate to (what is referred to in Systemology as) an "**Alpha**" **existence**—an 'Upside-Down', or the 'Other', 'Further', 'Astral', 'Shadow Lands', 'Beyond' and 'Outside'—that is *exterior* to (and in many ways considered coexistent and coterminous with) *this* Physical Universe. This "Physical Universe" (or "Beta-Existence") is simply what we are accustomed to perceiving exclusively at the sensory "level" of the stimulus-response driven package known as the Physical Body or "*Genetic Vehicle*"—and thus *agree* to as consensual *reality* for the "Physical Universe" *level* of **Game**-play. Understanding the nature of such systems as they relate to all *Life, Universes* and *Everything* is the core philosophical, spiritual and/or mystical pursuit of *our* Systemology.

Practical (or '*applied philosophical*') foundations of development for a *Pathway of* **Actualization** have proven self-evident in the past several years to an increasing number of *Seekers* and readers within the Mardukite Systemology branded genre. The original Mardukite Systemology material—"*Tablets of Destiny Revelation*" (LIBER-ONE), "*Crystal Clear: A Handbook for Seekers*" (LIBER-2B), "*Metahuman Destinations*" (LIBER-TWO) and "*Way of the Wizard*" (LIBER-3E)—all reflect fundamentals of the *Pathway-to-Self-Honesty*. This process or sequence of processes (mental exercises, &tc.) is also known (in Systemology vocabulary) as '**Beta-Defragmentation**'.

However, LIBER-011 resulted from an even more advanced gradient of work—first introduced in our "*Imaginomicon*" (LIBER-3D)—which is traditionally added onto the former, and which is generally referred to as the *Gateways-to-Infinity*. At this juncture (November 2022), "*Imaginomicon*" (LIBER-3D) is the direct precursor for this present work. An individual should, at the very least, have worked through (and have access to) *"Crystal Clear: A Handbook for Seekers"* (*LIBER-2B*) and *"Imaginomicon-Revised"* (*LIBER-3D*) prior to attempting to derive anything other than entertainment value from the information, techniques, suggestion and systemological **processing**.

On a more academic level, or within the structure of Mardukite Academy and the Systemology Society, *LIBER-011* is a supplemental *Pathway* discourse bridging between GRADE-VI and GRADE-VII (*both still forthcoming*), based on its **premise** and practical applications alone: GRADE-VI in pertaining to advanced Wizard-Level **treatment** of *'Universes* and **Games***'*; GRADE-VII in regards to *'Unlimited Self* and *Cause'*. This precise projected/planned gradient classification schedule is actually embedded in the GRADE-III text for *"Crystal Clear: A Handbook for Seekers"* (*LIBER-2B*), and was predicted by our initial groundwork for Systemology. Consider even what is originally laid out in the premiere professional publication of Mardukite Systemology: *"The Tablets of Destiny Revelation"* (*LIBER-ONE*). [Both of these titles are also available in the complete GRADE-III 'Master Edition' anthology: *"The Systemology Handbook."*]

Keep in mind that completion of GRADE-IV material only occurred relatively recently (Spring-Summer 2022). As a practical application or *'applied philosophy'*, this present work is ahead of itself—or *ourselves*, as an "Organization" officially. In fact, *LIBER-011* is not presently taught in the classrooms (virtual or otherwise) of Mardukite Academy and so it is offered by the Systemology Society only as an experimental report. Being *officially unofficial* and baring the semblance of something that is only intended as a source of entertainment to the general public, it is safe to say that "Projekt-011" is enshrouded in the type of covertly overt double-speak and overtly covert Systemology techniques that are appropriate to the entire scope of this book and the work it represents (that officially doesn't exist and is unofficially presented to fans of a unique brand of 'meta-fantasy-sci-fi-horror'.

LIBER-011 is not an episodic guide to the beloved series or a fan-celebration of its epic cast of characters. Such volumes and publications continue to flood the market—and it is assumed the fanatic reader or *Seeker* is in possession of one or two of those already. There is no point, nor respect earned, in being notoriously redundant or overly dependent on the plot-points of a previously established body of work. For those reader-*Seekers* that are not already in the position of having seen the *Stranger Things* series, it is expected that this book will inspire them to do so—thereby contributing to the *Stranger Things* "*zeitgeist*" rather than 'milking' it. For those existing fans who have watched the series (probably numerous times), THE METAPHYSICS OF STRANGER THINGS is sure to enrich their own experience and enliven their personal reflection on the show, rather than simply piggy-backing on the **extant** cultural momentum.

From the Eternal Twilight Shadows in the Upside-Down,

—Joshua Free
October 31, 2022
Borsippa HQ, San Luis Valley

PART ONE

STRANGER RESEARCH

:: PART ONE ::

— Stranger Research —

THE "STRANGER THINGS" MYTHOS

Stranger Things debuted on Netflix (online streaming service) in Summer 2016; an amazingly original science fiction approach to horror-fantasy (in a hybridized storytelling tradition of *H.P. Lovecraft* mixed with *Stephen King*). The show mixes sci-fi/fantasy-horror with nostalgic 1980's themes and 'coming-of-age' drama unique not only to the period, but to all those that have felt or considered themselves as "outsiders" **relative** to a mainstream pop-cultural experience of the *Human Condition*. It is equally a humorously comical and delightfully refreshing approach to the '*Young-Adult*' ("YA") genre, which that had otherwise only increased in popularity throughout this new millennium.

The "YA-genre," as such, evolved into a seemingly exhaustive approach to novel-series and multi-film mediums. Entering upon another age marked by **superfluous** '*retro-remakes*', many were left to wonder '*what hasn't already been done before*'? This, of course, left a gaping hole for more than a few **demographics**—one's that *Stranger Things* now seems to fill. It is obviously a throwback to the young *Gen-Xers* growing up during the early 1980's—but it is also appreciable to the older *Millennials* that remember partaking in the "electric-neon fantasy-kingdom aura" of the 1980's for themselves. Of course, coupling organic "word-of-mouth" popularity with liberal merchandising, its fanship is certainly not exclusive to those who were even alive during the 1980's.

Nostalgia inherent in the show is no accident. The dynamically surrealistic, yet stringently poignant, throwback style of production and filming intentionally and successfully captures a period of time almost unrecognizable by today's standards—and still it is recognizable. Acceleration of modern technologies (and specifically and blatantly their speeds) and the manner in which information and **perception** is handled, leaves a time only a few decades past that is treated as "vintage" and "retro"—yet, on another level, seems as though it could have been just yesterday. One wonders how those generations living in the 1920's might have reflected on life in the 1880's. How quickly things might progress from an **app-**

arent 'western-style cowboy' stasis toward a world rampant with 'planes, trains and automobiles'.

HAWKINS NATIONAL LABORATORY ("Hawkins Lab")

"Hawkins National Laboratory" ("HNL"; stylized "hnl" for logos) is a ("fictional") Post-World-War-II secret research center founded in 1953 (in the fictional town of *Hawkins, Indiana*). Although not excessively emphasized in the TV Series, the work conducted at HNL was originally sanctioned by the CIA (U.S. Central Intelligence Agency). This alludes directly to "Project MK-Ultra" efforts—those that originally "did not (*officially*) exist," but which later turned up to be an actual "secret" tax-supported U.S. Government effort toward "understanding" (clinically, e.g. "psychology") and (according to HNL's unofficial MK-Ultra motto): "expanding the boundaries of the Mind." Although a lofty goal on the surface, the entire focus of this type of work is usually weaponized and restricted to military purposes.

While *Stranger Things* is a fictional series in regards to plot and characters, the MK-Ultra research and experiments are a very real aspect of relatively recent American History. And while we cannot be absolutely sure of the exact details of MK-Ultra, there is no reason to believe that such work does not continue to this day— whether by governments or the private sector. Furthermore, although a specific operation (or "project") may have ceased under an existing classification or code-name—for example, once it received public attention—the same experimental research lines could continue on under other "guises" and "titles." Even in *Stranger Things*, operations at Hawkins National Laboratory are covertly continuing under-the-radar well into the 1980's, long after the official cancellation of "Project MK-Ultra."

In the show, "Sheriff Jim Hopper" uses a geologic and urban survey (or "map" if you prefer) during the second season to track reports of strange phenomenon to Hawkins National Laboratory. A facsimile of this map is found in new copies of "*Stranger Things: Worlds Turned Upside Down (The Official Behind-the-Scenes Companion)*" published in 2018. According to this map, HNL is located within woodland hills a mile south of Hawkins, on the same side as "Sattler's Quarry" and a large trailer-park. This part of town is the opposite side from, for example, the "Starcourt Mall" built in the outskirts to the north.

The actual location of the "Hawkins National Laboratory" site used for film production is the former 40-acre site of "Georgia Mental Health Institute" (GMHI) in Druid Hills, Georgia, just outside of Atlanta. The facility operated from 1965 to 1997 (with over 140 beds) as a psychiatric hospital. It is now used solely for academic purposes by the nearby Emory University, but the building carries a genuine history of psychiatric research, training and experiments. Most evidence would suggest that the subject of "mental health" has never been appropriately handled in human society. In fact, the field of "psychology" is hardly a "mental science," although it may have had that ambition at its inception. When the "Mind" could not be discovered empirically and put under a microscope, the entire pursuit degraded into a physical "brain science" theorizing only on "observable behaviors."

Fictional character "Dr. Martin Brenner" serves as the director of research at Hawkins National Laboratory from his arrival in at least 1968-69 until 1983-4 (considering events depicted within the plot of the TV series first few seasons). More specific data is introduced within the first official *Stranger Things* novel, a prequel —"*Suspicious Minds*" by Gwenda Bond (published in 2019), where HNL is the centralized location for "Eleven"/"Subject-011" ("Jane Ives"; later "Jane Hopper") and her mother's ("Terry Ives") backstory. The novel suggests Dr. Brenner's involvement with HNL begins in July 1969. He then recruits college-students for experiments, supplementing the research taking place on children residing at HNL full-time.

In the TV-series, Dr. Brenner is portrayed by *Matthew Modine*—an actor that earned increasing notoriety during the 1990's, gaining a cult following from such films as *Pacific Heights* (*1990*) and *Cutthroat Island* (*1995*). His character's scenes and involvement with the show primarily surrounds "Eleven." It is not surprising that *Modine* and *Millie Bobby Brown* became close during the preparations and filming of the series—he even reportedly stayed with the *Brown* family during periods of the COVID lockdown where the two could rehearse the scenes for season four, which are expected to be particularly dramatic. *Modine* has remarked on the challenges he was forced to overcome regarding his style of acting and **identifying** with a role, and the fact that Dr. Brenner's character is particularly cold, sadistic and heartless. *Modine* and *Brown* would also reassure each other of their friendship and that "this is all just acting" before shooting the particularly emotionally straining scenes in season four. This level of care and proper handling of "young stars" is seldom seen in the media industry as it should be—an industry notorious for viewing its talents as products and treating them as disposable objects, or at best, living dolls. Over the course of the series, *Brown* has even received helpful tips and pointers from co-star *Winona Ryder*, an actress experienced in what it means to be a "young female Hollywood personality" and who certainly knows a thing or two about it.

In Gwenda Bond's novel *"Suspicious Minds,"* we pick up where "Terry Ives" gets involved in MK-Ultra at Hawkins National Laboratory in Autumn 1969. It starts with her filling in for a friend as an experimental research subject for college credit and cash. There are also some other participants from nearby, or from her college, which demonstrate some traces of minor testable 'special ability'—sensing future events, receiving significant visions, being able to 'charm' individuals, &tc. Subjects for MK-Ultra were often recruited from colleges or experimented on in relation to some college involvement with the CIA, as noted by Senator Ted Kennedy when addressing the senate on August 3, 1977:

> "The Deputy Director of the CIA revealed that over thirty universities and institutions were involved in an 'extensive testing and experimentation' program which included covert drug tests on unwitting citizens 'at all social levels, high and low, native Americans and foreign'. Several of these tests involved the administration of LSD to 'unwitting subjects in social situations'..."

It also becomes apparent to the characters in *"Suspicious Minds"* participating in the research experiments are also taking place on young children and teens residing more permanently at HNL. These are children which, according to the *Stranger Things* graphic novels, *"Six"* and *"Into The Fire"* (also compiled together in a hardcover library edition), are especially **"gifted"** in various ways—but who have been outcast or misunderstood enough in their normal lives (or with their families) that they ended up, one way or another, in the care of Hawkins Lab.

"Suspicious Minds" draws attention to another factor that often goes overlooked: that *Indigo Children* may be the product of psychedelic research experiments involving their parents; that the 1960's

psychedelic revolution may in some way have contributed to an increase in *energetic sensitivity* or what most generally categorize as ESP. We've all heard the stories about children born addicted to certain chemicals used by their parents, so what about non-addict-ive **consciousness** changing substances, such as "LSD"? How might these affect the mental abilities of a child later on, if administered to the mother during pregnancy?

Certainly in the TV-Series, Eleven's ability is not being credited to something truly supernatural or as a spiritual gift, but as innate **faculties** of consciousness that have been activated by the work of Dr. Brenner and Hawkin's Lab intentionally and systematically. Terry Ives is pregnant with Eleven (Jane) during her LSD experiments according to the back-story. Given what we *do* know about "*MK-Ultra*" (and its other related projects), one might expect that this would be examined given that it is quite basic to experiment with (considering the type of invasive experimentation conducted). And as we might further expect, an individual like *Subject-011* born into the program would not be allowed a public life—if even allowed to live out a life at all.

Starting in season two, "Dr. Sam Owens" takes over the project at Hawkins Lab in Dr. Brenner's absence. He is, essentially responsible for "cleaning up the mess" and handling the "damage control" for events relayed in season one and consequences of the same, which spread throughout season two and the remainder of the series. Although "Dr. Owens" is still a scientist with a government-trained mentality, his approach to managing the aftermath and continuing events at Hawkins (and those civilians and children experiencing them) is notably softer and more genuine than Dr. Brenner's. Given that it has been decades since first seeing him on "*Mad About You*" and in the (relevantly related to *Stranger Things*) movie "*Aliens*," there is certainly something nostalgic about seeing *Paul Reiser's* return to the screen for this role—and his unique wit and mannerisms that we can all recognize shines through his "white-coat" facade for the show.

As many fans have discovered, there is a very real historical framework or foundation that directly inspires the presentation of "Hawkins National Laboratory" in the series. This is even gleaned from the official back-story of the show's initial pilot development. Before this monumental franchise carried the familiar name "*Stranger Things*," the *Duffer Brothers* originally titled their series and its pilot-script *"Montauk."* Conspiracy theorists will recognize the connection to various stories about Montauk Air Force Base/Coastal Defense Station (or else referred to as "Fort Hero" and "Camp Hero"—named after *Major General Andrew Hero Jr.*, and not for the more obvious reasons that one might conclude).

The U.S. Government commissioned the eerie concrete building in 1942. It was constructed near Montauk Point, already famous for its *Lighthouse*, built in 1792 partially to keep watch for the British during the American Revolutionary War of that period. As the eastern end-point of Long Island (New York), the site serves as a military tactical **vantage** point—even long before concerns of a potential German invasion arose during World War II. The end of the World Wars essentially marked the beginning of the 'Cold War', at which time the combined paranoia of global government agencies and civilian hysteria ushered in an age of questionable research and dark-natured experimentation—all in the name of 'expansive militarization' and 'defense of national security'.

During the post-World-War-era, humanity became increasingly suspicious of each other. In the wake of holocausts, genocide and attempts at global dictatorships, most populations were at least marginally 'shell-shocked' and fearful that such events could happen again. This prompted a general war-cry that "this must never happen again." As a result, more obvious approaches to the problem were attempted by establishing international organizations (and thereby increased **communication** between various political nations)—but, on the surface, the world was frightened into submission by wide-spread increased development of nuclear physics and atomic bombs.

The "Montauk Base" allegedly expanded its programs during the 'Cold War' and thereafter. It became the main focus for a rise in (what some refer to as) "conspiracy theories." This is something that has only gained more attention in the past several decades. Those pursuing such alternative interests and anti-Orwellian (and anti-**authoritarian**) ideals often cross paths with the occult scene and controversial lifestyle types. But after World War II, governments became increasingly paranoid about their citizens; and citizens began to fear that their "elected" leaders were conspiring against them. Right or wrong, this general attitude has reflected an increased consensus ever since.

Unofficial reports allege a surge in headaches and nightmares by the local population residing near the Montauk Base after the large long-range search radar dish (twice the width of the building it sits on) was installed on the roof of the tall square cement block of a building. Supposed 'conspiracy theorists' believe that the military investigated 'remote viewing', 'psychic potential' and 'time travel' at Montauk and that the base was involved in the legendary "MK-Ultra" project. Of course, the work conducted at "Camp Hero" is most famously culminated under an umbrella of reports and theories generally referred to as the "Montauk Project" by the public.

Government and military use of the base continued until 1981, when "Camp Hero" was decommissioned. In 1984, an attempted sale was blocked for environmental protective purposes and the area passed into the responsibility of the National Park System. Afterward, it eventually entered into the care of the New York State Park System, and remains so to this day. The radar and its tower (and "Camp Hero" proper) was abandoned-in-place within the heart of the park, towering above the surrounding landscape, but remains off-limits to the public as a security and safety risk. It is surrounded by many acres of forested terrain and does emit a striking resonance with the ominous aura of Hawkins National Laboratory on the series.

MK-ULTRA FLAVORED PSYCHOLOGY

As a shared common point or 'meeting ground', indirect allusions and "unofficial" parallels between fiction and fact form a crossroads for reality. The subject matter of *Stranger Things* intersects with some elements of our Systemology *Grade-VI* and *Grade-VII* material and ongoing experimental research at the Systemology Society for the Mardukite Academy. It would be illogical to assume that there are not other underground factions of mysticism and science that also continue similar pursuits—toward both the most lofty ideals and mundane goals.

Even though the "MK-Ultra" project, as so designated and named, was allegedly shut down, there is little doubt that a continuation of similar "top secret" efforts still takes place today internationally. In the past 150 years, fields of "psychology" and "metapsychology" and "parapsychology" have all become fast growing industries. "Contemporary psychology" or "psychiatry" often serves as an authoritarian agent and chemical **catalyst** for issuing other-determmined **control** of the standard issue Human Condition—potentially changing its **patterns** of thought and reasoning, **associative** considerations, compartmentalization of memory, and handling of **motor-functions**.

Unofficially speaking—and in regards to unofficial projects that "do not exist" according to public knowledge—we could safely (or unsafely) assume that *all* of "*top*" governments (particularly those not exclusively tied up in "third-world" "primitive" *beta-existence* survivalism) maintain some type of psychological (and parapsychological) experimentation programs. These might include investigations into effects of drugs, programming or **implanting** and, of course, what is generally referred to as "telepathy," "remote viewing" and "telekinesis"—just to name a few. Such programs would undoubtedly 'draft' subjects knowingly and unknowingly. Methods of testing the public would also be required to determine what sensitive individuals should be recruited, or rather what types of individual would be most suited for specific types of work. Where we have once witnessed Albert Einstein's equations transmuted into atomic bombs, it is interesting to see how all modern applications of a 'science of mind' have been coerced into a vehicle for control of civilization toward worldly ends.

In recent history, few academic figures and actualized individuals —particularly in the field of "psychology"—have made the same broad sweeping global influence that Carl Jung has. A physician and creative psychologist in Switzerland by the age of 25, Jung made vast literary contributions to growing fields of practical and philosophical *metaphysics*, "creative" or "theoretical" *metapsychology* and the inception of *transpersonal* psychological methods of therapy, including autosuggestion and using *GSR-biofeedback* devices during *word association*. Jung was never officially involved with any secret societies (as far as we know), but many friends and fellow academicians shunned him as a "natural born mystic." Growing up in a household filled with paranormal phenomenon paved the way for him to become a "sensitive." Upon waking each morning, he began a tradition of "centering" himself by drawing *mandalas*. He developed an inclination towards alchemical lore, **Gnosticism** and the Rosicrucians, especially that which concerned his work on dreams.[*]

---

[*] Several paragraphs here are excerpted from the Mardukite Grade-I (Route-A) Master Edition anthology, "*The Great Magickal Arcanum*"

While Carl Jung launched his medical career, Sigmund Freud published his famous treatise, "*The Interpretation of Dreams*." Although he disagreed with Freud's pointed emphasis on sexuality above all other matters and the resulting lack of spiritual dimension taken up in Freud's work, Jung found many of the suggestions could be used to support his own unique systemology of the mind. The two individuals were well acquainted and even began to travel together professionally starting in 1907. But, in 1912 Jung's publication of "*Symbols of Transformation*" forced a separation between them—yet Jung would ever after remain classified as part of the school (or field) of "psychoanalysis."

Carl Jung's classification of the *psyche* is referenced or cited frequently in New Age materials, contemporary mysticism and philosophy. He recognized that each of us lives according to patterns inherent in **archetypes**, or a "*persona*" used to play out 'roles' for the *Game of Life* in society. His writings indicate that this *persona* (and any *goal* motivated by it) may, but probably does not, relate to our "true" and "actual" or "neglected" Self, which he terms the "*Shadow Self*." Certain 'inclinations' seem dictated to us, or destined for us, in our lives—whether **manifested** in our path by an all-encompassing Higher Self or some other-determined "synchronicity" that seemingly occurs unbidden. In fact, Jung actually coined the term "synchronicity," defining it as: "parallel events, instances or thoughts that have no physical, **apparent** or observable causal relationship."

While many pass off the 'sign-posts' in their life as "coincidence," Jung found that strong 'links' or 'connections' of this nature continue to get stronger. They will eventually surpass simple classifications of "happenstance" or "coincidence" if so recognized. Lacking other "appropriate" terminology, Jung's descriptions of consciousness also parallel beliefs held by ancient mystics, shamans, seers and magicians, concerning a "universal stream" or Akashic field of interconnectedness. Even beyond the connections to esoterica and mysticism, Jung's presence in the realm of psychology allowed the field to retain some semblance of its original purpose and a pursuit of understanding the "mind" and the "spirit" that *is* the individual, while the remaining materialist fields of psychology turned exclusively toward "behaviorism" and the "brain." Psychology is now a "behavioral science."

---

by Joshua Free.

A historical perspective or **timeline** to represent 'real-world' events relating to *Stranger Things* and the activities of "Hawkins Lab" is difficult to pinpoint definitively. Project code-names are frequently short-lived, overlap with other integrated projects or have a specific focus blatantly spun-off to form a new project. For example, *"Project MKULTRA"* allegedly spawned nearly 150 sub-projects, much of which is still classified "Top Secret" (for reasons of "national security"). Accurate "start" and "stop" dates for various projects are also obscure. They each seem to evolve as their own entity—and each with a targeted emphasis. Researches and theorists have been compiling data (either leaked or declassified) for many years, which is generally made public thereafter—although most official documents are so redacted with black marks that their meaning can be nearly impossible to decipher. As a basic **chronological** outline of relevant covert operations in the U.S., the following is merely a suggestion:

PROJECT PAPERCLIP 1945/1946–1951

PROJECT CHATTER 1947-1953

PROJECT BLUEBIRD 1950 → *"Project Artichoke"*

PROJECT ARTICHOKE 1951-1953 → *"MK-Ultra"*

PROJECT MKULTRA (*"MK-Ultra"*) 1953–1973

OPERATION MIDNIGHT CLIMAX 1953-1964

PROJECT MKNAOMI (*"MK-Naomi"*) 1953–1973

PROJECT MONARCH (*"Monarch Programming"*) 1950s–?
(This project is still completely classified TOP SECRET.)

STARGATE PROJECT ('*Sunstreak*'; '*Scangate*') 1973/1978-1995

Our brief journey through surveying this dark side of American history appropriately begins in the aftermath of World War II, with *Project Paperclip* in 1945 (or 1946). Over half a century of covert and clandestine operations first emerged as a reaction to events in the war. The 'American-Soviet Cold War' immediately followed. Based on alleged intelligence gathered concerning soviet research and experiments, America didn't want to fall behind in their ability to interrogate and control. Thus, the excuse was made—and ultimate justification provided—to essentially do anything for any purpose, no matter what suffering would ensue or lives irreparably lost.

Project Paperclip involved clandestine immigration of Nazi German leaders and scientists and their employment by technology and intelligence offices of the U.S. Government. Reportedly this was conducted under the sanction of President Henry S. Truman. Seeking a tactical advantage in "population control," "rocketry" and the "space race," the ex-Nazi leaders were given a pardon for their war crimes in exchange for sharing their existing technological research, and advancing it, for America.

Perhaps the most famous example of those individuals brought to our side is *Wernher von Braun (1912-1977)*. He transferred his previous efforts and focus from the Nazi rocket program toward the inception and establishment of N.A.S.A. in the late 1950s. He even appeared on several of Walt Disney's television programs regarding the future of rocket technology and space travel. But this is not the only type of information that survived, migrated and evolved after the fall of Hitler's *Third Reich.*

Many of the ex-Nazi officers involved with *Project Paperclip* had been witness to, or even participated in, intense and diabolical human experimentation, manipulation and torture tactics used by the Germans in World War II. This type of information was of particular interest to certain factions or national intelligence agencies. By 1950, we began to see (or rather, *not* see, until declassification decades later) a rise in "projects" or "operations" aimed toward focuses on "*mind kontrolle*" for military and other covert purposes. It should not be so surprising that after importing this type of intelligence to America, *Project Bluebird* launched in 1950—a program aimed at understanding human conditioning, memory enhancement and methods of controlling an individual via intensive or unconventional **interrogation**. An emphasis on interrogation continued in *Project Artichoke* and *Project Chatter (MK-Chatter)*, but with an integration of hypnosis, sensory deprivation, sleep deprivation, **enforced** heroin addiction (and subsequent withdrawal)—and then finally, the clinical application of a newly discovered and little understood substance: "*LSD.*"

"*Lysergic Acid Diethylamide-25*" or "*LSD-25*" (often referred to simply as "acid" in counter-cultures) ranks famously high on any "drug list" as an extremely potent perception-altering hallucinogen (with metaphysical and spiritual applications according to many **esoteric** adepts in the past. While famous for its association with 1960's culture and social movements of that era, initial academic applications of LSD-25 pertained to creative psychology,

34

metapsychology, medicine/pharmaceuticals, and of course, the kicker of them all: political governments around the world seeking to expand military intelligence and ability during the American-Soviet Cold War.[*]

Discovery of LSD-25 (or simply "LSD") was perhaps an inevitability of our modern era—a synthetic antidote to a highly synthetic world. But what can heal can also harm—and if it were not for the government and military interest in LSD, it would likely have taken much longer to see the type of cultural swing we did during the 1960's. Those figures like Dr. Timothy Leary and Ken Kesey actually credited the C.I.A. and their "MK-Ultra Project" with igniting the spark for what later became the "anti-authoritarian hippie" and "new consciousness" revolution. Dr. Leary was introduced to LSD via experiments with graduate-level psychology students at Harvard. Elsewhere, a Stanford psychology graduate student invites Ken Kesey to participate in a psychedelic study funded by the CIA at Menlo Park Veterans Hospital (California). Combined, these two figures went on to pioneer the bulk of what is associated with the 1960's "psychedelic revolution."[‡]

Many people believe they know the "truth" about LSD, but this may or may not be so, as the present author has heard so many versions of things that it is clear that the matter is still quite esoteric. Only one man really knows: Albert Hofmann, a Swiss chemist employed by Sandoz Pharmaceutical Company, and fortunately he wrote about it in his book: "*LSD: My Problem Child.*" In the 1930s, he began a series of experiments with the alkaloid found in the nucleus of ergot, called *lysergic acid*. Funding for this specific medicinal pursuit regarded discovering a new "analeptic," a substance to stimulate respiration and blood circulation in the body.

Sandoz Laboratory originally deemed "LSD-25"—the twenty-fifth substance produced in the experimental *lysergic acid* series—to have no medicinal value; but other pharmaceuticals, like *Hydergine*, did result from this same cycle. Any "mystical" properties of LSD were, however, discovered entirely by "accident," though others say "**destiny.**" During the crystallization process, a small amount

---

* Several paragraphs here are excerpted from the Mardukite Grade-I (Route-A) Master Edition anthology, "*The Great Magickal Arcanum*" by Joshua Free.

‡ The subject of Dr. Timothy Leary or Ken Kesey and his Merry Pranksters make for excellent supplemental research.

of the substance was absorbed through Albert Hofmann's skin. He then went home early from work, reporting symptoms of dizziness, visual distortions and restlessness. Upon direct experimentation later, Hofmann found LSD to be quite active in miniscule doses. A single droplet could produce disorientation for hours. It was also colorless, tasteless and odorless.

Effects of LSD-25, as stated on one of the original medical documents, include: "hallucination, depersonalization and expression of repressed memories" with a chance of "intermittent disturbances for several days afterward." Of course, as we know today, the experience of *"flashbacks"* can take place many years afterward. And this is an interesting phenomenon for a Systemologist to consider, because it overtly demonstrates the very mechanisms involved in **imprinting** or *implanting* and the potential restimulation of this energetic **turbulence** when *facets* and **hot-buttons** are present or reintroduced to an individual's environment later. More traditional psychology treats its own understanding of this phenomenon with **semantics** as "conditioning" and "triggers" and "stimulus-response"—but we are still dealing with the *same* phenomenon.

In addition to *Project Paperclip*, the U.S. Government and military experienced complete restructuring following the end of World War II with the "National Security Act of 1947" (**enacted** *July 26*). The act served to unify the diverse branches of government and military intelligence and sanctioned forming a centralized agency to oversee this. Therefore, in 1947, what began during the World Wars as the O.S.S. (*Office of Strategic Services*) expanded and evolved into the C.I.A. or *Central Intelligence Agency*. As a new 'intelligence company', its first covert operation in 1947, called *Project Chatter*, primarily focused on interrogation and "truth-drug" experiments. This began at St. Elizabeth's Psychiatric Hospital (*Washington, DC*).

Certainly "interrogation" is a necessary part of maintaining the legal systems presently in place for the type of society we share as a reality. All useful information regarding systematic **methodology** for interrogation tactics falls under the category of "psychology"—although the science of this is embedded within Systemology work too. Certainly an experienced *Class-3E Professional Pilot* of Systemology would know a thing or two about the mechanisms at work governing human behavior—and of course, its manipulation. And one pursuit clearly feeds into or supplies data for the other, since by 1952, we read in a CIA memo for *Project Artichoke* (the immediate forerunner for *Project MK-Ultra* the following year in 1953) regarding objectives for the program: "can we get control of an individual to the point where he will do our bidding against his will and even against the fundamental **laws** of nature such as self-preservation"—which is to say "*survival.*"

Ideals of *MK-Ultra* splintered into, or were absorbed by, numerous other projects and operations. Most of them involved drugs, particularly LSD, but also psilocybin mushrooms, DMT, heroin, opium, and so forth—the list is endless. *MK-Naomi*, for example, focused on biological and chemical warfare. *Operation Midnight Climax* operated "safe houses" for drug-testing notably in New York and San Francisco, where "sexual manipulation" experiments targeted those on the fringes of society that wouldn't be taken seriously if found out or whistle-blowing. There is little doubt—given what we know of the human condition and covert handling of power—that additional sexual abuses took place and that individuals were coerced into engaging in activities solely for the benefit of private gratification.

Rather than "expanding the mind" for any lofty purpose, consciousness changing substances were only used toward ends of disrupting and **fragmenting** the psyche. *MK-Ultra* consisted of "operationally realistic" experiments on unaware American citizens—and this is not a matter of opinion or conspiracy theory, but a matter of public fact, even if we choose to ignore it. After over two decades, the existence of *MK-Ultra* was eventually made public in the national courts. By 1979, ABC News Washington D.C. produced an hour-long special edition report called "*Mission: Mind Control*" that detailed much of the available information at that time. Although more information continues to get declassified, CIA Director Richard Helms destroyed most of the *MK-Ultra* documents during the time of the Watergate scandal.

DUNGEONS & DRAGONS & DIMENSIONAL DOORS (...Oh, my!)

"*Dungeons and Dragons*"—often stylized "*D&D*" or written as "*Dungeons & Dragons*" with a draconic icon for the ampersand—is a fantasy role-playing tabletop game system developed by Gary Gygax in the 1960's. It first launched publicly in 1974 as a series of small boxed kits and booklets from Gygax's own kitchen. By the time of D&D's public release, Gygax was an established game-developer. His first medieval fantasy "miniatures" tabletop war-game—*Chainmail*—inspired formation of his group, "Lake Geneva Tactical Studies Association" in Wisconsin. The group later re-formed and rebranded to form an official publishing company: "*Tactical Studies Rules*," better known as *TSR*. The "Miniatures" battle games in many ways resembled more advanced variations on themes found in similar mainstream classics, such as "*Risk*." All TSR products emphasized practical use of **game-theory** in theoret-ical "play out" of military tactics and battle strategy.[*]

In 1977, TSR launched their first edition of "*Advanced Dungeon & Dragons*"—or *AD&D*—but what players would continue to simply call "D&D." This version of the game consisted of new expanded rules available in separate hardcover books—the "Core Rulebooks"—al-lowing for infinite expansion supplement possibilities, an aspect that TSR took full advantage of.

The "Core Rulebooks" generally required for the game (or at least in possession of the "Dungeon Master"; the person running or nar-rating the game) are "*The Player's Handbook*," "*Dungeon Master's Guide*" and the "*Monster Manual*"—all of which were originally writ-ten by Gary Gygax himself. This same model has continued to rep-resent the game for over 40 years, although various editions them-selves have been consistently updated by other writers. In fact, even the original release of the *Advanced Dungeons and Dragons* (AD&D) Core saw revision within its first year after debut cover artwork was deemed too "demonic" and controversial, so a more commercial feel was brought to the same books in 1978. Further titles later supplemented the core materials, including: "*Deities & Demigods*," "*Manual of the Planes*" and widely controversial "*Fiend Folio*."

While building in popularity underground, *Dungeons and Dragons* began to spark religious controversy almost immediately in the world-at-large. Most were concerned about "devil-worship," but other strange things started happening to psychologically unstable teenagers obsessed with occult elements and/or over-**identifying** with aspects of character "role-play." Certainly, these games obvi-ously expose players to metaphysical, fantasy and magical themes,

---

[*] Several paragraphs here are excerpted from "*Draconomicon: The Book of Ancient Dragon Magick*" by Joshua Free; also contained in the Mardukite Academy Grade-I (Route-D) Master Edition anthology, "*Merlyn's Complete Book of Druidism*."

but no more than an extremist personality might find exploring Grimm Faerie Tales and archaic mythologies. The one element these types of games do actually provide is a social community for those interested in these themes for any number of personal reasons or inclinations—including the practice of occultism. But they are hardly responsible for the inception of such personal interests.

The first real bout of public concern emerged in 1979 when a young player attending the University of Michigan—James Dallas Egbert III—disappeared for nearly a month. As media attention developed, so did the story: the young man's reality irreversibly merged with the game world, so he went into the steam ducts of the university for personal adventure and died. None of this turned out to be true and sales skyrocketed. Later it was discovered that Egbert was simply missing due to his own psychological instability—but he did commit suicide a year later. Throughout the 1980's, it was commonplace for the news media to associate D&D with all manners of misdirected youth activity—satanism, cults, suicide or even murders. The book and movie "*Mazes and Monsters*" (starring *Tom Hanks*) was based on this same hysteria.

Negative attention enshrouding the *Dungeons and Dragons* brand in the early 1980's eventually did influence a noticeable decline of sales. Many executive shareholders for TSR decided to "get out." But Gary Gygax had faith in his vision, commissioning a Saturday-morning "*Dungeons and Dragons*" cartoon. It aired on CBS from September 1983 until November 1985, adjusting adult themes inherent in the game to provide a greater appeal to younger audiences. When the series released to DVD, the special edition included a gaming supplement allowing players to adapt elements and characters from the animated series into their tabletop gameplay.

In 1989, TSR produced a new "2nd Edition" of *Advanced Dungeons and Dragons* (*AD&D*) corresponding with a complete revision of all rules and supplements. As the company struggled to manage ongoing financial problems, it sought to not only retain existing players, but to attract a whole new generation with a revitalized look and feel to the product. Yet, a decade later, TSR faced bankruptcy, and their design patents and trademarks were purchased by *Wizards of the Coast*—a company responsible for another widely successful quasi-occult fantasy game system called "*Magic: The Gathering*" (or "*M:TG*"). *Wizards of the Coast* went on to release a new streamlined version of *Dungeons and Dragons* as a "3rd Edition" in 2000—returning the core game title to simply *"Dungeons and Dragons."* This debut of a new edition coincided with the first feature-length *"Dungeons & Dragons"* motion picture ever, followed by a sequel in 2005: *"Wrath of the Dragon God."* The company *Wizards of the Coast* has since been purchased by the *Hasbro* toy company, and as of writing this, the game system is currently in its "5th Edition."

With the release and successful reception of *Stranger Things*, a resurgence of interest in the *Dungeons and Dragons* game ensued. In 2018 *Hasbro/Wizards of the Coast* commissioned a retro-80's styled *"Dungeons and Dragons Starter Set"* modeled after the original nostalgic "red box starter set" released at its commercial inception. Like the original and other "starter basic sets" released prior, the *Stranger Things D&D Starter Set* introduces the fundamentals of game-play, elementary statistics for the first couple of player 'levels', and provides an introductory-level adventure. In this case, the adventure is a facsimile of the same game that the boys are playing during the beginning of the first episode and at the end of the last episode (of the first season), when Mike is the 'Dungeon Master' for encounters involving troglodytes and, of course, the *"Demogorgon."* These scenes literally serve as a launch point for game-specific semantics and vocabulary used throughout the remainder of the series.

It is true that the *Stranger Things D&D Starter Set* does make for a nice piece in a nostalgic collection—and it is quite appropriate for a new up-and-coming generation of players. However, for those more seasoned players (experienced with the current "5th Edition" game-core), a more traditional (and advanced) approach could be taken that even involves confronting *troglodytes*, but also taking on the legendary *"Demogorgon, Prince of Demons"* of the actual 'D&D Pantheon', a creature of such epic proportions that it more closely resembles the "Shadow Monster" (of the second season). The name of the 'campaign manual', first released for 5th Edition in September 2015, is *"Out of the Abyss: Rage of Demons"*—and the adventure takes place in, what is called, the *"Underdark."*

"Underdark" originally started as part of the popular *"Forgotten Realms"* 'campaign setting' ('world', 'plane' or 'universe') for *Dungeons and Dragons*. While it does contain portals to other 'planes', Underdark is physically beneath-the-surface—a subterranean place of 'darkness, shadows and evil' created by an ancient malignant deity ("Torog") who found himself sealed away from accessing the 'Surface World'. There are innumerable parallels between the "physically underground" portion of the *Upside Down* (from *Stranger Things*) and Underdark—though one could draw comparisons between the Otherworldly aspects of the show and many of the other inter-planar concepts contained within the *Dungeons and Dragons* multiverse, including the *Abyss* and *Astral Sea*.

One of the more notable (and relevant) inhabitants of the Underdark is the *Mindflayers* (or "*Mind-Flayers*"), an intelligent and sadistic race of tentacled quasi-Lovecraftian squid-faced humanoids ('*Illithids*') known for feeding on the brains of their enemies (which is basically everyone) after "flaying their minds" using '*psionic*' will-bending and sanity-shattering abilities. Of course, "Mindflayer" is the term chosen by the group of young *Dungeons and Dragons* players within the *Stranger Things* mythos to denote the ominous tentacled **inter-dimensional** "Shadow Monster" plaguing main characters (well, mostly Will) in the second season. In the *Dungeons and Dragons* mythology, *Mindflayers* sought to enslave all the diverse races (that would submit) occupying the Astral Plane (and may have originated there) before a portion of their population migrated to *Underdark*.

The "psionic" game-variant on traditional "magic" appears since the earliest days of *Dungeons and Dragons*. Unlike the 'wizard' or 'sorcerer' that studies the occult, or even the priestly 'cleric' that prays for, or invokes, the powers of their patron deity, the '*psion*' taps inherent power of the "mind" or "Self." This character class is a practitioner capable of what we might consider the more spectacular "psychic" phenomenon imaginable. There are, of course, specialized disciplines within this wide encompassing field—'telepathy', **'psychokinesis'** and 'clairsentience' (to name a few). It is accurate to say that the domain of 'psionics', far more than 'magic', constitutes the bulk of what a person might deem "supernatural" within the *Stranger Things* saga. Of course, by definition, what is considered "supernatural" to the ignorant may very well be driven or governed by an, as yet, undetermined, unrecognized or otherwise misunderstood "natural" 'principle' or 'law'.

The area of Underdark closest to the Surface-World is referred to as the "Shallows." There is one particular spot of note, where *Torog* thrashed about enough to create a significant portal to other planes/dimensions. It is called the "Dark Lake **Ziggurat**," which is set next to a 'bottomless black lake' and described [in the campaign game supplement published in 2010 for 4th Edition] as: "a four-sided stepped pyramid rising above the black waters of the lake, also duplicated below the lake surface, so the whole structure is an eight-sided shape." The plane on which each of the eight primary chamber-rooms crosses with is constantly shifting, and each occupies a separate plane from its adjoining chamber-rooms. One might be reminded of the "tesseract" or "hypercube" described in the science-fiction/fantasy story by Robert Heinlein, "...And He Built A Crooked House." The Ziggurat is connected to other significant planes within the *Dungeons and Dragons* "multiverse," such as: the "Astral Sea," the "Elemental Chaos," "Feywild" and "Shadowfell"—all of which carry inter-dimensional qualities relevant to the *Stranger Things* mythos. Other scattered points of inter-connectivity with these planes also exist elsewhere in the Underdark and throughout the various worlds.

While the original presentations of *Dungeons and Dragons* offered a mostly generic approach to "sword and sorcery" fantasy gaming loosely inspired by the works of *J.R.R. Tolkien*, it did not take long for the cumulative creative efforts of countless individuals to fashion a cohesive **cosmology** and pantheon for the 'multiverse'. For example, a reference to the name "*Vecna*"—a figure from the TV-series, emerging in the fourth season—may actually be found deep within dark annals of Underdark mythology, and even those dedicated to the "*drow*" [rhymes with "*cow*"] or 'Dark Elves'. This race occupies "The Deeps" of Underdark—a network of tunnels and large urbanized caverns that is further beneath-the-surface of "The Shallows." Although not usually a *drow* diety, "*Temples to Vecna*" may be found, where permitted, among certain *drow* populations. Otherwise, 'Dark Elves' primarily practice a **religion** solely dedicated to the evil goddess "*Lolth-the-Spider-Queen*." Rather than large obvious temples, *Vecna*'s followers are generally congregated in isolated cultist cells that pride themselves on secrecy—for they do serve a god of secrets and espionage.

Vecna is one of the 'lesser deities' of evil, necromancy and conspiracy that shares a "D&D Pantheon" common to all 'Outer Planes' of the "D&D Cosmology." The 'meta-thought' behind this cosmological structure has crystallized with deeper facets with each progressive edition with increasing consistency. Originally a mortal king, *Vecna* ascended the pantheon as a '*lich*' or "evil undead sorcerer-like priest" (and classified, in game-terms, for the 3rd Edition

"Deities and Demigods" manual, as a dual-classed '20th-level Wizard' and '20th-level Cleric').

Within the "D&D Cosmology," the "Epic of Creation" back-story also mirrors historical **Babylonian "cuneiform"** tablets[‡] in many respects: it takes place during a primordial era of cosmic development; it involves dragons or dragon-like gods, even a primary one among them with the ability to create expressions of life by infusing primary elemental energies with mortal **simulacrum**; and finally our "Epics" are always set beyond the material realm, at the furthest reaches of pure **existence**—spaces between the spaces we see in our **condensed** solidified experience. Additional similarities to ancient mythologies may be gleaned from even a small portion of the actual *Dungeons and Dragons* narrative:[*]

> "During the *Dawn Wars* between the 'primordials' and the gods that followed the world's creation, *Io* and his children stood at the forefront of all mortal beings in the fight to preserve creation from the unchecked elemental forces of the angry primordials. *Io* fought and defeated many primordials, but one of them, *Erek Hus*—the King of Terror—slew *Io*. Just when the primordials seemed on the verge of victory, from the halves of *Io's* shattered body, two new gods arose: *Bahamut*, the Platinum Dragon; and *Tiamat*, the Chromatic Dragon. *Bahamut* and *Tiamat* together defeated the King of Terror, but then *Tiamat* turned against the noble *Bahamut*, attempting to seize dominion as Queen of All Dragons—she could not suffer the existence of any equal or allow any other creature to reign over dragonkind. But, the Platinum Dragon defeated *Tiamat*, and she retreated to the dark depths of Tytherion, the *Endless Night* or *Abyss*."

Another unique deity-like monster from the *Dungeons and Dragons* multiverse famously borrowed for the *Stranger Things* mythos is

---

‡   Referencing the Mesopotamian Tradition explored as an integral part of *'Mardukite Zuism'* and the "Arcane Tablets of *'Mardukite Systemology'*; also contained in the Mardukite Academy Grade-II Master Edition anthology, *"Necronomicon: The Complete Anunnaki Legacy"* by Joshua Free.

*   Commentary in this paragraph excerpted from *"Draconomicon: The Book of Ancient Dragon Magick"* by Joshua Free; also contained in the Mardukite Academy Grade-I (Route-D) Master Edition anthology, *"Merlyn's Complete Book of Druidism."*

the *"Demogorgon."* However, the gargantuan "Shadow Monster" of the TV-series is referred to as "The Mind Flayer." In 'actual D&D' terms, *mind-flayers* are an entire race of *'psions'* approximately the size of a very tall athletic human. Of course, the "Shadow Monster" is called a *mind-flayer* because of its 'psionic' ability and not for its relative "difficulty class," "challenge rating" or "statistics" within the *Dungeons and Dragons* game by traditional standards. In fact, the epic *"Demogorgon"* of actual *Dungeons and Dragons* reflects the "Shadow Monster" of *Stranger Things* far more accurately than its portrayal of humanoid *"Demo-dogs"* &tc.

The Demogorgon (with a capital "D"; as opposed to ST's *demogorgons*) is a very specific entity within the *Dungeons and Dragons* paradigm; therefore, not a race or creature-type. He is given the title "Prince of Demons"—also 'Sibilant Beast' and 'Master of the Spiraling Depths'—throughout many *Dungeons and Dragons* editions. As horrific as the scrapes with bloom-faced human-sized *demogorgons* of *Stranger Things* might be, a run-in with *The Demogorgon* abyssal fiend of 'true D&D' would be an unparalleled epic-level encounter, such as we find better represented (again) with the large "Shadow Monster" of season two—approximately '475 *hit-points*' and all the powers of an inter-dimensional demon-fiend, versus the '30 *hit-points*' attributed to the more familiar humanoid *demogorgons* (of the *Stranger Things D&D Starter Set*). According to *"The Book of Vile Darkness"* by Monte Cook [published in 2002 for 3rd Edition]:

> "The Demogorgon is 18 feet tall and bizarre in appearance even by demonic standards. He has two heads, each like that of a hyena. His body is long and serpentine, covered in dark, blue-green scales. His necks are long and snaky. Rather than arms, Demogorgon has two long, sinuous tendrils not unlike the tentacles of an octopus. His legs are lean and muscular, and his long tail is forked."

This description matches the playing-token or "miniature" of the monster used for the game portrayed *on* the show. The original game-piece is, in fact, modeled after *The Demogorgon* as originally depicted in *Dungeons and Dragons*. But, of course, this contrasts significantly with "Mike Wheeler's" version of a *demogorgon* (as based on the creature developed for the series) given in a nostalgia-styled replica of Mike's adventure book *"Hunt for the Thessalhydra"* in the *Stranger Things D&D Starter Set*—a set which includes a plastic *demogorgon* game-miniature based on the show:

"A demogorgon is a monstrosity the size and shape of an adult human, but its mouth fills its face and opens like a blooming flower. One currently lives in the Upside Down, and no one knows where it came from originally. It's incredibly strong and can heal itself from damage it takes. Like a shark, a demogorgon is drawn to the scent of blood, and goes into a frenzy when blood is near..."

Part of the shared "D&D Cosmology" common to the entire multiverse is 'The Abyss'—and the 88th level or layer of *The Abyss* is referred to as the 'Brine Flats' or 'Gaping Maw'. But the portion of this level where the *Demogorgon* makes its lair is called "*Abysm.*" It is from here that the *Demogorgon*—"the embodiment of chaos, madness, and destruction"—seeks to "corrupt all that is good and undermine order in the multiverse, to see everything dragged howling into the infinite depths of the Abyss" (quoting "*Out of the Abyss,*" 5th Edition).

OPENING THE GATEWAY

Dungeons and Dragons is not the main subject or upper-level focus of this present book, but there are innumerable aspects that overlap with the TV-show and even *Systemology;* and for decades—ironically, since the same era that *Stranger Things* takes place—the game materials increasingly developed an unspoken reputation for being the authority on "rules" or "guidelines" of "Fantasy." As stated during the naming of the '*Mindflayer*' in season two of the TV-show, lacking alternatives, the game provides the "*best analogy*" for the metaphysical phenomenon experienced by the characters. Of course, our Systemology library did not exist during the 1980's to help them out.

The *Dungeons and Dragons* paradigm includes treatment of various '*Planes of Existence*' beyond *this* "Physical Universe" (or the '*Material Plane*' that we are most familiar with—or else "*Beta-Existence*" in *Systemology* vocabulary). The game-system tends to employ a cornucopia of elements drawn from variegated folklore and mythologies from around the globe spanning thousands of years. It tends to do this indiscriminately, of course; but what the "D&D Cosmology" *does* take into account, resonates strongly with the metaphysics inherent in *Stranger Things,* in addition to facets of other science fields and mystical traditions, not to mention the '*Standard*

Model' and '**Cosmic History**' explored in *Systemology*.

Among the many traditional wilderness environments and castle-dungeon settings for game-play, we discover an integral and diverse mythology embedded in the "D&D Cosmology." Here we find homelands for deities, dark spaces for fiends and demons, bright places for celestials and demigods, domains for the elementals, and, of course, a means for traversing this multiverse and moving between planes. A direct relationship between planes is generally classified in two different ways, as:

— "Coexistent" (*overlapping planes*); or

— "Coterminous" (*sharing interconnected points*)

An "*Astral Sea*" is connected to all planes, enveloping and encompasses each—thus permeating and connecting all planes together in commonality. This means it is a "transitive plane"—a '**threshold**' or 'veil'—allowing access to "*Outer Planes*" or even as a catalyst for alternate spatial travel across distances of the '*Material Plane*'. A "*Wildspace*" (*Outer Space*) zone or region separates each '*Material Plane*' (on all sides) from the '*Astral Sea*' (or *Astral Plane*). '*Wildspace*' and the '*Astral Sea*' are treated as primary focuses in the *Dungeons and Dragons* "*Spelljammer*" campaign setting, with a new version of the original "*Adventures in Space*" boxed set just recently released (August 2022) for 5th Edition.

In addition to the '*Astral Sea*', there is the '*Etheric Plane*' (or '*Ethereal Plane*') and '*Plane of Shadow*', both of which are also considered transitive planes. They are coexistent (overlapping) and are coterminous (having interconnected '**terminals**' or 'portals'/'gateways') with a '*Material Plane*'—for example, the standard "Physical Universe." Of course, this refers to *any* 'Material Plane' and not only *this* "Physical Universe." The 'Material Plane', as we are accustomed to experiencing via the Human Condition, is still used as a baseline for basic comparative understanding of these various existences—but it is only one manifestation of a "*Beta-Existence*." Portals to other planes appear in the '*Astral Sea*' (or '*Astral Plane*') as '*Astral Pools*' of various colors. Each is linked to a specific plane—for example, the '*Plane of Shadow*' is represented by a black-spiral and pools for the '*Ethereal Plane*' are indicated by a white-spiral.

The '*Plane of Shadow*' is probably the most appropriate parallel for the "Upside-Down"—and the young gamers practically refer to it as the "*Vale of Shadows*" in season one before it receives its upgraded more famously known name. Given the sheer amount of *Tolkien*-esque qualities providing the original standard for fantasy role-playing even prior to the rise of *Dungeons and Dragons*, one might draw parallels to the coexistent/overlapping 'Realm of Shadow' entered by an individual (for example, in "Lord of the Rings") whenever *The Ring* is put on and worn. Elsewhere in *Dungeons and Dragons* lore, it goes on to explain:

> "The Plane of Shadows is a world of black and white... in many ways the dark duplicate of the Material Plane. It is (a) toxic plane of darkness and power. It is the hidden place that hates the light. It is the frontier of worlds unknown. The Plane of Shadows is a darkly lighted dimension (that) overlaps the Material Plane much as the Ethereal Plane does. Landmarks from the Material Plane are recognizable on the Plane of Shadows, but they are twisted warped things—diminished reflections of what can be found on the Material Plane. While the Plane of Shadow is not evil in and of itself, it is home to a variety of creatures that hate the light and the living."

To be all inclusive in this account of our survey of Fantasy-based source material, it is interesting to note that the *Dungeons and Dragons* 'Ethereal Plane' also shares many points of commonality with the "Upside-Down" of *Stranger Things*—though perhaps without as many of the darker overtones. The description provided in the "*Manual of the Planes*" [published in 2001 for 3rd Edition] reads like something right off season one script pages for the TV-show:

> "It is a plane out of **phase**. It is a place of ghosts and monsters. It is right next to you, and you don't even see it. The Ethereal Plane is a misty, fog-bound dimension... The Material Plane itself is visible from the Ethereal Plane, but it appears muted and indistinct... as though viewing it through distorted and frosted glass..."

This "Otherworld" zone is never really officially defined by the scientists of Hawkins National Laboratory—although they acknowledge they opened up a "Gate" and that it was a mistake. The popular name erupts during the first season, when asked *where* "Will Byers" is, Eleven answers by flipping the game-board over so its backside is facing up and the designation is ever after: "*The Upside-Down.*"

"Mike Wheeler's" description of '*The Upside Down*' given in the "*Hunt for the Thessalhydra*" adventure book for the *Stranger Things D&D Starter Set*:

> "The Upside-Down is a kind of alternate dimension—an echo of the Material Plane (where we all live)... in some ways very similar to our world, but in others completely different. The Upside-Down is a cold, dark place. It's always night there, and the air is always cold (like just before a snow storm)... In places where our world and the Upside-Down touch each other, the Upside-Down looks like our world—the same buildings, trees, and other structures—but they're always broken and ruined. These are the places where you can cross between planes, if you know how... In places where the worlds don't touch, the Upside-Down looks like a haunted forest..."

According to background provided in Nadia Bailey's "*Stranger Things Field Guide*" (another unofficial fan guide), contact with "The Upside-Down" is **inadvertently** made during the experiments at Hawkins National Laboratory; specifically those involving Eleven's "remote viewing" of secret Russian intelligence conversations in November 1983. [Of course, some of the details on this shift in season four.] In reality, this type of work became an entire subset of the infamous *MK-Ultra* program, ironically called "*The Stargate Project*"—an exploration of the "potential for psychic phenomena in military and domestic intelligence applications." Although not officially launched until 1978 as a "*psychotronic*" (seeing and/or influencing people at a distance) research program of the U.S. Army in Fort Meade (Maryland), its development and applications were conceived of many years prior—again involving experiments conducted by the Stanford Research Institute in Menlo Park (California), the same location where Ken Kesey was introduced to LSD in *MK-Ultra* decades earlier.

As with most 'projects' of a similar nature, the official details of *Stargate* are obscure. In fact, the very origins for the experiments and the development of training protocols has been misplaced for half of a century. Even after government funding lifted and the mere existence of the project was declassified, those participating in pioneering the effort continue to mislead and misdirect about the details all the way up to present time. It seems strange that since the 1940's, hundred of millions of dollars would be spent on decades of various types of research, of which it is claimed that not a single one of these covert projects "officially" revealed any useful information or could be implemented in actual practice in any way. Undoubtedly, there are some individuals that would prefer to believe as such.

The "Stargate Project" is the subset of MK-Ultra that carries the greatest similarity to not only those events taking place at 'Hawkins Lab' on Stranger Things, but also the underground connections to prior Mardukite Org work, the Systemology Society and several streams of experimental research that we have explored over the years. None of our research is based strictly on the "Remote Viewing Training Program" pioneered for "Stargate Project" because we are well acquainted with the original sources. And although the nature of the 'project' is certainly in-line with the type of interests maintained by the "intelligence community," it would seem that government involvement and design of the program was initiated by individuals propositioning the C.I.A. for its funding—and not the other way around. And on paper, the CIA only funded the program for a few years in the 1970's before other "contractors" (including military) began to finance its continuance.

Among those individuals that consider themselves 'Elite', there is a long-standing tradition to hide the identity of sources in order to preserve their esoteric secrecy, in fulfillment with the "knowledge as power" motif. Some of the oldest 'occult' or hidden information regards what is known as "Cosmic History"—and it is not exclusively specific to this Universe. There is also data concerning the origins, design and original purposes behind the "Human Condition" and the reality that has been **engineered** for them here on Earth. Additionally, we find lore and teachings that pertain to achieving or actualizing higher states of Knowingness and Beingness then are currently outside the **realizations**, and therefore **parameters**, of the standard-issue Human—however innate these may be. An individual can only actualize to the point that they have realized, as demonstrated in Grade-III Systemology material.‡

Starting with the basic surface knowledge of the "Stargate Project":

---

‡ Referencing "The Tablets of Destiny Revelation" (Liber-One) and
"Crystal Clear (A Handbook for Seekers)" (Liber-2B). "Systemology:
The Original Thesis of Mardukite New Thought" (Liber-S1X) and
"The Power of Zu: Applying Mardukite Zuism and Systemology to
Everyday Life" (Liber-S1Z) are also recommended.

—the program for *"remote viewing"* was mainly led by Harold "Hal" Puthoff and Russell Targ, but which included, from its inception in 1972, Ingo Swann and Pat Price. Much of this, again, involved Stanford Research Institute (SRI) in Menlo Park (California). The team (which also included Cleve Backster of the CIA) developed what is publicly considered the first "Remote Viewing Training Program" in existence. A slow release of related information (and that of its original sources) over the decades is mainly responsible for the general public understanding of this new terminology, which is actually based on 'New Thought' applications of "remote **viewpoints**" that date from decades earlier.

Of course, the *"Stargate Project"* is not the first time that 'New Thought' methods have been usurped for sensitive projects or by the Intelligence Community without offering credit to their originators and sources; it is not even the only time. Let us consider Cleve Backster, once an interrogation specialist for the CIA and whose name shows up in connection to the *"Stargate Project."* Supposedly on a whim, in the late-1960's, Cleve Backster attached polygraph equipment to plants to demonstrate that they are receptive to emotion. This information was famously presented in *"The Secret Life of Plants,"* a book written by Peter Tompkins and Christopher Bird, published in 1973. Why would we expect this to be anything other than openly criticized when its true sources have also been tainted? And what are the true sources of this experiment and the methodology undertaken in the *"Stargate Project"*?

Without drawing conclusions, let us consider that *a decade prior* to Cleve Backster's "findings," another man did the same thing—demonstrating fluctuations in the "galvanic skin response" (**"GSR"** or *electrodermal*) of plants using a much more sensitive metering device than even the "polygraph," but similar in many respects.[*] This other man, worked with others on this project in a private greenhouse at St. Hill Manor in England and the results were presented to the public (and attending members of his organization) at an assembly (now known as the *"Theta Clear Congress"*) in Washington, D.C, July 1959. This man was *Lafayette R. Hubbard.*[†]

---

[*] Additional details regarding systemological applications for GSR-Meters may be found in the text: *"The Way of the Wizard: Utilitarian Systemology"* (*Liber-3E*) by Joshua Free.

[†] As stated in *"The Way of the Wizard"* (*Liber-3E*):—"Legal

In late 2017, a forum primarily for ex-Scientologists (*scientolipedi-a.org*) uploaded a three-part podcast series titled: "*Remote Viewing: The Scientology Connection*" as hosted by David LaCroix with his guest Robin Adair. While the theatrical nature of the podcast (still available on YouTube) is a bit lackluster, the actual details and points of fact explored are all verifiable—and for those who *do* actually understand scientological concepts, such as "exterioriz-at-ion," "remote viewpoints," "**anchor** points," "tone-40 on an object" and "theta clear," it should not be surprising that this caliber of "operating thetan" or "OT-level" work developed by *Hubbard* in the 1950's (and codified for his organization in the 1960's) constituted the definitive foundations of the "*Stargate Project.*"

If we assume for the moment that Cleve Backster had very little to do with the original "Remote Viewing Training Program" based heavily on regimens developed by *Hubbard*, it might seem we have very little case for making the connection. But, Backster was only mentioned here as an example—the one involving plants. His coincident connection to the '*Stargate Project*' seems almost trivial, by comparison, when we turn our attention to those who were actually involved in initially developing such a program directly for the Intelligence Community, starting as early as 1972.

The "OT" or "operating theten" levels are not a part of the "Bridge to Clear" and are instead administered after an individual has '*gone*' "Clear"—meaning after they have handled the problems of *this* lifetime *and* managed to either 'erase' or '**confront**' the considerations carried from *past* lives. Prior to being radically altered in the mid-1970's, the seven original "operating thetan" levels emphasized development of what would otherwise be considered '*psychic*' abilities and '*spiritual*' potential. It is probably no sheer coincidence that these levels were changed, as were any materials pertaining to them—such as we see with revisions to the book "*Scientology 0-8*," where the goals of the "OT" levels are no longer described in the section regarding "States Attained" after 1975. This

---

complications allegedly prohibit reference to '*Lafayette Hubbard*' by his more commonly recognizable name, which is apparently trademarked by "The Church" he established in 1953/1954. Usage of the name appears in the present text for educational purposes only and is not intended to infringe on any legal trademarks or the organizations that hold rights to them."

is all relevant because it specifically relates to the **experiential** background shared by those pioneering the "*Stargate Project*" independently of *Hubbard* and his "Church."

Ingo Douglas Swann (*1933-2013*) was once actually well known in the underground '*psychic*' community and is among the most famous innovators and participants in the "*Stargate Project.*" He demonstrated skills in both "remote viewing" (RV) and "telekinesis"/ "psychokinesis" (PK) and assisted in drafting the regimen for a training program. One of his better documented skills involved viewing planets, such as when he gave specific details about the planet Jupiter and its moons in 1973 that were not verified until the Voyager probe visit in 1979. This is interesting, because viewing planets in this wise is a part of the "exteriorization" exercises given in a book by *Lafayette R. Hubbard*, published in 1954, titled "*The Creation of Human Ability*" (originally "*The Auditor's Handbook*"). What's more interesting is that "*Advance*" magazines, published in the early 1970's by the Advanced Organization of *Hubbard's* Church, list *Ingo Swann* as an "OT-VII" (the highest officially released level of advanced work). There is even an interview in "*Advance*" magazine where he attributes the attainment of his '*psychic*' abilities to the work done in the organization.

If this is not convincing enough, let us consider the primary initiator for funding of the 'project'. Harold E. Puthoff (b. *1936*) has a professional background in naval intelligence and work for the "<u>N</u>o <u>S</u>uch <u>A</u>gency," &tc. and even a Ph.D in physics. We find Puthoff at the forefront of "remote viewing" experiments at Stanford Research Institute (SRI) and even going on to lecture about the (now-disclassified) 'project' thereafter—although there are still points of inaccuracy in his accounts, obviously to protect identities, sources and results from the 'project'. He does not openly acknowledge that origins for the research and his own abilities undoubtedly came from, again, involvement with techniques developed by *Hubbard*. This is apparent because by 1971, Puthoff is also listed as achieving "OT-VII" prior to alteration of the material.

Another Scientologist, Pat Price (d. *1975, questionable circumstances*) —"OT-III"—was also contracted for participation in the project. Reports of Price's success were discussed on the *scientolipedia.org* podcast and are mentioned in various forums throughout the internet. For example, in one experiment with Ingo Swann, the team was asked to "remote view" the inside of a house belonging to a particular NSA agent. Instead, they 'accidentally' remote located a classified NSA facility and were able to actually read parts of documents there, titles on folders and even the code-name for the installation. This immediately spawned interest in the realities of "metaphysical" ("occult") "warfare"—but specifically the state of 'national security' in the light of 'psychic ability'. Harold Puthoff comments in a lecture that the C.I.A. was more interested in the threat **assessment** of such activities far more than their practical implementation—and they weren't pleased that the 'project' *was* actually yielding any positive results.

In a different example, Pat Price conducted a "remote viewing" experiment with Russell Targ in 1974 that involved spying on, and determining the functional purpose of, a soviet base suspected of constructing atomic/nuclear warheads. Price was able to quite describe and draw a very specific type of eight-wheel gantry crane and other features of the base. Somehow he was able to determine that the activities were related to a "space program" and not nuclear war. Many years later, after the 'Cold War', satellite photography and in-person inspections proved that his findings were accurate. Of course, "officially," nothing of any use was learned or applied by anyone in the *"Stargate Project"* for over two decades of its existence.

H.P. LOVECRAFT & THE NECRONOMICON

While we have briefly considered metaphysical and psychological facets of the *Stranger Things* mythos in view of the facts surrounding *"80's"*-nostalgia, *Dungeons and Dragons*, psychedelic research, *Project MK-Ultra* and its subsequent *"Stargate Project,"* there is one additional theme to consider before progressing onward to the sections regarding the sciences and practical experimental research. While many are familiar with the fantasy-horror and gothic-style storytellers and media creators of the modern age, not everyone is as well acquainted with how the genre began and just how much influence it has maintained in the century since its origination in the early 1900's—and a man named *Howard Philip Lovecraft.*

H.P. Lovecraft resided in Brooklyn, New York, where he developed a new genre of fiction writing called "fantasy horror" (or "dark fantasy" to some folks), originally brought to the public via the

"*Weird Tales*" literary periodical. Lovecraft wrote fiction and although he touched upon some real philosophies and even created an entire cosmological and anthropological mythology, he claimed there was no real validity to any of his work. As far as we know, he was not a member of any secret society or practitioner of any magickal craft or tradition. He said he only wrote for money, which is ironic because he was quite poor his entire life—which is typical of many writers. Most of Lovecraft's literary following developed after his middle-aged death (from intestinal cancer). His legacy survived as the "*Cthulhu Mythos*," which other authors eventually contributed to.*

Most *Lovecraftian* literature is in short-story or novella form, usually collected and published as anthologies of related works. Each story contributes to his mythos, though they never directly imply this (except in the passage of a familiar name or idea). Characters and places change and new manifestations of Ancient Ones constantly appear—though much of it surrounds the town of *Arkham* and the cultists worshiping a primordial tentacled deity named *Cthulhu*. However, "*The Silver Key*" and its companion "*Through the Gates of the Silver Key*," both share a character—and the stories also allude to the *Gate to the Outside*, a prominent theme connected to the legendary and fabled grimoire: *The Necronomicon*.

The writings of H.P. Lovecraft prompted a new type of 'consciousness' for the mystical movement—one obviously enshrouded in the freedom gained in fiction compared to what less artistic and creative occultists would only 'dream' of attaining in their plethora of undertakings. It was alluding to something that many misunderstood—as was undoubtedly the intention of intelligences that prompted his visions. Lovecraftian stories describe a malignant force of "*Ancient Ones*" that at one time reign supreme in the **Cosmos** but are later defeated by a younger generation of "*Elder Gods*"—those claiming responsibility for the creation of humans and **systematization** of the inhabitable ("civilized") earth. At one juncture, the *Ancient Ones* are sealed away behind "*Gates*" by the *Elder Gods*—yet there are ceremonial cultists that continue to develop rituals and rites to summon the *Ancient Ones* back into our dim-

---

* Two paragraphs here are excerpted from the Mardukite Grade-I (Route-A) Master Edition anthology, "*The Great Magickal Arcanum*" by Joshua Free.

ension, or "level" of reality.[‡]

The lure of a *Cthulhu Cult*—or any similar "cult" following—is essentially the promise of a communion with the "*Other*." We all instinctively know it's "out" there—that *this* isn't *all* there is—even atheistic minds among you (preferring semantic taunts of science to religion) still remain amazed about how many **apparent** "levels" there are even in this physical "*Beta-Existence*," and most individuals are suspicious to the untold secret power that is sealed away within the Physical Universe, the "Other," the "Veils" between—and a perfect understanding of the same. That there was something significant taking place on Earth "before" the inception of our modern civilization remains beyond the scope of popular opinions, public consensus and adherence to false ego-centric worldviews.

In a cosmology of reality separated into "levels" of **fragmented** existence, the "*Gates*" so often referred to in our literature, represent the routes, avenues and bridges of **communication** and power "between the *Veils*." Beyond these *Veils*, all of "*Beta-Existence*" experiences its own **entangled** and unified nature with the "ALL." This is demonstrated in the "Standard Model of Systemology" and "*ZU-Line*." But, the true "wizard" does not **succumb** to an "illusion of power," falsely believing himself a superior being exclusively from pride, but instead realizes that it is the ability to communicate and facilitate communication with the "fabric of space" that causes manifestation—by powers from the "*God-Source*" or "I-AM" (which in Systemology is referred to as the actual "*Self*" or "**Alpha-Spirit**"). This is what has been concealed in the dark and "shadowy" side of the "occult"—for the more self-deluded that "magicians" and "dabblers" become in their own **conceptions** of enlightenment, the less likely they are to see the forest for the trees—and the deeper they are enslaved to their own systems. We are, perhaps, being too esoteric for the general reader. The next parts of the book will journey much further into metaphysical and spiritual systems pertaining to the science and systemology of reality and methods used toward developing the type of abilities demonstrat-

---

‡   Several paragraphs here are excerpted from "*Novem Portis: Necronomicon Revelations and the Nine Gates of the Kingdom of Shadows*" (*Liber-R+9*) by Joshua Free; also available in the complete Mardukite Grade-II Master Edition anthology, "*Necronomicon: The Complete Anunnaki Legacy.*"

ed by "Eleven" in *Stranger Things* as sought after by the "*Hawkin's Lab.*"

The questions of *sanity* and *reality* are two primary themes **prevalently** erupting in all of H.P. Lovecraft's work. According to Lovecraft's **existential** perceptions, arcane esoteric knowledge is very dangerous, especially when we factor in the fragmented human element, aspect or **condition**. So long as characters accept what they have been given as the "norm" of society (via social imprinting or "conditioning") there is no question of *sanity*—and reality is **one-to-one** with the consensus of the Realm. But what if this were not the case? What if things are only "real" from a matter of perspective—with a deeper truth veiling the way things are as an Absolute? Or, perhaps there are no absolutes—this would also be a very "maddening" realization as well: *things are only the way they are because that is how we see them.*

There are *forces* extant in the universe—active principles of "**Cosmic Law**" in perpetual motion. They are actually quite amoral—without mundane **morality**—and exist solely to feed the continued operation of "existence" as it is, or to feed it back to *entropy* and reduce the *order* to *chaos*. The material world is fashioned to function by necessity, systematically. The way in which this is subjectively perceived and interpreted has little to do with the fact that the systems of the "Physical Universe" must function, and continue to function, *with or without* our agreement. At least this is the way the nature of the "Physical Universe" has been impressed upon us. Of course, a systematically fractured universe requires a degree of intricacy to keep it in operation. Polarized forces seem set against each other to keep the appearance of a dualistic program active. But, they are opposite only in their outer natures—meaning, as they are perceived. In truth—they are the same—two sides of the same **degree**. That the human mind wishes to partition some aspects as "good" and others "bad" is simply an individual's own way from which to view the world—or else a "paradigm."

H. P. Lovecraft's "*Cthulhu Mythos*" is therefore not "reality" as it necessarily *is*, but a reality based on how some humans have interpreted their experiences. And Lovecraft's writings are certainly not a sufficient basis for traditions or religions—although they do exist in the underground. The *Mythos* simply offers us a glimpse of one man's fragmented experience of universal forces and how they relate to one another as a functional (or dysfunctional) system.

Quoting fantasy role-playing game developer, *Monte Cook*:—

> "These forces taken together are not the Cthulhu Mythos, however. They are simply reality, the way things are. The body of knowledge known as the Cthulhu Mythos is the result of human attempts to make sense of this reality. We interact with these forces in tentative ways, and come away with suspicions about their true nature. Like medieval physicians who believed that stomach aches were caused by a small imp lodged in the belly, we look into the night sky and think we know what's there. We're wrong, because we can never truly know the darkness."

From his own subjective perceptions, "Lovecraft's Universe" was essentially *bad*. Color this however poetically with "*black seas of infinity*" and other word pictures—essentially, from the viewpoint of humanity, bad things happen for no reason, or bad things happen causally from human actions (such as opening the mind to the knowledge of the *Necronomicon* or by opening some other Gateway to the 'Beyond'), but ultimately in the end—*bad things happen.*

Nihilism grows like a tumor on Lovecraft's psyche the further he delves into the nature of his visions for the sake of his readers—or, perhaps as a practice of self-healing or personal coping. His perspective is very clear though—celebration of the *Old Ones* is bad; celebration of the new religions is bad; pursuit of the spiritual is bad; materialistic hedonism is bad... and when you factor in all of the rest we might add to this, the end result is always the question: *why are we even here?!?* Given this sentiment, or any systematic **realization** of this, the very idea that Lovecraft's characters seek to use the *Necronomicon* to "live forever" or "bring discarnate beings back" to this wretched existence *is* clearly *insanity!!!*

Many esoteric mysteries beyond our understanding of "Cosmic Law" bare no readily discernible answers for a fractured human psyche—but, nonetheless the quest ensues, and humans are left to fight amongst themselves with multifaceted interpretations. The lure of H. P. Lovecraft's *Necronomicon* is: just one more moment of power; just one more incantation; just one more deciphered word —will grant the Seeker a key out of the system—the "*Key to the Outside.*" And this type of "gambler's **fallacy**" runs rampant in most "New Age" traditions.

Within the *Cthulhu Mythos*, Lovecraft's pantheon of gods appear to do little to soothe any human fear—and, in fact, they use it to their benefit—cloaking themselves in obscure anonymity until the "stars are right" for their return. Will they even return...? Did they ever truly leave...?

> "It seems that the evil legends about what they have offered to men, and what they wish in connection with the earth, are wholly the result of an ignorant misconception of **allegoric-al** speech—how totally we had misjudged and misinterpreted the purpose of the Outer Ones in maintaining their secret colony on this planet..." —*The Whisperer in Darkness*

H.P. Lovecraft once explained to his beneficiary, *August Derleth*—"I have something to say, but can't say it..." And it is at this moment that the horror really hits us, for we now know for certain that Lovecraft knows well more than he is letting on. We have experienced it before—because his prolific writings, as insightful as they might be, continue to only be written by the truth of Lovecraft's own experiences—veiled from the reader's casual experiences concerning the "stories" themselves. "The books you read are safe," we remember the bookseller telling Bastian in *The Neverending Story*—"*This* book is *not* for you."

But, originally, there are no efforts directly made to compile a "pantheon" or synthesis of his mythology, and H.P. Lovecraft never once used the phrase "*Cthulhu Mythos*" to refer to his own work. This term is actually later coined by *August Derleth*. Lovecraft acknowledges that his interpretation is a primitive understanding at best, shaped by the fears of men—part of the evolution in human understanding of what has been hidden—resting in the shadows of cultural mystery and occult esoterica for thousands of years.

For moral or religious purposes, and political justification, opposing forces are always demonized as monsters and "savage beasts"—lesser than or antithetical to whatever "we" are—that must be destroyed to further the superior advancement, or even just the material survival, of a more "civilized" race. Differing widely from historical viewpoints concerning **Mesopotamian** Anunnaki,[*] the

---

[*] See also "*Sumerian Religion: Introducing the Anunnaki Gods of Mesopotamian Neopaganism*" (*Liber-50*) by Joshua Free; also available in pocket-paperback as "*Anunnaki Gods: The Sumerian Religion*" or in the complete Mardukite Grade-II Master Edition oversized hardcover anthology, "*Necronomicon: The Complete*

Lovecraftian interpretation regards two distinct races of alien intelligence—"*Ancient Ones*" and "*Elder Gods.*" In a time before *men*, after what can only be described as a "primordial battle in heaven"—very similar to what is depicted in Babylonian cuneiform literature and the later Semitic scriptures derived from the same— the *Elder Gods* "seal" the *Ancient Ones* away and entrap their powers into a "*Gate*-system" that divides the material cosmos and creates hidden "spaces between spaces." In the end, the *Elder Gods* are 'allowed' to rule the local universe—the same figures that comprise the mythologies of our ancient ancestors, which have since faded from our Awareness, locked away in the deep recesses of our consciousness.

Anunnaki Legacy."

PART TWO

STRANGER
SCIENCE

:: PART TWO ::
—Stranger Science—

THE METAPHYSICS OF STRANGER THINGS

"Part One" of THE METAPHYSICS OF STRANGER THINGS introduced the more basic "on-the-surface" information, the visible tip
of the iceberg as it were; that which reflects the observable
themes, actions and shifts in social culture, its people, its places,
and **correlating** events taking place. In a certain sense, we might
treat the previous part as the most "physical" or "material" level
of our presentation of these subjects. On the outside, we might
consider the final part ("Part Three") that comes later, as a handling of the methodology specific to Systemology teachings and related "spiritual" techniques—and by "spiritual" we mean exercises
pertaining to the actual *Self* or "Alpha Spirit." These methods are
based on *"Willpower"* and acting from *"Self"* as 'cause'; they are *not*
reliant on any manner of 'religious' devotion, &tc.

We presently turn our attention to the type of experimental research and development that is at the forefront of consideration
for anyone considering the metaphysics and reality of the work at
"Hawkins Lab" on *Stranger Things*—specifically the type of abilities
that *"Eleven"* demonstrates. The data relayed here is precisely for a
reader or *Seeker's* consideration—and it pertains to our relay of the
subject at a "mental" (or "psychological" if you prefer) level of
treatment. "Part Two" concerns "thought"—and things to "think"
about and "know." This middle part of the book—on metascience
and philosophy—could just as accurately be titled: *"What Every
Hawkins National Lab Technician Should Know."*

PART ONE	PART TWO	PART THREE
"Stranger Research"	"Stranger Science"	"Stranger Systemology"
-Physical	-Thought	-Spiritual
-Material	-The Mind	-Alpha Spirit
-History	-Theory	-Practice
-Observa.	-Considera.	-Application

The word *"science"* denotes *Knowingness*—from the Latin *'scire'*, meaning *"know."* A *science* is a systematized paradigm. While *"Systemology"* could also fall under this category, it also encompasses an objective understanding of all fields of science and philosophy as a methodology for systematizing knowledge. Systemology is that which validates paradigms and effectively observes, calculates and **holistically** handles a higher level of understanding of any science...*systematically.* There are already ten books (as of Autumn 2022) that collectively support a more complete understanding of what specifically underlies our *Systemology.*‡

Each flavor of knowledge systematization—*philosophy, mysticism, material science, religion*—treats its own "level" of observation, calculation and understanding. Each is a compartmentalized view out into the world. Each is its own experience of the same phenomenon of a Physical Universe (*"Beta-Existence"*). Principle fundamentals of our Systemology—that which singularly and universally rings true—have all been considered *philosophy, mysticism, material science* and *religion* at one time or another across history.

As a holistic applied philosophy and intellectual pursuit, our *Systemology* does not 'exclude' that certain types of 'exclusionary' understanding exists—usually called *"fields"* of science, or *"schools"* of thought. Various individuals across the **Backtrack** of time and space have each applied their own semantics and social understanding to the phenomenon of *Life, Universes* and *Everything.* Most of the pursuits begin as broad sweeping pursuits and then later become more and more restricted by a particular direction of "tunnel-vision"—and thus we now see a host of specialties and subsets of every scientific pursuit that confine its focus to a particular facet of existence at a specific level of observation and understanding separate from the others. This **fragmentation** of knowledge—or else understanding—has contributed to keeping the true condition or "spiritual" state of an individual enshrouded in darkness; the standard-issue Human still consistently stumbling in the dark in pursuit of *Self* even here in the 21st century.

---

‡ *"The Way Into The Future"*; *"Systemology: The Original Thesis"*; *"The Power of Zu"*; *"The Tablets of Destiny Revelation"*; *"Crystal Clear (A Handbook for Seekers)"*; *"Metahuman Destinations (Volume One)"*; *"Metahuman Destinations (Volume Two)"*; *"Imaginomicon"*; *"The Way of the Wizard"* and *"Mardukite Systemology: Mardukite Master Course Academy Lectures (Volume Four)."*

In order to properly communicate the subjects at hand in this discourse, it is necessary to examine each part making up the total understanding available at this time. Of course, due to space restrictions and anticipating the attention span of the reader, this will be something of a **crash-course**. To achieve an appropriate instruction, we again draw from a pool containing 6,000 years of written accounts and esoteric experimentation. From inter-dimensional mysticism and spiritual abilities, to the handling of science, experimentation, quantum physics and handling the faculties of the Human Condition... there are many parallels between this collection of information in the broadest sense and its use as a catalyst toward a better understanding of, quite literally, THE METAPHYSICS OF STRANGER THINGS.

Newcomers to the higher **echelon** of knowledge contained within our *Systemology* may not recognize the full significance of these parts until are examined as a whole—and even then, perhaps, only after a period of intensive study and practice—and preferably in relation to other *Systemology* books available. Those who are not newcomers, who are quite **exponent** and adept at their ongoing *systemological* pursuits, may find some facets explored in this part of the book are something of a back-step when we simultaneously categorize this full scope of work as upper-level *Grade-VI* to *Grade-VII* material. Nonetheless, we are taking a middle route between the two extremes of reader (or *Seeker*) that is likely to happen upon this book. It is, however, specifically prepared for any reader (or *Seeker*) that is interested in experimenting with advanced applications of our *Systemology* and 'systematic processing' in a way that is representative of the "*Stargate Project*"—or else the subset of "*MK-Ultra*" depicted on *Stranger Things* with regards to 'Hawkins National Laboratory'.

METAPHYSICS AND THE CONTROL OF REALITY

Characters on the *Stranger Things* series are repeatedly confronted with circumstances that make them question *reality*. What's more, these characters frequently discover that these experiences are not easily *communicated* to others—particularly those that have not experienced the *strange things* for themselves. The question of *reality* is often accompanied by considerations about *sanity*. This is a prevalent theme in *sci-fi/fantasy horror*, one that is clearly evident in *Lovecraftian* writings—where an investigator or unsuspecting individual is confronted with such reality-shattering experiences that their sanity is threatened, quite often permanently. This is a critical component of *Lovecraftian*-styled "fantasy role-playing games" as well—such as "*Arkham Horror*" and "*Call of Cthulhu*"— where a player is not only keeping an eye on their physical damage, but also their mental health or sanity. Going *insane* can cause a player to lose the game (or play at a disadvantage in an ongoing campaign) just as significantly as being struck dead by a crafted weapon or demonic tentacle.

Humans like to believe that they have a pretty good 'handle' on *reality*—that they 'know what they know' about any particular aspect, and that knowledge is based on their own previously perceived "experience." They continue to validate things from within that knowledge and things continue to be real within that experience. That's "*reality*." That's what you perceive to be "*real*," meaning that your way of perceiving the world will continue to conform to your beliefs about the world. We consistently prove and validate our own "truths" to ourselves time and time again. Energetic currents—"metaphysical" in nature, if we wish to use this term—are what is behind all *things* and *Life*. This is what you experience at its most **condensed** states here in the "Physical Universe" (*Beta-Existence*) of solid forms. Therefore, until all personal filters are cleared in *Self-Honesty*, an individual cannot actually perceive things for what they really are. Semantics and **symbolism** serve as a substitute for true *Knowingness*.[*]

This whole question of what is "*real*" or "*not real*" is a philosophical concern, but the issue also enters the realm of "psychopolitics"— management of the state, control of an individual and, of course, mass control of the general population. The matter of "reality" is not specific to just the esoteric occult mysteries or fields of metaphysics. All of science, philosophy and religion are concerned with answering the very question of "*what is real?*" The word "reality" comes from an **Proto-Indo-European** (*PIE*) root "*reg,*" (as in "*regal,*" "*region,*" "*regular*") which relates to a "measuring device" or "ruler" (also as in a "*ruler*" or "*king*"). The word "*sane*" is related

---

[*] Two revised paragraphs here are excerpted from 'An Introduction to Anunnaki Bible Studies' as found in "*The Complete Anunnaki Bible*" (or its alternative edition release, "*Necronomicon: The Complete Anunnaki Bible*") by Joshua Free; also available in the complete Mardukite Grade-II Master Edition anthology, "*Necronomicon: The Complete Anunnaki Legacy.*"

to what is "clean" or "healthy" and functionally it was the purpose of the king or "ruler" of the "real world" or "realm" to set the boundaries of what is "real" and "not real"—and by this, "sanity" among the population might be judged. The conclusion: those who are in agreement or consensus with the realm are healthy and clean and those who are not are mentally ill or insane.

Psychopolitics plays a role not only in the secret projects of "Hawkins Lab," but also the tactics employed by the Russians, starting in the middle of the series. When we consider full legal implications of "reality and sanity," we find that the "insane" have no legal 'rights' and are not considered 'citizens'. How could they be when we consider just how many 'mental health' patients were unknowingly subjected to MK-Ultra experimentation (or one of its subsets) in the past century. An individual can be detained against their will in the name of 'mental health'. What's further, when one also takes into account just how easy it is to make a person either actually insane or to appear insane—via drugs, hypnogogic implants, torture, &tc.—the world-at-large can become a dangerous environment to exist in, existence for those refusing to be 'part of the system' or that do not 'conform', or worse, actually speak up and become activists or freedom-fighters against injustice. Consider when "Jim Hopper" is first captured and interrogated at Hawkins Lab, they give him drugs and dump him back on his own couch at home: just another junkie no one would believe. But to take this a step further: how easily it would be to take the bodies of the most brilliant minds and spirits on the planet and destroy their ability to play the Game here on Earth by surgically lobotomizing their machinery or short-circuiting its wiring with electric-shock!

Broadly speaking, "metaphysics" (literally, "beyond" or "above" physics) is a philosophical (and often spiritual) pursuit to determine and understand the 'truth' and nature of "reality." While conventional physics (as a material science) seeks to understand the "how" of "material things," metaphysics examines qualities of these same "things" with a greater emphasis on "why." It is concerned with that which is outside or exterior to 'Causal Law' of the Physical Universe; meaning that it considers what might be unobservably **perturbing** existence into being. Metaphysical philosophy, regardless of how it is applied, will not achieve the status of a "material science" any more than a true "psychology" did. Consciousness, as it is understood, is not empirically observable, nor are any of the other **thought-forms** or "higher" dimensions that might be 'measured' to calculate a material science.[‡]

In many regards, the realm of *Quantum Physics* has taken steps in the direction of peeling back the Physical Universe to better understand what is happening beneath the surface of standard-issue Human perception—though it required a rejection of its parent school, "quantum mechanics," in order to do so. Quantum mechanics still sought to fit the subatomic world into the same **clockwork** "Newtonian" paradigm that the "new science" was trying to rise above.

Metaphysics is also philosophically dangerous business for less obvious reasons. Methods toward true reasoning and true knowledge, as Descartes describes in his **epistemology**,[†] requires a complete annihilation of all previous experience-based reactivity and anecdotal knowledge stored as a substitute for true *Knowingness*. Facets of knowledge may be replaced in a personal **data-set**, one-by-one, but only after vigorous scrutiny and analytical reasoning. Since the whole of emotional reactivity and stimulus-response takes place at varying levels of '**unconsciousness**'—separate from one's conscious *Actualized Awareness*—then all of what is truly significant to an individual, where they are knowingly at 'cause' or playing the *Game*, takes place at the analytical levels of the *Mind-System* and not the reactive ones. Yet, beneath the surface of conscious *Awareness*, there is an entire host of reactive imprinting and response-mechanisms that just as equally affect an individual's experience of *reality*, if not more so.[*]

Plato suggests that what we see is real as far as we can perceive it, but even this data is probably just a shadow of something's "true nature." This famous *"Plato's Cave"* example is taught to every entry-level philosophy student. The short version is that a caveman watches the light of fire dance against the back wall of his cave. In this example, his vision and sensory perception is always fixed there on the back wall of the cave; this is the limits of his "whole reality" or parameter-range of **Awareness**. Three figures pass behind him—between him and the unseen fire. Their shadows are projected on the 'wall' of his *reality*. Although he can see a fac-

---

‡ Several revised paragraphs here are excerpted from the Mardukite Grade-I (Route-A) Master Edition anthology, *"The Great Magickal Arcanum"* by Joshua Free.

† See *"The Way of the Wizard"* (*Liber-3E*) by Joshua Free.

* See *"The Tablets of Destiny Revelation"* (*Liber-One*) by Joshua Free.

simile of the true nature of the figures' existence, hear them speak in his direction and even communicate verbally with *some thing*, when the caveman's attention is fixed as it is, the "whole reality" is still limited to this sub-par version of the truth. The shadows and impressions are all that is *real*—while the whole origination, source or cause, the true nature of the existence, remains in a relatively 'unseen' dimension. Even the true source of the firelight goes equally "unseen" in this model.

Metaphysics is generally not taught in the world of contemporary academia. Critical thinking and questions of *reality* are not what the traditional social educational system are concerned with. An individual isn't meant to question; they are expected to accept the facts as they are given and to memorize an unending string of vocabulary words, so carefully defined within the specific paradigm, that they do support the existence of a paradigm but provide very little other universal application. An individual is also not let in on, what is apparently a big secret holding the fabric of this Physical Universe together, that they are a participant in the creation and manifestation of *Life, Universes* and *Everything*. What we perceive, we are also **projecting**. In fact, we can not actually understand, behold or receive a communication about anything that we are not already able to create within our own "Personal Universe." Without such a context, the waves and colors and sounds and **sensations** would have absolutely no meaning or significance to experience. Even the physical "drugs"—which are apparently "**external** agents"—actually mimic and trigger **internal** manufacture of various **neurotransmitters** and other chemical processes within the body, which the body is actually prompted to do by being 'triggered' or 'reminded' to do so.

Although we speak of "*metaphysics,*" philosophers of the past have found it folly to completely disregard the idea of a tangible world of "objects out there." But this world or reality does not really "exist to you" until you have "internalized" a communication with its "forms" and brought it to an internal world of "thought" or consciousness. This apparent "dualism" between the "**external**" and "internal" has always been a problem to science (and "psychology") and thus remains in the domain of "philosophy." The interconnected relationship between mind and body—or the Mind-System and any external form in *Beta-Existence*—is metaphysical (or non-physical) in nature, and likewise concerns an *Alpha* quality of existence. Whatever we "perceive" of an "outer world" using the sensory faculties restricted to a body (or *genetic vehicle*), we cannot hold with absolute certainty that our experience consists of the entirety of what *reality is* on all levels of a systematic existence.

An individual can certainly **acknowledge** that "forms" exist as **conceptions** cohesive to "objects of matter." One might even consider that apparently solid (though deceptively not-solid, in actuality) "forms" are essentially a condensation of thought. But the considerations themselves are senior to (or of greater importance) to the mechanics or apparent qualities of "form" (as they pertain to our agreements about what *Is* concerning the Physical Universe/*Beta-Existence*). It would, however, be incorrect to assume that the perception held in the mind is equivalent to (*one-to-one*) with the totality of what *Is*, especially where we are relying on faulting **channels** of sensory communication between a body (*genetic vehicle*) and the *Self*. Certainly, we cannot assume that the totality of existence is taking place in the day-to-day *reality* experienced exclusively within the standard-issue range of the Human senses. There are obvious social difficulties when an individual even attempts to communicate their experiences outside the "norm" of what is generally understood commonly.

Throughout Cosmic History and (as a microcosm) the history of Earth, beings have maintained a "shared" *reality*, paradigm, worldview or *Universe* as their fellows—those located closely geographically and via personal **affinity**. Although certainly each of us is in possession of an individual *reality* we think of as *"real,"* the process by which *reality* is even considered (as a Human) is learned, imprinted and socially conditioned. Surely, the realm of light and sound, particles and waves, and energy and **vibration** composes the most fundamental aspects of reality as we can describe on paper. But for it to be a useful model or objectively real, an individual must be able to relay the semantic knowledge coherently to their 'neighbor'. This is why language and **syntax** become important if we are to call *"A for A"* and *"B for B"* and others will know of what we speak. And we have seen how critical this is concerning cultures and nations. The brain seems wired to process that "if *A* has the properties known of *A*, then it is associatively *A*."

To maintain holistic and systematic intellectual integrity: when we speak of "truth" and "reality" and "observers," we must specify what semantic "level" of truth and reality we are referring to. It is clear that it is "your reality" that you perceive, but who is the observer? Is "you" the "I" of your consciousness (awareness), the brain or the sensory cells on the outside of your body? Or is it your nerves, cells, atoms or subatomic particles? Each level has its own truth or potential understanding—its own reality and its own paradigm from which an entire practical system (or material science) can be drawn. When a fisherman casts a net, he is projecting a perception of what is "possible," which is determined by the concentration (or size of the gaps) of the netting. Different spacing will allow different sized fish (or other debris) to be trapped in the net. When the net is retrieved, it satisfies the expectations. A better example would be the idea of a "filter." Regardless of what you are filtering (air or water), the concentration or denseness of the filter-screen is going to determine what the filter traps and what is allowed to pass through.

The level of reality observed is determined by the Observer. As a basic illustrative example, consider the following **thought-experiment**: stop and write down every single idea and concept that the word "TREE" conjures in your mind. Surely, you will agree that "*trees*" exist, but what exactly do we imply in our personal beliefs and communications when we take such an existential statement for granted? Certainly one individual's concept of a "tree" and another's is going to differ. But, it is a basic word—a *noun* to label an object—and we simply assume that everything encompassing our conception of "tree" is the same as the other person's, when we communicate about "trees." For one individual, "tree" may be associated with 'life', 'nature', 'green', 'forests', 'animals', 'the earth' and so forth. But, for another, "tree" may simply mean 'wood', 'lumber', 'logging', 'property', &tc.

"Forms" and "energy-masses" are treated as "*terminals*" of communication in systematic **processing** techniques. Although it would be more accurate—at a certain level of understanding—to handle the *energetic* turbulence an individual carries with them as the "*energy*" that it is, it is just as therapeutic (in application) to handle the *forms* and *figures* themselves. By handling the emotional reactivity and mental-image-pictures associated with the **presence** of a *form* or *mass*, and treating it as a "*terminal*" of this Physical Universe (*Beta-Existence*), an individual is able to regain their own power of choice on handling the considerations and energy connected with the *terminal*. In this instance, the *considerations* or *postulates*, in themselves, handle the energy. And yet, when we take an individual that is not seasoned in handling energy and then use advanced energy-handling techniques in processing, there are less gains. Once an individual has increased their own personal and spiritual "horse-power" in the direction of **confronting** and handling on their own *Self-determinism*, then they can eventually be introduced to "energy-handling" and become quite proficient with it.

In our previous example, *"trees"* are a *"terminal"* of the Physical Universe. At some point, you socially learned the word "tree" for the English language. Instantly you then attached semantics (meaning) to the **mental-image** you formed in your mind to associate with what is "defined" with the word "tree." Using this label, you were able to mentally store an entire schema or data-set in your 'knowledge-banks' concerning your ongoing and cumulative experience with the terminal known as "tree." Simultaneously, you check this knowledge and experience against a socially established (or conditioned) norm or "baseline," most likely impressed by whatever culture you were educated in or spent your early developmental years. To the materialist that says a "tree is just a tree," there would be no reality on the idea that a tree could serve as a "doorway" to the *Upside Down*, such as we see in season one of *Stranger Things*. Such defies the social and scientific understanding that is *agreed* to in this civilization regarding communicating the qualities of this thing called "tree."

Regardless of what causes the "metaphysical *why*" or what "source" is behind the package of vibrations and sensory stimuli existing as "tree," you learn to recognize it as "tree" whenever consciousness encounters that specific assemblage of energies. The form of "tree" perceived with normative senses (of the standard-issue Human Condition) still reveals nothing about the underlying nature of "tree." An external reality can only be said to exist where your internal world of thought or Personal Universe "collides with" the external world of form that is agreed to as the **continuity** or baseline foundation of 'substance' in the Physical Universe. In this light, *reality* is a matter of *"Awareness"* and *"agreements."* And so it is.

PSYCHOLOGY AND CONTROL OF THE INDIVIDUAL

Once upon a time, the highest intellectuals of former cultures—the

Druids of the Celts, the Magi of Babylon and Persia, the Socratics and Pythagoreans of Greece, the Tahuti wizards of Egypt, and so on —all studied a singular and holistic understanding of the Physical Universe called *Natural Philosophy*. This included everything from physics and mathematics to sociology and biology—as we would understand them today. But they had not yet been compartmentalized and fragmented into singular paradigms. However, this *Natural Philosophy* went on to evolve into the various 'material sciences' still emerging today. Everything not visibly related to the Physical Universe and its 'forms' remained as "philosophy."

Then, during the 1800's, another split occurred—a "science of the mind" separated from its parenting school—though we now realize that "psychology" is a science of anything but the "Mind" proper, joining up with the neurosciences and departing heavily from its original purpose. Those who practice the type of experimentation alluded to (or blatantly depicted) on *Stranger Things* are only concerned with the most material (profitable or military) gains and ends regarding any application of "psychology." And yet, it is the field of science that best applies to these types of pursuits. "Dr. Brenner" and "Dr. Owens" undoubtedly carry an academic background in contemporary, clinical and/or abnormal psychology. In fact, Hawkins National Laboratory operates protocols that are quite comparable to any normal mental health facility (combined with the security considerations typical of a prison).

In many respects, given what "psychology" and "psychiatry" commonly means today, the terms no longer seem appropriate in describing many of the applications regarding "higher faculties" **capable** to an individual. Even if we did determine some (positive coefficient) relationship between various metaphysical (or spiritual) phenomenon and certain observable readings or measurements on scientific devices, we still cannot be certain of the true nature of these abilities and the source of their qualities when restricting our understanding exclusively and internally to the Physical Universe (*Beta-Existence*) as presented by material sciences and as determined or observed within the range of standard-issue Human sensory receptors and filtered perceptions.

Just because a particular part of the brain (such as the "*Sylvan Fissure*") might 'light up' with a physiological response when an Alpha Spirit (the individual "*Self*" or actual "I-AM") communicates an **intention** to the body from a point exterior to the Physical Uni verse, this does not mean that the true source of ability ultimately originates from the Mind-System or the brain. Does a car move simply because it is consuming fuel, or does it operate because an individual has engaged the transmission gears by consciously pressing down on the accelerator? The power of choice and the actions of the individual (which are a part of 'Game Theory') are not commonly considered as part of the 'material' equation. Yet without the operator, the machine does nothing automatically that is not already a part of its basic preset existence.

In the late 1990's, prior to establishment of Systemology semantics proper, the present author advocated for the same direction of work under the guise of "metapsychology." It seemed the most appropriate application of terminology at the time. Psychology no longer handled the "psyche" or "Self" and handled bodies instead. Parapsychology seemed to be a 'New Age' codification used by the ghost-busting demon-hunting UFO-chasing types—or is it the ghost-hunting demon-chasing UFO-busting types (I forget precisely how they classify themselves). This is not to poke fun at those who study and pursue knowledge of the 'Other'—but only regarding the semantics applied to distinguish or differentiate a 'label' for their paradigm. So, in the face of an extant 'psychology' and 'parapsychology', we originally adopted 'metapsychology'—just as we treat a distinction between 'physics' and 'metaphysics'.

Metapsychology is not really a new discipline, but a return to the philosophic roots of modern psychology, much of which has since been rejected in favor of "behaviorism" now dominating the realm of psychology. Dr. Timothy Leary once alluded to the idea that 'you have to go outside of your head to properly operate your mind'. But this is far too mystical of thinking for conventional psychologists who would rather determine the truth about humans by studying rats. —And isn't that just a wonderful outlook to have about the Human species. This is not, of course, the view shared by a small niche of humanists still out there; but there has been little effort in recent past to properly return the "psyche" to the field of psychology.*

As every "psychologist" working at Hawkins Lab would know, Wilhelm Wundt is generally agreed to as the "father" of their field.

---

* Several revised paragraphs here are excerpted from the Mardukite Grade-I (Route-A) Master Edition anthology, "The Great Magickal Arcanum" by Joshua Free.

Another individual, Edward Tichener, emphasized the structure of the mind in early 'European psychology', but when Tichener died in 1927, his "structuralism" collapsed under the weight of William James's 'American Behaviorism' (called "functionalism" at the time). This new "Darwinian" slant on psychology emphasized the mind only as far as it relayed to an external environment; meaning that which could be overtly observed. In other words: behaviors. Needless to say, this effectively limited the field of contemporary psychology to a physical science and not a mental one.

Though many problems existed for Sigmund Freud, both professionally and personally, even Carl Jung had to admire the man's emphasis on the psyche amidst a wave of behaviorism, and so he has remained a unique and recognizable name a century later. Freud argued for the existence of an "unconscious," which possessed all the thoughts, memories, desires and surface thoughts, but also more importantly, the "beneath-the-surface" consciousness that influences behavior. Freud founded the idea of "internal **conflicts**" being expressed at the mental level of existence as "psychological disturbances." While much of the emphasis on motivation of behavior was later placed on survival of the individual through sexuality, the originating conflicts and emotional experiences from birth also seem to play out cyclically later in life, following the pattern of a **recursive** spiral.

Psychologists like Carl Rodgers and Abraham Maslow (who codified the famous 'Maslow's Pyramid')[‡] had more optimistic views of human nature and eventually were known as "humanists." They acknowledged that the 'behaviorism' approach to psychology was quite dehumanizing and preoccupied with "animal reactions" and sexuality as motivation for behavior. Rather than treat humans as animals, 'Humanist Psychology' is the first subset of that science to promote beliefs in *"Self-Actualization,"* with an emphasis on motivations driven by free will, the power of choice, individuality of *Self* and **logical** reasoning. As such, there are many parallels between 'New Thought' and 'Humanism'. This is one of the only fields of psychology that directly assisted not only the development of Systemology, but also would represent necessary considerations for any type of personal metaphysical-ability programs developed at *Hawkins Lab* to either develop (initially) or restore (as in season four) the type of "powers" demonstrated by *Eleven*.

---

‡ See *"Crystal Clear"* (*Liber-2B*) by Joshua Free.

The *axioms* of metapsychology (or the 'New Thought') are actually not *new* at all. Most of the "spiritual", metapsychological and transpersonal (or motivational) gains of the past century are rooted in very ancient concepts—such as the '*Arcane Tablets*' explored (and Self-honestly exploited) in our Systemology.[†] Esoteric practitioners and mystics have made practical use of metapsychological and 'New Thought' concepts for thousands of years. From it, we have seen sporadic underground occurrences of "Wizards" using 'Hermetic Philosophy', 'Theosophy', 'Rosicrucianism' and the 'Law of the Mind' throughout history. Although the education and practice of these principles may be restricted or controlled—or at the very least not shared equally among the population prior to Systemology—that does not mean that little known sects, secret societies and other factions have not made use of this data for their own purposes covertly behind the curtains of what is visible in the Realm.

While the distinction between *magic* and *psionics* (at least in *Dungeons and Dragons* terms) is treated in the former section of this book ("Part One"), there are numerous times where characters in *Stranger Things* refer to *Eleven* as the "mage" of their 'real-life' adventure-party. In the game, this role might be played by "Will-the-Wise"—but he is mostly absent throughout the first season when *Eleven* joins the 'party'. Of course, by this time, the *Game* has gotten real, and the roles are played out by the characters as part of their everyday life during the ongoing battle against the "evil" that was unleashed, and continues to spread, from the *Upside Down*. In essence, *Eleven* is a "wizard"—and not just for their board-game—and it is probably by no coincidence that we examine this metaphysical lore from within the "wizard levels" of our own Systemology paradigm.

The "*Self-Actualized*" individual is a "Wizard" in comparison to the standard-issue Human Condition. Such a "Wizard" is often defined in mysticism and spirituality as one that has mastered some "metahuman characteristic" or demonstrated some outward expression and/or *reality* (at the very least to themselves) of being "more than human"—and thus fulfilling the humanist's promise that an actualized individual can "rise above" or "transcend" the *mundane*. To do so, esoterically speaking, is to be a 'Master' of the '*serpent*

---

† See "*The Tablets of Destiny Revealed*" (*Liber-One*) by Joshua Free.

knowledge' or '*dragon-mind*' that is alluded to in the old occult texts. The ultimate goal of any true *Self-Honest* "magickal work" is to open the avenues (or "*Gates*") by which routes of **Ascension** may be traveled. Within such texts, the sequence of these 'routes' is sometimes referred to as the 'Right Way' or the 'Pathway' or the 'Ladder of Lights' or some kind of 'Bridge'. Various secret societies and underground magical orders throughout the ages have often represented the same sequence of progression as 'levels' or '**degrees**' marked by 'Initiations' and **symbol**-specific ceremonial rites. Whether or not these groups actually delivered their initiates to promised destinations is beside the point.

> The basic tenet of metapsychology and 'New Thought' is: "*Energy flows where attention goes.*" This means that your focus of *Awareness* determines where your energy is connected or having its communicative exchange. While this seems incredibly basic and 'fluffy', the phenomenon of *telepathy* and *psychokinesis* are fundamentally dependent on its truth.

The average individual simply has too much internal 'noise' resonating from their environment and/or patterned thought to maintain the type of focus generally required for a consistent success of 'psychic phenomenon'. A **compulsive** or obsessive preoccupation with mundane worldly matters—money and sex, pleasure and pain—is going to keep your focus and energy restricted locally. Yet the truth is that the actual *Self* or "I-AM" (called the "Alpha Spirit" in Systemology) is an *Awareness* that is not located or fixed locally, except by consideration.

We frequently refer to a physical body as a '*Genetic Vehicle*' in Systemology, because the driver is not the car. The driver is a consciousness or *Awareness* that is above and beyond the existence of the car; they are having an experience of operating the car on a road. If you take away the road and the car, there is still a driver—the individual remains and is not dependent on the existence of anything else for its own *Beingness*. Such is the analogy by which we can not only understand the metaphysics of *Life*, but also the unlimited potential or ability that is capable to an individual that has actually mastered their own *Self-determinism* of postulates and consideration.

THE SYSTEMOLOGY OF CONTROL

Control is a basic property of 'order' and 'creation'. In fact, the fundamental *Game* of actualized *Alpha Spirits* is an ability to create and un-create at *Will*. At each turn of the *Pathway* for Systemology we find increasing personal realization of abilities—and along with it, the education regarding applications of *Games* and *Systems* toward management of our *beta-existence*, which is also to say our environment—the Physical Universe. Every step of the way we are working **successively** toward *Actualization* (a total *Awareness*) of the *Alpha Spirit* as "I" and *Self*. All of these aspects, conditions—and even the very *Processing* and exercises themselves—point toward one centralized theme: CONTROL.*

It is not altogether surprising that a civilization so *fragmented* on the concept of "control" should produce populations (of standard-issue Humans) that maintain an exceptionally low level—or *no* level—of "*Self-control*." The factors of "control" are actually quite necessary to carry out operations toward whatever we might *do*, *think* or *be*, and have them be *Self-determined*. Reactive-responses and **inhibitions** concerning "control" are most likely the result of experiences regarding improper handling and management of "control"—both *toward* you and *by* you.

The very idea of "control" is likely to spark emotional reactivity and illuminate fixed considerations. This should be "processed-out"—meaning that the emotional and analytical "**charges**" are reduced or discharged via 'systematic processing'. The 'systematic processing' methodology presented in "***Crystal Clear: Handbook For Seekers***" (*Liber-2B*) and referred to as "ROUTE-2" may be used to "**process-out**" any personal 'stores' entangled with a particular concept or terminal. Similarly, the 'systematic processing' formula provided in a forthcoming section ("Part Three") concerning considerations for "*psychokinesis*" (PK) may be used to **defragment** postulates and considerations regarding any former agreement with the Physical Universe (*Beta-Existence*). And such exercises require a certain handling of "control" to even be effective.

---

* Two revised paragraphs here are excerpted from "*Crystal Clear: Handbook For Seekers*" (*Liber-2B*) by Joshua Free; also available in the complete Mardukite Grade-III Master Edition anthology, "*The Systemology Handbook.*"

Systemology observes a functional difference between the kind of obsessive, automatic and unknowingness elements that are contained in "bad control" versus the knowingly *Self-directed* communication of control and **command**. The kind of "obsessive control" so rampant in the world is actually brought about by failure to control. This is why only "bad control" is generally exercised in civilization—and why the population eventually takes on an allergy or aversion to handling and confronting control in any way. It becomes a "bad" *word.* Of course, as a result, you yield a population incapable of *Self-directing* proper control of themselves—and by that we mean control and command of the body ('*genetic vehicle'*) and the Mind-System *as* "Self"; because these other systems are not *Self*, in spite of the over-identification that takes place in the course of one's *Life-Track.*

The inability to properly manage, handle and exercise control is what causes an individual (or family or group, *&tc.*) to 'press harder' in the direction of control. This ultimately becomes a sort of 'enforced control'—and this is what we see with the authoritarian-totalitarianism and fascist states and so forth. Systematic Processing methods (including 'ability enhancing' exercises) are maintained under the control of a *Pilot*, but this is done properly and only toward the ends that a *Seeker* or *subject*, themselves, is progressively developing a proper systematic control and command of the Mind-Body connection *by practical demonstration.*

Proper application of 'Systematic Processing' is towards "freeing up" an individual's 'power of choice' over their postulates and considerations (**Alpha Thought**) on a **gradient** incline or scale of ascent—hence the Systemology *"Grades."* Exercising personal abilities to the extent of *psychokinesis* (PK) and *telepathy* (RV or *psi*) very much requires a *Seeker* to observe full control and command as the 'actual' *Self* at the observer-viewpoint or cause-point. This means operating *exterior* to locality considerations for this *Beta-Existence.*

An individual that has difficulty maintaining true fluidity of—or an ability to freely change—their postulates and considerations will undoubtedly be facing many additional challenges with regard to 'higher-level' work. As a precursor to what you will find contained in the present book, materials comprising *Grade-III* (*Mardukite Systemology*) and *Grade-IV* (*Metahuman Systemology*) illustrate the basic *"Beta-defragmentation"* procedures/processes. Very often an individual has fragmented or entangled their '*Beta-Awareness*' with that of the Physical Universe and the periods or events that we consider "stuck" points are, in fact, times when an individual could not handle and/or confront the lack of control in a situation. In most cases, this is when an individual *failed* to "stop" something from happening. As a result: fragmentation and fixedness of related considerations and their association with other data.

Awareness and **attention** essentially is, or rather directs, a particular pattern or "*flow*" of energy. These "flows" are communications along 'conduits' or '**circuits**' between 'terminals'—operating very much in the manner that we might describe electricity or even a running current of water. Notice that when we begin to deal with communication of control using words like 'conduit' and 'circuit' and 'current' and 'catalyst', we are treating existence in its energetic terms. In advanced systemology applications, the same is treated as "beams." As such, we also know that a "flow" mainly operates in one of two directions: *in* and *out*. In *Systemology Grade-IV Professional Pilot Training*,[√] the communication flows monitored on circuits to terminals (for any person, place or object) in "ROUTE-3" systematic processing, include:

Circuit-1 : Self *to* others/terminal (*out-flow*)

Circuit-2 : others/terminal *to* Self (*in-flow*)

Circuit-3 : others/terminal *to* others/terminal (*cross-flow*)

Circuit-0 : Self *to* Self (*Alpha-flow* or *Alpha-Thought/* "postulate")

Ability to command attention is probably one of the more commonly ascribed traits or characteristics to those who are considered successful or charismatic or confident... or dare we say it, "powerful." To what else are we basing our considerations for comparison of such traits if not for the "ability to command attention"? Here then we discover an important key to the success of controlled communication—which is to say, the "*systematic processing session,*" or else the protocols for techniques of our brand of applied philosophy. Additional details and basics for structuring a "systematic processing session" may be found throughout former Systemology materials, such as "*Crystal Clear (Handbook For*

[√] See the "*Metahuman Destinations*" volumes by Joshua Free for the original Grade-IV '2020 Professional Piloting Course'; also available in the complete Grade-IV anthology, "*The Metahuman Systemology Handbook.*"

Seekers)," the "***Metahuman Destinations***" volumes and "***Imaginomi-con.***"[*]

Although methods of Self-processing are frequently used by *Seekers* in Systemology,[‡] a majority of the work conducted by the Systemology Society (upper-levels of the Mardukite Academy) is "piloted." This means the "systematic processing session" is operated and *controlled* by a trained Mardukite or Systemology "Pilot." The *Pilot* is responsible for the control of a *Seeker* in 'systematic processing' in much the same way that a *subject* in similar applications and experiments might be controlled. This is a 'systematic control' that is handled with specialized protocols that a *Pilot* learns to handle; this is not 'bad control'.

Control is necessary to conduct a *proper* "session." Whether "*piloted*" or "*solo*," a session must be *controlled*; and the operator (*Seeker*) must be under *proper* control, their own or otherwise, but controlled. It is a lot to ask, given the current state of the Human Condition, for a *Pilot* to say, "we will now begin the session" and suddenly everything outside the session goes out of view and the *Seeker* is "present right there with full attention" (which we call "***presence***" in Systemology). Of course, a proper command of the communication line with clear intention would make this possible —and in some respects is a goal for high-horsepower processing— and yet we are not restricting the potential of our methodology to only cases that have already assumed the state of **Homo Novus**.

"Low-Level Systematic Control" is of greater interest to a *Pilot* processing a random individual off the street, or even a physician interested in rigorously intensive mental science experimentation, but not necessarily a *Seeker* that is actively interested and willingly studying Systemology. Such an individual usually carries enough *Actualized Awareness* to want to "see themselves through" to higher points of *Beingness*. The entire idea of "pushing" the "secret realizations" of Systemology (the personal discoveries intended behind transmission of the exercises given throughout the various books) or even "forcing" processing on someone that does not want to

---

[*] Several revised paragraphs here are excerpted from the Systemology Grade-IV *Liber-2C+2D*, "*Metahuman Destinations (Volume One: Communication, Control and Command)*" by Joshua Free; also available in the complete Grade-IV anthology, "*The Metahuman Systemology Handbook.*"

[‡] See "*Crystal Clear*" (*Liber-2B*) and "*Imaginomicon*" (*Liber-3D*).

provide their *presence* to the session is too **counter-productive** for our intentions. But a communication of proper control is necessary for effectively undertaking any of the '*processing*' or applications suggested in this book (and elsewhere throughout Systemology literature).

However, to give one of our textbook examples: an individual who cannot at first follow the command to pick up a "**bell, book or candle**,"† might be able to mimic an action. You say, "watch what my hand does, okay?" and they should respond in some way—even with a facial twinge. Then you pick up a [*bell*] and ask them, "did you see that?" and if you had their attention before—if you had enough intention on the line for them to look—they will indicate a response. You can experiment with—and perhaps actualize a few realizations on your own—by trying the most socially recognized example of mimicry out in the world laboratory: "waving your hand" simply with an intention of communicating "*Hello!*" See what happens with others.

A *Seeker* is systematically processed (using techniques and exercises) toward a greater certainty of *Self-determinism*. This is a critical component of the development and/or rehabilitation of innate 'spiritual abilities' (or however an individual might label these faculties of the '*Alpha Spirit*'), such as what is encouraged in Dr. Brenner's work at *Hawkins Lab* and is clearly evident by *Eleven*'s experiences with him throughout the *Stranger Things* series. But in regards to the standard-issue (fragmented) Human Condition, even the most basic actions and communications are not carried out deliberately or by true freedom of choice; they are instead the product of imprinted, socially installed, automaticities (response-mechanisms) and learned tendencies.

Control may be (and should be) executed by postulate rather than handling of energy as it pertains to the Physical Universe; postulates (*Alpha Thought*) are senior to energy and can even create energy (contrary to supposed 'laws of conservation'). Often, it is the use of energy and effort at the continuity-level of the Physical Universe that can get one stuck. In fact, there is an energetic mechanism at play where one develops a relationship with—or rather, 'be-

---

† The "*Bell, Book & Candle Systematic Procedure*" is described in Systemology Grade-IV "*Metahuman Destinations*" volumes by Joshua Free; also available in the complete Grade-IV anthology, "*The Metahuman Systemology Handbook.*"

comes'—that which one had failed to control. To some degree, *Awareness* (attention) fixedly snaps-in on, or *"interiorizes"* into, what is not being controlled, or more accurately, what one had *failed* to control. This is where we find a "problem" generated as an energetic-mass when an individual *must* "control" but is *unable* to. These pre-programmed (*implanted* imprints) **personality** logic circuits of "must but can't" and "enforcement but denial" are what can really 'spin-in' an individual into low-level considerations and agreements about the Physical Universe and therefore reality.

The type of loyalty imprinting discovered with prisoners, detainees and other subjects in various case studies reveals that overt/empirical enforced social control is not always a matter of blatant violence or painful coercion. There are many techniques employed 'out in the open' every day that are social communications aimed at manipulating, altering or negating an individual's considerations, reality-agreements and/or beliefs. When we take the ideas behind "psychopolitics" into consideration, it is not difficult to observe how the "masses" (meaning large populations) are controlled by the same type of 'selective directed attention' worked with in 'systematic processing'. In the world-at-large, however, there is an increased tendency toward using this knowledge for furthering "enslavement" of an individual's 'consciousness', rather than its liberation. All of the fear-based hypnosis, targeted advertising and lobbying by shareholders with **invested** capital interests, specialized use of harmonics and frequency in audio medias, visual cues and trigger phrases littered throughout our society is really just waiting to catch each individual with their *Awareness* down around their ankles.

A "snap-in" *"interiorization"* effect—regarding control of the mind-body connection and the ability to confront *Life* as it actually is—precludes the *Seeker's* ability to be knowingly and willingly apart from, for example, a "body." This fixation on *having* to *have* a "body" or to be restricted to its viewpoints (**point-of-view**, &tc.) is an emphasis of defragmentation at the 'wizard-levels' of Systemology, such as we introduced for "*Imaginomicon*" (*Liber-3D*) in 2021.

The whole issue stems from the obsessive need that ensues toward controlling a body that has not been under proper control of *Self*. This area of 'systematic processing' will also be an emphasis for our present purposes in a later section of this book ("Part Three") in order to render this relay of teachings, exercises and techniques more effective for any reader-*Seeker* studying this book independent of additional supplemental instruction.

THE SYSTEMOLOGY OF INTERROGATION

In the Mardukite Org, Mardukite Academy and/or Systemology Society, a *Pilot* or staff member makes quite a business of understanding the systemology of communication and interrogation, even if just for conducting interviews and basic processing. In essence, the steps for conducting a 'session' of systematic techniques and exercises (otherwise referred to as 'processing') are drawn from the same basic communication formula as the interview/interrogation knowledge and skill-set referred to in this section.*

Here we could supply a very long list of skills that are beneficial for a *Pilot* or *interrogator* to have and/or to develop for effectively managing "sessions." Such a list would not necessarily prove very valuable by itself, particularly concerning "how to be a good interrogator." Experience has shown that these skills are best learned via demonstration and intensive practice, rather than book learning. However, for our present purposes, we will consider that there are at least a few 'critical skills' or 'preferred traits' that we might systematically **assess** for any professional pilot, interrogator, case-handler, staff-member, publication officer, minister, counselor, &tc. with regards to our own Organization and paradigm. These include:

- a practical understanding of the mind, body and spirit
- functional experience with systemological techniques
- an increased awareness (beta-awareness)
- personal defragmentation (calm, patient, flexible)
- personal integrity (**ethics** checkout)
- personal manners (etiquette)
- handling of interpersonal communication and control
- emotional integrity (composed without display)
- ability to 'read' an individual ('silent communication')

---

* All of which are minimally prerequisite for a *Class-6 Systemology Pilot* (a forthcoming gradient tier of professional application—pertaining to *Grade-VI/VII*—not yet in operation).

'Effective communication' *is* 'effective communication.' Very little difference exists between the structure of a session (and its handling) for a *Seeker* to improve in personal/spiritual ability versus one that interrogates for purposes of accessing a 'confession' or some other piece of desired data. In terms of "*Personal Integrity Processing*" and "*Ethics Processing*," a distinctive contrast between the two types can quickly fade to gray.† Any differences are related specifically to the purpose or goal in mind. The same aspects used for an effective 'systematic processing session' may be applied across the boards for other purposes—and actually have innumerable times in the past.

The very fact is that the formulas and training spread across Systemology literature can be (and have been) used to hinder and fragment the population, just as we use it to undo the same. By keeping the data hidden, it is more easily weaponized. The type of information accessible via a complete study of Systemology is only dangerous *if* it remains in the possession of a small minority. As such, there are four main types of interrogation for which the 'Systemology of Communication' is theoretically applicable for:

—interrogation for systematic processing
—interrogation for research purposes
—interrogation for counterintelligence
—interrogation for matters of state (policing)

Even at a more intensive security level, such as depicted on *Stranger Things* and the high-power faction of secret government operating at *Hawkins Lab*, the matter of 'detention' (arresting and detaining) and 'illegal interrogation' are critical factors to consider. Even among voluntary subjects of intensive experimental research for extensive periods of time, there are matters (and costs) associated with 'room and board' to attend to. For matters of personal development, 'isolation' is frequently employed, such as we see with hermitages and monastical retreats; and for interrogative purposes, 'isolation' serves to establish that an *interrogatee* has no external lines of communication for support or salvation. Likewise, for this purpose and to prevent interruptions, no phone should be present in an *interrogation* room.

"Game Theory" may be applied to interrogation efforts, but is dependent on whether we are treating the case of a *Seeker* willingly

---

† See "*The Way of the Wizard*" (*Liber-3E*) by Joshua Free.

participating in a 'systematic processing session', or handling a *subject* as a counterintelligence '*interrogatee*' that is operating with totally different "goals" than the *interrogator*. In the first instance, we have a mostly 'cooperative game', even if a *Seeker* is initially maintaining **hold-outs** from the *Pilot*. But, in the second scenario, there is a greater need for attention on "control" handling. A *Pilot* is trained to simultaneously observe a Seeker while keeping a written record of the session; however, for counterintelligence interrogations, a session should be recorded on video to alleviate an interrogator the necessity of keeping notes. Of course, one of the first conditions in any case is to have a *Seeker* (or *subject*) actually '*present*' in order to have a session (*game*) at all.

Locating/**acknowledging** the *Seeker* as an individual—by name—is the first step of communication to 'open' (or 'start') a session. No matter what the nature of the session/interrogation, the *Pilot* or *interrogator* must treat the *subject* as an '**identity**' and not a piece of 'matter'; there is no gain in objectifying or dehumanizing (but this should not include befriending or emotionally connecting with a counterintelligence subject). Attention given to a *Seeker* or *subject* should include silent assessment of their emotional state (for example, on the '*Beta Awareness Scale*'[‡]). It is helpful if a *Pilot* or *interrogator* has had supplemental study (and experience) involving identifying personality patterns that may be useful in determining a particular 'approach' to the session (the nature of the session). Various types of '*pre-screening*' (assessment) may be conducted by other less experienced staff-members (*interviewers, &tc.*) prior to a formal session (or in between multiple sessions) with an *interrogator* or *Pilot*.

As relayed in the "KUBARK Counterintelligence Interrogation Manual" (CIA-C01297486, July 1963, Approved For Release 2014/02/25):—

> "Once questioning starts, the interrogator is called upon to function at two levels. He is trying to do two seemingly contradictory things at once: achieve rapport with the subject but remain an essentially detached observer. Or he may project himself to the resistant interrogatee as powerful and ominous [...] while remaining wholly uncommitted at the deeper level, noting the significance of the subject's react-

---

‡　See "*Crystal Clear: Handbook For Seekers*" (*Liber-2B*) by Joshua Free.

ions and the effectiveness of his own performance. Poor interrogators often confuse this bi-level functioning with role-playing. The interrogator who merely pretends, in his surface performance, to feel a given emotion or to hold a given attitude toward the source is likely to be unconvincing; the source quickly senses the deception. Even children are very quick to feel this kind of pretense. To be persuasive, the **sympathy** or anger must be genuine;[*] but to be useful, it must not interfere with the deeper level of precise, unaffected observation. Bi-level functioning is not difficult or even unusual; most people act at times as both performer and observer unless their emotions are so deeply involved in the situation that the critical faculty disintegrates. The interrogator who finds that he has become emotionally involved and is no longer capable of unimpaired objectivity should report the facts so that a substitution can be made. Not the reaction but a failure to report it would be evidence of a lack of professionalism."

The best approaches are for an interrogator to take the mind set of "How can I get them to *want to* tell me what they know?" rather than "How can I *force* them to talk (tell me what they know)?" Non-coercive interrogation is meant to generate and build up (and eventually relieve) internal pressure in the interrogatee, whereas the traditional "Hollywood" style of coercive interrogation is intended for an interrogatee to buckle under external pressure. The non-coercive approach requires much more skill, such as we would minimally expect of a *Class 3E Systemology Pilot* that has professionally completed Grade-IV. One factor established in a 'systematic processing session' that may not be the case in other forms of interrogation is that a *Seeker* is secure knowing that information disclosed will not be used against them. A **willingness** to communicate with the *Pilot* is critical for success.

Non-coercive methods are technically and systematically more manipulative—but they also lack in generating the fragmentary imprinting that takes place via pain and unconsciousness.[‡] For example, an individual might be "tricked" into believing that more is known about a situation (or themselves) than actually is. A common tactic is to throw a thick file onto the table with the subject's

---

[*] See 'Unit Five' in *"Crystal Clear"* (*Liber-2B*) by Joshua Free.
[‡] See *"The Tablets of Destiny Revelation"* (*Liber-One*) by Joshua Free.

name across the front of it. This can be effective even when the file actually contains little more than a stack of blank paper. If there is more than one individual involved, they should be interrogated separately. The suspicious tactic of saying that "your buddy confessed" or "pointed the finger at you" is likely to be useless, but it can be more believable if there is a way of showing a recording (even if it is edited) that would indicate the same. [Although the Mardukite Org and Systemology Society do not employ these methods internally, the matter of their effectiveness is studied.]

An ability to measure shifts or gauge changes in **"biofeedback** responses" may also be of beneficial use to an interrogator. The 'Systemology of GSR-Meters' (meaning "Galvanic Skin Response" devices or *Electrodermal Metering*) is introduced in the Grade-IV text *"The Way of the Wizard: Utilitarian Systemology-A New Metahuman Ethic"* (*Liber-3E*).$^{\sqrt{}}$ Dozens of pages of training material need not be repeated here. The book also relays an interesting history of 'GSR-Meter' use for 'therapeutic' purposes that extends back to the days of Carl Jung and his 'word association' experiments.

By the 1930's, the field of criminology began utilizing a "GSR-Meter" for the main component of what is otherwise better known as a *"polygraph"* machine. The standard "polygraph" (referred to somewhat inaccurately as a 'lie detector') also measures heart-rate, temperature, blood-pressure and respiration (breathing)—whereas the *GSR-Biofeedback* device measures changes in electrical resistance across the surface of the skin. The "GSR-Meter" is the most important and sensitive component of the complete apparatus, whereas good visual observation (of a *Seeker* or *subject*) can override the necessity for measuring other factors.

It is advantageous for an upper-level Systemology *Pilot*—or an *interrogator*—to make use of a *GSR-Meter*. There is a long-standing tradition of using such meters to conduct 'security checks' among personnel of sensitive organizations. Most 'intelligence companies' require GSR-metered interviews for employment applicants. Such screening would have been likely for any staff-members at *Hawkins National Laboratory*—which would have likely also conducted follow-up interviews with its employees at regular intervals.

Expert use of GSR-technology renders interrogation possible on a

---

$\sqrt{}$ Also available in the complete Grade-IV anthology *"The Metahuman Systemology Handbook"* by Joshua Free.

subject that cannot or will not speak. The sensors ('electrodes', usually metal cans) may be held, but they can also be strapped to a subject's feet, &tc.—so long as good consistent skin contact is made. A baseline can be established by asking neutral questions (about the weather, food, nothing of particular significance to the interrogation)—of course expecting no vocal response by the subject. It may be necessary to realign the individual's attention with neutral questions periodically in the case of increased irritability or when an individual seems to be 'running down'. The purpose behind this is very similar to why a *Pilot* will periodically break from subjective techniques and instruct a *Seeker* to perform **objective** exercises during a single 'systematic processing session'.

A typical "no" or "don't know" type of answer will not cause a drop in resistance (measured on the meter in *Ohms*). A twitch of the needle or small drop can indicate a "maybe" or that the questioning is 'getting warmer' so to speak. Generally, when the correct answer is reached (or the answer *is* "yes") a large fall will register on the meter. When listing out various possible answers, the *Pilot* or *interrogator* is looking for the biggest 'read' on the meter. Questions may be directed to determine clues and then this data may be used to question them with a list of likely possibilities. Generalities can be used to guide the questioning. *Do they live in the Western half of the country? Central part?... Do they live in Colorado? Kansas? Oklahoma?... Does their name start with a letter in the first half of the alphabet?... Was it A? B? C?...*

Much like 'systematic processing', the use of a *GSR-Meter* for interrogation requires as much skill with the meter as it does the ability to select and communicate the right questions while simultaneously holding the individual's attention and presence in the session. After an individual's attention has been steered to 'contact' an event, location or person in 'mind', try to work 'present-time' into the question format: *"Does"* or *"Is"* rather than *"Did"* or *"Was."* Given what we have discovered in '*Systemology Grade-V*' about the *"Backtrack"* (a continuation of the **spiritual timeline** as experienced by an individual Alpha-Spirit), questions must be specifically worded to pertain to *this* lifetime. 'Timing' is a critical component of how memory is stored from this lifetime and past lifetimes (on Earth or elsewhere). Rather than asking the subject if they *"have ever"* done something, a parameter should be inserted into the question, such as *"in the past so-and-so years."* As with many aspects of both Systemology and the types of information presented in this book, only practice and experience will make it real for you.

THE NEW AGE 'ASTRAL PROJECTION' CONNECTION

An increase in public attention on "remote viewing" (RV) spiked following a declassification of the *Stargate Project* in the 1990's and official approval to release many of the less-sensitive C.I.A. documents related to the same—including those involving experiments at Stanford Research Institute (SRI)—in the early 2000's. While the pointed experimental use of directed non-local *Awareness* of *Self* may be a more recent development, along with the terminology surrounding "remote viewing," the efforts were not a 'shot in the dark'. They reflected a curiosity regarding phenomenon that has been with us, a part of our *Beingness*, since the beginning of time. The 'New Thought' movements of the early and mid 1900's—and even the 'Magical Orders' of the mid and late 1800's—were reviving a very ancient and esoteric interest in the metahuman aspects of the Human Condition that included unlimited potentials of the 'Spirit'.

Although the *Dungeons and Dragons* conception of an "Astral Sea" is treated in a former section ("Part One"), this does not necessarily reflect the spiritual and mystical lore of an "astral plane" extant in New Age teachings, traditions and techniques. And while we might be systematically technical in saying that the *Stargate Project* type of "remote viewing" is developed and applied differently (and usually) for different purposes than "astral projection," the two phenomenon share many qualities and are undoubtedly related in many respects. It may even be difficult to draw the lines between the experience of one from the other as suggested in *Stranger Things* with the numerous occasions when *Eleven* puts on a blindfold and pierces the veil of what many would consider the "astral."

The 20th century witnessed a publication of countless books, training materials and lecture-workshops emphasizing ideas regarding "astral projection" and "mental travel." Although these 'New Age' concepts and practices are traditionally integrated with intensive spiritual traditions and mystical lifestyles, it has been demonstrated many times over that these abilities are simply inherent, innate, or otherwise natural state, qualities of all individual 'Alpha-Spirits' (the actual *Self* as an *Awareness* or "I-AM").

Practice of "remote viewing" and other phenomenon (such as "astral projection") is not restricted to an adherence to a specific mystical, spiritual or religious paradigm. The reason they tend to go hand-in-hand is that contrary to exclusion of the 'spiritual component' in paradigms of material science, the factors that make any use of (what is referred to as) E.S.P. (&tc.) possible are dependent on metaphysical consideration. This understanding must extend beyond semantics and restrictions of even the most intricate of material sciences—such as "quantum physics"—although correlative data may be found to validate a connection between material science and metaphysics.

In the 'New Age', "astral projection" consists of a number of various techniques and practices intended to cause a deliberate shift in personal consciousness (or "*Awareness*") from the mundane "sensual" experience of "self" (as a '*genetic vehicle*') 'out' into an "astral body" for experiencing an "astral plane." Much as is the case in the Physical Universe (*Beta-Existence*), both the "astral body" and "astral plane" are mental or energetic constructs. Waves, particles and beams of energy form "**energy-signatures**" or "patterns" that are then interpreted internally and experienced subjectively. The actual "*Self*" is a non-local *Awareness*, so any consideration of a body or the laws governing the 'plane' are a matter of postulate. The considerations are senior to the mechanics; and the truth of the knowledge is senior to any application formula. An individual may have also had an experience come unbidden or unexpectedly that is termed an "out-of-body experience" (or OBE)—and while the phenomenon may be correlated to what we discuss in this book, such terminology is generally reserved for unintentional occurrences and even "near-death experiences" (NDE).*

Whereas the lore and recorded personal experiences extend back to ancient times, the vocabulary pertaining to "astral projection" is relatively modern, based primarily on a **western**ization of **Eastern** mysteries as explored by the "Theosophical Society" of England in the late 1800's. This society, and its founder *Helena Blavatsky*, are also responsible for incorporating a lot of Eastern-styled energy-work into Western Mysticism (and the evolution of the 'Western Magical Tradition') and popularizing the idea of the "*aura*" and "*chakra*" system for the 'New Age'. Similar concepts

---

* Several revised paragraphs here are excerpted from the Mardukite Grade-I (Route-A) Master Edition anthology, "*The Great Magickal Arcanum*" by Joshua Free.

may be found throughout the Hermetic schools, ancient Druidism, Egyptian religion and other forms of spiritual-mysticism, but common terminology used today is imported from the Ancient Near East.

There are two figures which contributed quite significantly to our modern "metapsychological" understanding of astral projection. *Sylvan Muldoon* (*1903-1950*) spent the majority of his physical lifetime quite ill and bed-ridden. Consequently this afforded him an extensive opportunity to innately explore means of accessing "astral travel." He published his experiences in "*The Projection of the Astral Body*" (*1929*). Then, eight years after Muldoon's death, a television executive, *Robert Monroe*, found that he was starting to have intense "astral" experiences right before falling sleep (during the 'hypnogogic state'). In addition to writing several books, Monroe's experiences led him to found a research institute—"The Monroe Institute" (TMI)—dedicated exclusively to this phenomenon. Based on the declassified documents for the "*Stargate Project*," it is clear that in the past several decades, The Monroe Institute (TMI) became much more active in exploring practical use and training for, specifically, "remote viewing" (RV).

There are as many 'New Age' techniques for accessing the 'Astral Plane' as there are publications on the subject. "Astral projection"—much like "remote viewing"—is a very individual 'effort'. Here again, in both cases, considerations take precedence over any specific rote techniques. Because in the two decades developing this research and in the examination of successful case-studies on these subjects, no ultimate '*end-all be-all*' procedure presented itself. Each individual innately developed their own unique style that was proved to themselves, by experience, to be successful—thus earning the **validation** to almost instinctively or unknowingly duplicate the same sequence of postulates or considerations again. Consider how many different manners of "walking" or "eating" there are and yet each person finds one that satisfies the basic goal in agreement with their own inclinations or personality, &tc.

All of the related metaphysical and metahuman or spiritual techniques are dependent on the operator—the individual or *Seeker* themselves—and not any type of external technology or whether or not the 'stars are aligned' in order to be effective. As a result, we discover much of the same emphasis on 'breathing', 'meditation', 'clearing the mind' and so on, as prerequisite for success. 'New Age' techniques for "astral travel" do tend to differ from the 'New Thought' and *'Stargate'* techniques in one respect: the 'New Age' methods usually incorporate some visualized form (or mental imagery) representing a 'portal' or 'threshold'. "Doorway" or "gateway" symbolism is intended to trigger a separation of 'consciousness' (*Awareness*) from a fixation on the material body (*genetic vehicle*).

UNDERSTANDING 'ZU-VISION' AND 'REMOTE VIEWING'

When *"Eleven"* puts on a blindfold and/or uses other 'sensory-blocking' methods to access information or contact places (and people) 'remote' from her physical body, she is seeking to access what is defined as *"Zu-Vision"* in our Systemology. Although we have alluded to this concept in Systemology (and earlier Mardukite 'Gate' work) for quite some time, a commitment to the "ZU-VISION" terminology occurred relatively recently, in the developmental stages of Grade-IV and inception of the 'Wizard-Levels'. Actual use of the word first appears in *'Liber-2D'*, based on a lecture in early 2020:[‡]

> "Our present focus concerns demonstrations with physical objects—their identities, associations and control. This same methodology is also applied to higher 'Actualized Technician' ('A.T.', 'Wizard' or 'Ascension Technology') levels operated exclusively in *Zu-Vision* as Self, clear and free of any limited considerations of a physical body or astral form in order to spiritually exist. But, for now, we shall focus on our treatment of the 'objective' universe."

This excerpt implies that many 'objective processes' used in Systemology may also be practiced in *"ZU-Vision"*—without actually moving the genetic vehicle or relying on the eyes of any body—

[‡] *"Liber-2D"*—first released in June 2020 as *"Command of the Mind-Body Connection"* for the Systemology Society's original Grade-IV 'Professional Piloting Program'; later integrated into *"Metahuman Destinations"* as 'Unit-2' in October 2020 and reissued for the Mardukite Academy edition of *"Metahuman Destinations (Volume Two): The Universe & Mind-Body Connection"* in October 2022; also contained in the complete Grade-IV anthology, *"The Metahuman Systemology Handbook."*

even an 'astral one'. The actual "I-AM"-*Self* or *Alpha-Spirit* is an *Awareness* with unlimited potential of consideration—and *all* "bodies" are considerations. Elsewhere from the same lecture we find techniques introduced that later went on to establish 'Wizard Level-0 **Creative Ability Training** (CAT)' for "*Imaginomicon*" (*Liber-3D*):

> "As an 'A.T.' exercise, you can have the *Seeker* make a duplicate copy of the object for their own 'Personal Universe' that occupies the same space-time as the actual object. Eventually the *Seeker* can even be directed to send their *Awareness-POV* 'in-to' and 'out-of' the object; an exercise that will encourage future Spiritual '*Zu-Vision*' practices."

As a result of these lectures, "Zu-Vision" required a proper definition for our cumulatively collected glossary-dictionary:

> **Zu-Vision** : the true and basic (*Alpha*) Point-of-View (perspective, POV) maintained by *Self* as *Alpha-Spirit* outside boundaries or considerations of the *Human Condition* "Mind-Systems" and *exterior* to beta-existence reality agreements with the Physical Universe; a POV of Self *as* "a unit of Spiritual Awareness" that exists independent of a "body" and beyond entrapment in a *Human Condition*; "spirit vision" in its truest sense.

The applied spiritual philosophy of Mardukite Systemology is rooted on one primary axiom: that the *Self* is a point or unit of *Spiritual Awareness* that we refer to as the *Alpha-Spirit*—the first-form or primary principle of "I-AM" that exists as a center of our true Alpha-Existence. The *Alpha-Spirit* has *one* true lifetime or continuous eternal Alpha *Beingness*, which is only separated by consideration of individual life-cycles (*incarnations*) that it has located its point-of-view (POV), and identified its *Beingness*, to some level or plane of common communication: in order to *do* something, in order to *have* something.[†]

Self-Actualization, as it applies to our *Metahuman* and *Spiritual* "Systemology," is a higher state of *Beingness*, *exterior* to the *Human Condition*, that includes a true *Self-Honest* perception and realization of the "I-AM." Although the concept has appeared in the

---

† Several revised paragraphs here are excerpted from "Imaginomicon" (Liber-3D) by Joshua Free; also available in the complete Grade-IV anthology, "*The Metahuman Systemology Handbook.*"

semantics of many spiritual philosophies and mystical religions in the past, the *map* is not the *territory*—and in the past 6,000 years we have found few demonstrations of these higher ideals experienced by individuals still entrapped within the POV of the *Human Condition*. In short: former attempts have not delivered satisfactory results.

It is true that many who remain suspended within "parameters" of the *Human Condition* cannot *actually* conceive of *Self* as a "Spirit" operating *exterior* to states of "feeling" (sensation) and "thinking" (associative reason), which have far too long substituted actual states of "*Knowingness.*" Even magicians, mystics and priests—with their "*astral bodies*" and "*mental bodies*" and "*etheric bodies*"—are still yet unable to *realize* a *Self* that is not tied to forms and bodies. We have experienced phenomenon of *Seekers* in processing: some of which are stuck in a body POV; some of which are stuck in a head POV; some of which are stuck apart from wanting anything to do with control of "bodies," leaving the one they identify with to run completely on its own stimulus-response impulses.

Many ongoing "Alpha-Defragmentation" experiments at the Systemology Society are born from archaic "New Thought" formulas found in old forgotten corners of dusty esoteric libraries—many of which bare similarity to various methods of "Eastern Tradition," but we emphasize *Self-Actualization* as an Alpha-Spirit (a point of pure *Spiritual Awareness*) that is not the same as an "Astral Body" or even a "thought"—although it is capable of *creating* both "thoughts" and "bodies." The very fact that *Self* is able to *observe* all these faculties should suffice to *realize* that the actual I-AM is above, superior to, and fully able to control and command its own *creations*. Even when we are presented with something *externally*—creations of others—the actual *facsimile* "copy" we store in our databanks and all associations we identify with it are completely our own *creations* to manage.

The basic methodology and "esoteric exercises" suggested in "*Wizard Level-0*" (and above) are meant to assist a *Seeker* in more fully *realizing* the *Awareness* of "Spiritual Individuality" as opposed to the "*beta-personality.*" The total *realization* of "I" as *Self* as Alpha-Spirit *is* a prerequisite to the attainment or *Actualization* of that high-level *Awareness*. This is not "word-play"; the fundamentals of this principle are outlined more clearly in the Grade-III text "*Crystal Clear (Handbook for Seekers)*" and many other works collected within the complete Grade-III "*Systemology Handbook*" anthology. An actualization of these same fundamentals is also necessary for a *Seeker* or "*Master*" to achieve the highest goals for "*Wizard Level-0*" (*Grade-IV*) in Systemology.

The most critical component to operating "out" and *exterior* to this *Beta-Existence* is to attain a "crystal clear" certainty and realization —complete reality agreement—that the I-AM, *Self*, is: not the Mind, not the Body (or any *genetic vehicle*), but *Self* is commander and operator of these instruments in *Beta-Existence* from a point of true *Spiritual Awareness* that is not directly identifiable within the boundaries or parameters of the Physical Universe; it simply operates the machinery there. As an individual *Alpha-Spirit* becomes increasingly fragmented by "associative thought," the circuitry of the Mind-System offers POV that make it seem as though the individual *is* confined within those Systems as its point of *Beingness*. But these "implants" are not truth.

When *Self* is operating as an *Awareness* "outside" sensory perceptions and energetic rigidity of a "material body," it may, in effect, *look into* the *genetic organism* and view its workings—practice in which will demonstrate that the "I" or *Self* is not identical or identified *as* the "body." For some it is easier to consider that they are operating *exterior* to this Physical Universe, but are "**projecting**" their *Awareness* to a POV that *is within* another form or "body" to experience a *Beingness*. Desired states and goals for the 'upper-level' aspects of Systemology are not altogether different than the very gradients defining efforts by 'The Monroe Institute' and their 'Hemi-Sync' states of awareness such as described by participants[*] of the "Gateway Voyage" or 'Remote Viewing Practicums':

> RV-10 :: "you realize you are more than the physical"
> RV-12 :: "information seems to flow in from wherever you aim your attention"
> RV-15 :: "time and space cease to be limitations"

Practice of *exterior* "Zu-Vision"—the *Awareness* POV from *Self* independent of a "body" in *Beta-Existence*—ensues until a *Seeker* has an increased *realization* (reality) on the matter; and such practice req-

---

[*] The Monroe Institute (TMI) hosted its first 'Remote Viewing Practicum' September 28 through October 4, 2002; the states of Awareness are described by Katie Letcher Lyle in TMI Focus, Vol. XXIV, No. 1-2, Winter/Spring 2003.

uires "**Imagination**" and *Creative Ability* for that *realization* to become *actual*. Here, an individual should not **invalidate** their own experience—or a *Pilot* to invalidate a *Seeker*—concerning exactly what is happening within the realm of one's "Imagination" and Personal Universe. An individual "*imagines*" **potentiality** of something until it is *realized*, from which it may then be made *actual.*[†]

For a long time, it was assumed that 'remote viewing' was entirely "passive"—completely undetectable—but this may not be absolutely accurate. It is difficult to ascertain (based on 'intuitive sensitivity' of the subjects) if an individual can sense "being watched" (or another "presence" is there) in an active 'remotely viewed' location. However, because of the specialized usage of these tactics by "Intelligence Companies," the matter required serious investigation. "Intrusion Detection" became the subject of a 35-page technical document from the mid-1980's, when the "*Stargate Project*" is referred to by the special access program title: "*Grill Flame.*"[‡] It describes a replication of experimental protocols used by the Chinese physicists that discovered measurable "photon production" (an increase of light particles) taking place at a target site upon positive connection/contact by a "remote viewer" ("*RVer*").

> "We have conducted a conceptual replication of work published by physicists in the People's Republic of China (PRC) in which they claimed that 'effects' upon physical systems can be observed during successful remote viewing [and that] light is emitted in the vicinity of correctly identified RV target material. The overall results (summed across all RVers) indicate a weak statistical effect, which supports the Chinese claims that correct RV acquisition of information perturbs physical systems [and] the statistical correlations we observed represent the first evidence that intrusion detection may be possible—even in principle. Therefore, this work must be continued..."

[†] See also "*Imaginomicon*" (*Liber-3D*) by Joshua Free.
[‡] CIA-RDP96-00789R003800320001: Stanford Research Institute (SRI) Project 7408-10 for Defense Intelligence Agency (DFI), May 1985, covering the period of October 1983 to October 1984; Approved For Release 2003/01/17.

HANDLING ENERGY-MATTER IN SPACE-TIME

Humans often speak casually of "mind over matter"—not realizing, of course, that everyone is **participating** in the *reality game* of this universe. At the very least, we find a strong 'psychokinetic component' inherent in the "Observer Effect" (especially at 'quantum levels'). We are affecting the **probability** of events in our lives every day—simply by the act of applying our attention-*Awareness* to the energy-matter of the Physical Universe. At a material level, *psychokinesis* ("PK" or *telekinesis*) is the ability to affect 'physical' systems without direct 'physical' interaction—which is to say, to *perturb* it from an *exterior* point. And although proficiency in one does not automatically generate experience with the other, the mechanics and systemology behind *remote viewing* and *telekinesis* share many metaphysical fundamentals and mutual interest by the "Intelligence Community."

As we have seen at the close of the last section, even giving something concentrated attention and 'contacting' or 'connecting' with it at a distance has the ability to affect (or increase) the amount of 'light' emitted in the area—even if only detectible by highly sophisticated machinery. The fact that we should be able to affect energy-matter with our Observation was a startling enough truth for quantum physicists to play with; but the fact that we should be able to affect energy-matter at a distance—any distance—remotely from the physical body is quite remarkable (particularly if considering it exclusively within paradigms of material science). As stated by Gerald J. Schueler, in his occult interpretation, "*Enochian Physics*":—

> "Levitation is usually viewed as a violation of the law of gravity. However, there is considerable doubt as to exactly what the law of gravity is. In fact, Einstein's general theory of relativity has cast significant doubt on gravity being a force at all. The occult explanation was stated by Master Koot Hoomi as, 'there is no gravitation properly speaking; only attraction and repulsion.' However, one must consciously oppose the collective idea that levitation is impossible. One must 'believe' that levitation is possible and that one can do it. The belief itself will open up those mental **channels** necessary for success."

Psychokinesis begins to play an iconic role in *Stranger Things* from the moment "*Eleven*" flips the HNL van over 'using her mind' from the back of *Mike's* bicycle in season one. As the series progresses, particularly into season four, *PK/TK* and *levitation* take greater prominence in the display of 'power' demonstrated by both *Eleven* and *One/Vecna.* While the action on the show is colorfully **dramatized**, it does reflect a key 'spiritual ability' (or 'innate' quality of the actual *Self*) that is highly worthy of examination. Yet, apart from 'stage-magic' and a stream of covert government research experiments (only relatively recently disclosed), the whole subject of "levitation" in general has mainly been restricted to archaic *religio-mystical* discussions and lore.

In his book, *"Deepteachings of Merlyn,"* Douglas Monroe illustrates many examples of psychokinetic (PK) research. In addition to religious annals of the Catholic Church regarding the phenomenon of "levitation" not only with *Jesus Christ* but many of the saints as well, Monroe presents more modern examples such as the case of *Monica Nieto Tejada.* "At fifteen years old, the young Spanish psychic could bend metal strips sealed in tubes simply by thinking about it. Extensive testing by researchers around the world have verified the phenomenon as real, with special attention by *Dr. Elmar Gruber.*" Various other case studies of interest are also supplied, including:

• *Felicia Parise*, 1981, New York—"demonstrates 'small object movement by mental force' at Maimonides Medical Center."

• *Mark Briscoe*, 1982, England—"a teenager accomplished the feat of bending 'memory metal' (Nitinol) into permanent shapes without touching it; certified by *Professor John Hasted* of the University of London."

• *Subbayah Pullavar*, 1936, London—"*P.T. Plunkett,* a critical reporter of the London News, gathered 150 witnesses and photographed the yoga-guru levitate."

• *Joasia Gajewski*, 1984, Poland—"teenage girl caused a metal fork to fly across the room during a filmed Japanese documentary. Her specialty was causing untouched light bulbs to explode at will."

• *Alla Vinogravada*, 1970's, Harvard University—"showed she could make objects weighing up to 3-ounces roll across a tabletop without touching them."

Then there is the obvious matter of a certain famous slumber-party 'game' played by children, generally referred to as:

"Light as a Feather; Stiff as a Board." This 'levitation' exercise involves a subject laying flat on their back (on a floor), whereas a popular variation has them sitting in a chair. The subject is usually surrounded by four individuals; for example, one per leg of the chair. The group is evenly spread out around the subject's body and together, each individual puts one (or two) fingers underneath it (or under the seat of the chair at one of the corners). The functional purpose of this 'game' is to demonstrate being "cause" over considerations of space-time energy-matter in the Physical Universe (*Beta-Existence*).

In the version of this 'game' popularized by the motion picture, *The Craft (1996)*, the young witches perform it while chanting: "*Light as a feather; stiff as a board,*" and then gently lift their friend into the air. Most experimental material-scientists directly observing this phenomenon seem to conclude the most **rational** explanation: that a successful "lift" is accomplished only by precise timing of physical efforts by all participants. Of course, to be true, this would mean that each of the four participants, if evenly dispersed, is receiving a load-weight of between 30 and 50 pounds to lift the average adult—which really is a significant amount of mass to comfortably balance on a finger or two. Of course, we usually hear of this 'game' as played by children, which are considerably 'lighter'—but relatively speaking, among the young it is probably just as great of a physical feat to accomplish.

The 'game' actually has a lesser-known darker edge to it, from its origins. The imagery invoked is that the subject (sometimes called the "victim") is, or becomes, a 'dead body'. Those gathered around might call-and-repeat a series of lines, such as "she's looking ill," "she's looking worse," "she's dying," and "she's dead." In "*The Diary of Samuel Pepys,*" a 17th century British naval officer accounts the experience told to him by a friend (*Mr. Brisband*), who witnessed some children playing "Light as a Feather; Stiff as a Board" in Bordeaux, France during the 1600's. Pepys writes:—

> "He saw four little girls, very young ones, all kneeling, each of them, upon one knee; and one begun the first line, whispering in the ear of the next, and the second to the third, and the third to the fourth, and she to the first. Then the first begun the second line, and so round quite through, and putting each one finger only to a boy that lay flat upon his back on the ground, as if he was dead; at the end of the

words, they did with their four fingers raise this boy high as they could reach..."

Of the chant that is spoken in this 'game':—

> Here is a dead body (*voici un corps mort*)
> Stiff as a stick (*raide comme un baton*)
> Cold as marble (*froid comme le marbre*)
> Light as a spirit (*leger comme un esprit*)
> Lift yourself, in the name of Jesus Christ!
> (*leve-toi au nom de Jesus-Christ!*)

* * * * * * *

— <u>FINAL THOUGHTS</u> —

"Part One" and "Part Two" of THE METAPHYSICS OF STRANGER THINGS is intended to strongly suggest many things for the *Seeker* (reader) to consider. 'Telepathic' and 'telekinetic' abilities are *not* "supernatural" (if we assume the common use of the term) but they do lay dormant—hidden and forgotten—most of the time. In view of the fact that many individuals have been, and continue to be, unknowingly subject to various forms of abduction, experimental research, 'sleeper-cell' implantation—lives are laid out to ruin in the name of 'national security' or to protect some corporation's financial interests, an individual's mundane enforced control or the perversions of some niche group. Even those that we might believe originate the "conspiracy" against us are, themselves, prey to some even higher-level 'alien agendas' that they are seldom fully aware of.

Many of those individuals subjected to 'research' or 'training' regimens seldom retain conscious memory of it—although just about anything might 'trigger' some recollection. But most are suggestively implanted (conditioned) to generate a feeling of 'illness' (&tc.) when presented with such stimuli later, in order to encourage avoidance of these sensitive "terminals" altogether. Others who are more aware or have recovered awareness of their experiences also report that popular medias were used during imprinting efforts. Alleged examples include "*The Wizard of Oz,*" "*Alice in Wonderland,*" "*Avatar*" and "*Harry Potter*" (just to name a few)—all of which graphically depict sudden extraordinary shifts in consciousness from one reality to another. It is probably only a matter of time until *"Stranger Things"* is added to the list—if it hasn't already been used this way. Innumerable "triggers" and "codes" are supposedly embedded throughout most mainstream medias, including advertising, film, music and the speeches used by politicians and other contemporary authorities.

There is, perhaps, one major fundamental 'bright side' to the last hundred years of research, experiments and developments... the essential revelations are still with us.

"Part Three" discloses what has been discovered or developed by the 'Systemology Society' and its pursuit of understanding the systematic rudiments of how the more "psionic" or "psychical" aspects displayed in *Stranger Things* are actually possible. Now, with the publication of THE METAPHYSICS OF STRANGER THINGS, a person does not need to actively participate in some little-known underground organization in order to access critical information, collected exercises and spiritual techniques used toward effectively 'awakening' ability or 'accelerating' development of:

—receiving and projecting mental images;

—receiving and projecting frequencies in the emotional **band**;

—advanced *Knowingness* and elevated *Beingness*;

—attracting and repulsing particular types of energy-matter;

—using the "mind" and esoteric energy work to heal or kill;

—the ability to open dimensional-doorways; and

—increasing acute mental skills (problem solving, technical), *&tc.*

There are ongoing projects, still today, maintained by corporate organizations and privately funded research teams—it's not just "Big Brother" that is involved with such matters (although they do their best to monitor these other activities). Even our own 'Mardukite Office' on-line computers and cellular communications are frequently (if not constantly) targeted for monitoring. Of course, most of the work for this—and for what was planned for a decade as "Mardukite Phase-10"—took place 'off-grid'.

The "Mardukite Research Org." ("Systemology Society") began underground development of a secret *'Mardukite Phase-10' 'Systemology Grade-VII'* research program in 2017, codenamed *'Stargate'*. Although this part of our operations remained mostly dormant and unnoticed during a public revival of "Mardukite Systemology" in

2019 (with release of "*The Tablets of Destiny Revelation*" and "*Crystal Clear: Handbook For Seekers*"), investigations resumed in late 2020 as 'Projekt-011', while refining "*Imaginomicon: Accessing Gateways to Higher Universes*" for publication. A complete collection of disclosed research was approved for inclusion in "*Liber-011*"—debuting in late-2022 as THE METAPHYSICS OF STRANGER THINGS.

'Systematic Processing' employed for "*Liber-011*" is concerned with 'breaking agreements' with the Physical Universe—and in doing so, postulating (considering) *new* 'reality agreements' rather than opposing the *old* ones by force, which is futile. In fact, personal entrapment in the Physical Universe occurs by an individual being "tricked" into using force—and the more 'effort' applied (or received) in this existence, the more "spun-in" one is to the idea that this is the *only* 'existence', or even the *truest* 'reality experience'. Keep in mind, that at basic, above and back of all else, *Self* is always occupying the same **static** point, *exterior* to the Physical Universe, but with near-unlimited potential to consider itself as a body locatable in space-time. Hence, in season four, we discover the true nature of *Vecna*'s universe and its affect on the 'Physical Universe' when agreed to.

The readings throughout early parts of this book—and especially the exercises and techniques to follow—should, if nothing else, reinforce a certainty that *Self* is the 'Alpha Spirit' of our systemological equation, exactly as described in "*Imaginomicon*" (*Liber-3D*) and other Systemology materials. This 'Alpha Spirit' has nearly unlimited potential to create its considerations and consider its creations—all by 'postulate'. The individual 'Alpha Spirit'—the actual *Self* or "*I-AM*"—occupies, has always occupied and will continue to occupy what is best described as a 'Personal Universe', completely *exterior* to the 'Physical Universe' (or *Beta-Existence*). The postulates (considerations) and agreements about the 'Physical Universe' are *superimposed* over one's own 'Personal Universe'. This is what is treated as *your reality*. If you can realize these things than you may find great success with the "Infinity-Level" goals suggested in this 'Grade-VII' literary treatment of "*Liber-011.*"

PART THREE

STRANGER
SYSTEMOLOGY

Approval For Release: 2022/10/31 (Liber-011)

THIS FILE-FOLDER CONTAINS LIMITED ACCESS MATERIAL
OF THE MARDUKITE RESEARCH ORG. / SYSTEMOLOGY SOC.
CLASSIFIED RESTRICTED, CONFIDENTIAL and TOP SECRET

LIMITED ACCESS REQUIRED

Access to these files will be restricted to those
persons specifically indoctrinated to the individual
Limited Access Systemology Program indicated below:

STARGATE // PROJEKT-011

MARDUKITE RESEARCH ORG. / SYSTEMOLOGY SOC.
MARDUKITE BORSIPPA H.Q., SAN LUIS VALLEY, COLO.
GUARDIANS OFFICE, RESEARCH AND DEVELOPMENT

---C-O-N-F-I-D-E-N-T-I-A-L---

RE: projekt-011 (disclosure2022)
CC: stargate//projekt-011 folder
BCC: disclosure inquiries on file

31, OCTOBER 2022

GREETINGS AND SALUTATIONS SEEKERS
(and readers of "Liber-011")

We have received your inquiry into Projekt-011 and
repeated requests for disclosure of Org files.

As you know, Projekt-011 has been an extremely
sensitive part of 'Operation Eridu' since its inception at the 'SLV Babylon Site' in early 2017.

Relative to our other work, extraordinary funding and
attention went into development of Phase-10, and
ultimately resulted in the founding of the present
'Borsippa HQ' in San Luis Valley.

The amount of security and confidentiality that
surrounds this work has ensured its unhindered
development in private for over five years.

Although some of the information contained in the
Stargate//Projekt-011 file-folder was silently leaked
Spring 2021 for "Imaginomicon" (Liber-3D), an
approval for release of the complete files is
authorized on this day 31, October 2022 for inclusion in the Autumn/Winter 2022 publication "The
Metaphysics of Stranger Things" (Liber-011).

A facsimile version of the file-folder is included
here for viewing and your own experimental exploration of what otherwise is Systemology Grade-VI/VII
material intended exclusively for specially trained
Systemology Class-6 Professional Pilots.

Joshua Free
approval for release
auth. by Joshua Free
projekt-011 director

STARGATE//PROJEKT-011

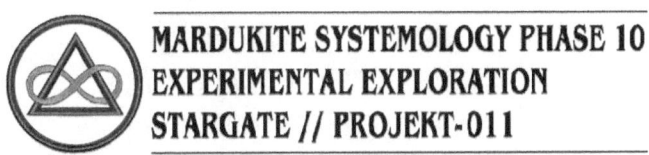

MARDUKITE SYSTEMOLOGY PHASE 10 EXPERIMENTAL EXPLORATION STARGATE // PROJEKT-011

LIST OF MARDUKITE STARGATE PROJECT BULLETINS
[*Renumbered for this approved release.*]

STARGATE SERIES

1	03 MAR 17	#B011-A	Establishment of Mardukite Phase-10
2	30 APR 17	#S011-A	Direct Access to Information
3	11 MAY 17	#S011-B	Mind-Body Connection-Separation
4	23 MAY 17	#S011-C	The Bird's-Eye View (RV) [*omitted*]
5	12 JUN 17	#R011-A	Establishing the Self (Alpha-Spirit)
6	20 JUN 17	#B011-B	Mardukite Phase-10 (Summer 2017)
7	05 JUL 17	#S011-D	Secret Doctrines of the Cosmos
8	10 JUL 17	#B011-C	Hermetic Philosophy & W.W. Atkinson
9	14 JUL 17	#S011-E	Hermetic Principles & Cosmic Laws
10	19 JUL 17	#S011-F	Secret Formulas of the Cosmos
11	27 JUL 17	#R011-B	Systemology Technique 1-8-0, Issue 2
12	04 AUG 17	#B011-D	Basic Training (Summer 2017)
13	16 AUG 17	#S011-G	Astral Planes & Ascension [*revised*]
14	01 SEP 17	#B011-E	Mardukite Phase-10 (Autumn 2017)

PROJEKT-011 SERIES

1	13 OCT 20	#B011-F	Mardukite Phase-10 Restart Proposal
2	20 OCT 20	#R011-C	Stargate Training (Autumn 2020)
3	17 NOV 20	#R011-D	Imagination Tech (Grade-IV) [*revised*]
4	15 DEC 20	#S011-H	Remote Viewing (RV Training Example)
5	09 JAN 21	#B011-G	"ZU-Vision" Academy Lecture [*abridged*]
6	18 MAR 21	#R011-E	Spiritual Entities & Fragments
7	30 APR 21	#B011-H	Beta-Defragmentation Schedule (v.1.3)
8	01 MAY 22	#S011-J	Mardukite Phase-10 // "Projekt-011"
9	06 JUN 22	#R011-F	"Projekt-011" & Psychokinesis (PK)
10	08 JUL 22	#R011-G	Processing Toward Psychokinesis (PK)
11	01 AUG 22	#B011-J	Proposal for "Liber-011" (2022 Edition)

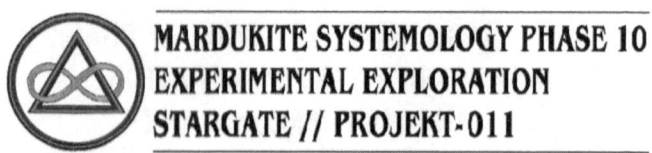

MARDUKITE SYSTEMOLOGY PHASE 10 EXPERIMENTAL EXPLORATION STARGATE // PROJEKT-011

MARDUKITE STARGATE PROJECT BULLETIN OF 03, MARCH 2017
BABYLON SITE, SAN LUIS VALLEY, COLORADO

TECH BRIEFING # B011-A [*Restricted (IV)*]

ESTABLISHMENT OF MARDUKITE PHASE-10
Stargate Series - 1

SUMMARY
The 'Council of Nabu-Tutu' met frequently during Nov-Dec 2016 to discuss establishment of
'Mardukite Phase-10', a proposal-plan that has
been with the organization since its 2008 inception. It is the final 'step' toward solidi-
fying our basic position in the 'New Age' and
among other esoteric organizations. Success of
'Phase-10' ensures our Seekers have a certainty
on the proposed 'Pathway'; that there is 'somewhere' to 'go' or actual upper-level work to
aspire to. The proposed 'codename' for 'Operation-Eridu' is "STARGATE".

PROPOSAL
Three members of the 'Council of Nabu-Tutu'
convened several times (and communicated remotely with other council-members) in late 2016
to establish an agreement on protocols for implementing 'Mardukite Phase-10' in 2017. These
meetings took place (in Golden, Colorado) at
our present mobile Office-HQ ("The Marduk
Temple") a 29-foot recreational vehicle that we
moved into in May 2016.

The details of this proposal include: acquisition of vacant rural land (in San Luis Valley,
Colorado); building three temporary structures
(a library-office, an outpost for experimental

research and a utility storage); acquisition of solar-power, generators and other 'off-grid' supplies; relocating the mobile Office-HQ to the site; preparation of the structures for appropriate use; and the establishment of 'Phase-10' development of our post-Mardukite Systemology.

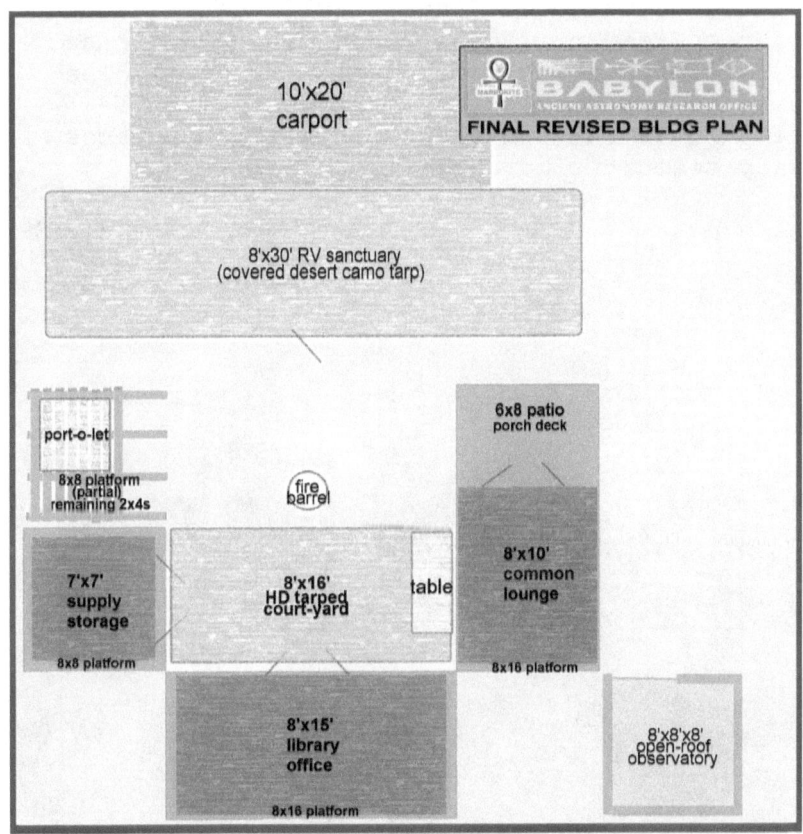

The budget requested from the 'Mardukite Fund' is as follows: $4500 for land; $4500 for construction; $1000 to tow mobile Office-HQ; $1000 for generator and portable solar-power; $1000 to restock research in the library; all amounting to $12000, a five-figure allocation that is expected to completely exhaust the present 'Mardukite Fund'. The site will be referred to

as "BABYLON" and official coverage is that the
site will be used for 'astronomical observation' under the title "Mardukite Babylon Ancient Astronomy Research Office".

IMPLEMENTATION
Acquisition of a five-acre site in San Luis
Valley occurred in January 2017. Construction
of temporary buildings began two days ago and
will continue until completion in April. The
site is expected to receive the mobile Office-HQ at the end of April. All other necessary resources have been acquired.

APPROVAL FOR RELEASE:
31, OCT 2022 (Liber-011)
Joshua Free, project director

Mardukite Babylon Site A, Office-Library, March 2017

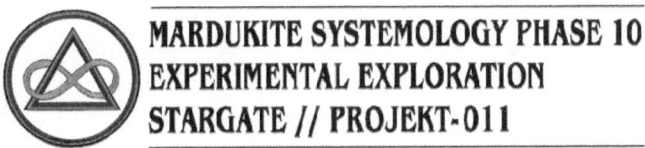

MARDUKITE SYSTEMOLOGY PHASE 10 EXPERIMENTAL EXPLORATION STARGATE // PROJEKT-011

MARDUKITE STARGATE PROJECT BULLETIN OF 30, APRIL 2017
BABYLON SITE, SAN LUIS VALLEY, COLORADO

TECH SUMMARY # S011-A [*Confidential* (VI)]

DIRECT ACCESS TO INFORMATION
Stargate Series - 2

SYNOPSIS
This is a summary of Chapter 17 'Direct Access
of Information' in Barbara Ann Brennan's "Hands
of Light: A Guide to Healing Through the Human
Energy Field" (1987). [A copy is retained at
the Office-Library for additional reference.]

TECH SUMMARY
Direct access to information is accomplished by
connecting directly to (and receiving) the information. The surface world categorizes this
as ESP or psychic (psionic) phenomenon. Most of
this phenomenon relates to heightened sensory
perception of traditional (known) faculties:
hearing sounds, seeing pictures, tactile, &tc.
Different individuals will connect to information via one or more acute or preferred senses.
For example: hearing the sound of a person's
name, touching an article of their clothing, or
smelling a perfume (cologne) they wear; these
can all be used to connect to an individual
over distances.

TECHNIQUES
The author provides basic exercises to enhance
perceptions; variations of the typical Hermetic
'Body of Light' formulas and objective processes involving awareness on the body as a
method of progressive relaxation. Different

parts of the body are given attention and 'reached' for, first physically and then 'mentally'. The same is done for the ambient space (environment, room, &tc.), remaining seated but 'reaching' with "beams" (attention-energy) toward different locations (spaces) and objects (energy-matter) in the room. Similar practice with visualization (visual and audio) is also taken up.

CITATIONS

"The best measuring of the process of direct access of information is the work done on remote viewing by Russell Targ and Harold Puthoff of Stanford Research Institute. They found that a viewer in the basement of the lab at Stanford could fairly accurately draw a map of the location of a target team of people, who were sent to various predetermined points. Targ and Puthoff began their experiments with known psychics and then found that anyone they chose, even the most skeptical, could do it."

APPROVAL FOR RELEASE:
31, OCT 2022 (Liber-011)
Joshua Free, project director

Mardukite Babylon Site A, construction, April 2017

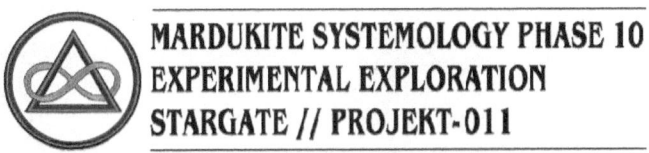

MARDUKITE SYSTEMOLOGY PHASE 10 EXPERIMENTAL EXPLORATION STARGATE // PROJEKT-011

MARDUKITE STARGATE PROJECT BULLETIN OF 11, MAY 2017
BABYLON SITE, SAN LUIS VALLEY, COLORADO

TECH SUMMARY # S011-B [*Confidential (VI)*]

MIND-BODY CONNECTION-SEPARATION
Stargate Series – 3

SYNOPSIS
This is a summary of Chapter 7 Meditations 'Mind Out of Body' in Douglas Monroe's "The Deepteachings of Merlyn: 13 Quests Into The Deeper Secrets of the Druids" (2011). Joshua Free was also a contributor to this book. [A copy is retained at the Office-Library for additional reference.]

TECH SUMMARY
Various terms are recognized throughout history for a 'second spiritual body' or else the one 'other' than our physical: 'Ka' (Egyptian); 'Atman' (Hindu); 'Neshamah' (Judaic); or 'Astral Body' (Western), &tc.

SYSTEMOLOGY CLARIFICATION
Systemology takes the position that the individual (the 'Self' or "I-AM") is not, and has never been, one-and-as the physical body (genetic vehicle); only that it can 'consider' itself so (as an 'identification') and be entrapped to only 'consider' from a fixed viewpoint (POV), e.g. 'the physical eyes'. The 'Self' ("I-AM") is also not the "Mind" but makes use of a 'Mind-System' (just as it makes 'use' of a "Body") though its 'considerations' for 'identity' can also be entrapped within a "Mind". [Ref: "Systemology: Original Thesis".]

THE FACT FILES

The 'double' is usually fully-clothed. This suggests a 'residual self-image' or 'mirroring' an expected appearance of a body during 'astral projection'. This 'astral body' may presumably affect (perturb) the physical world via "psychokinesis" (PK) in the same wise as a more 'material' body can.

TECHNIQUES

This is a summation of 'New Age' techniques:

 * "The Aleister Crowley Technique"
The projector, eyes closed, imagines a closed door in a black wall. Inscribed on the door is a symbol or glyph which is significant to the person. When ready, simply open the door mentally and move through.

 * "The Robert Monroe Technique"
Choose a day when the weather conditions are clean and dry with temperature between 70-80 degrees F. Humidity and electrical storms not preferred. Do not eat 6-12 hours prior. Avoid high protein foods (dairy, meat) for 24-hours prior. Be warm and relaxed in bed with head-North and feet-South. Breathing: heavy rhythmic, followed by holding breath as long as possible, then relax completely. To 'loosen the astral matrix' use the following imagery: 1) yourself as a point floating in space; 2) yourself as a cloud; 3) yourself as a stream; 4) yourself as a star twinkling in space; 5) yourself flying; 6) yourself as a whirlpool, squeezing down then out; 7) ...out into a tank filled with water, yourself floating on top as a point of light; then 8) find a small hole in the side of the tank and pass through.

 * "The Skullgate Technique"
Massage with two fingers in a clockwise direction, the Right Temple Lobe (outside the 'Sylvian Fissure' area of the brain, the right temple indention just beside the ear). Do this for five minutes, then stop and visualize an

'open gateway' in this section of your brain. Squeeze your consciousness through slowly.

* "The Fox Technique"
Very similar to the technique described just above, except the 'third eye' (chakra center) is used as a doorway, which 'Fox' equates to the 'pineal gland'. [Focus and stimulate this area with heat, massage, herbs, &tc.]

* "The Yram Technique"
This method involves laying down comfortably and imagining yourself 'rising up through innumerable bodies of lesser and lesser density the higher you rise'. [Also known as the 'egg within an egg' technique.]

* "The Muldoon Technique"
Which he called 'rising to sleep'. His idea is to hold consciousness up to the very moment of sleep (or 'hypnogogic state'), using willpower to take control of that moment. He suggests holding one arm up in the air, so you will awaken the moment it hits the bed upon sleep.

* "The Carrington Technique"
Place a lighted candle in your bedroom just before bed. Put it in comfortable sight on the far side of the room. As you fall asleep, visualize moving ever closer to the light.

APPROVAL FOR RELEASE:
31, OCT 2022 (Liber-011)
Joshua Free, project director

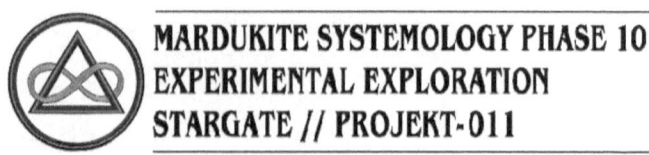

MARDUKITE SYSTEMOLOGY PHASE 10 EXPERIMENTAL EXPLORATION STARGATE // PROJEKT-011

MARDUKITE STARGATE PROJECT BULLETIN OF 23, MAY 2017
BABYLON SITE, SAN LUIS VALLEY, COLORADO

TECH SUMMARY # S011-C [*Confidential (VI)*]

THE BIRD'S-EYE VIEW (RV)
Stargate Series – 4

SYNOPSIS
This is a summary of Chapter 8 'The Extended
Eye' in Lynne McTaggart's "The Field: The Quest
for the Secret Force in the Universe" (2001).
[A copy is retained at the Office-Library for
additional reference.]

TECH SUMMARY
Stanford Research Institute...

  [Although the Title and Synopsis for this
  bulletin is listed in the STARGATE **catalogue**-index, a complete record is missing
  from the file archives and therefore cannot be duplicated for this facsimile.]

APPROVAL FOR RELEASE:
31, OCT 2022 (Liber-011)
Joshua Free, project director

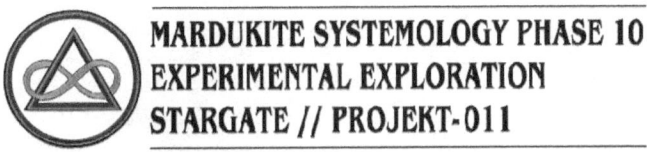

MARDUKITE SYSTEMOLOGY PHASE 10 EXPERIMENTAL EXPLORATION STARGATE // PROJEKT-011

MARDUKITE STARGATE PROJECT BULLETIN OF 12, JUNE 2017
BABYLON SITE, SAN LUIS VALLEY, COLORADO

TECH REPORT # R011-A [*Top Secret (VII)*]

ESTABLISHING THE SELF (ALPHA-SPIRIT)

Stargate Series - 5

PREMISE

Applied spiritual philosophy of Mardukite Systemology is rooted on one primary axiom: that
the actual "Self" is a 'point' or 'unit' of
'Spiritual Awareness' -we refer to it as the
'Alpha-Spirit' (first-form) or primary principle of "I-AM" extant as a center of our true
Alpha-Existence. A secondary axiom is: an Alpha-Spirit has one true 'spiritual lifetime' (a
continuous eternal Alpha Beingness), which is
only separated by consideration of individual
life-cycles (incarnations) where it has located
a fixed POV and identified its Beingness to
some level or plane of communication: a "body",
in order to do and have on that plane (Universe).

SUMMARY

The most critical component to operating 'out'
and 'exterior' to Beta-Existence is crystal
clear certainty (a complete reality agreement)
that "Self" (I-AM) is: not the Mind, not the
Body (or any 'genetic vehicle'), but commands
and operates these instruments in 'Beta-Existence'. The 'point' of true 'Spiritual
Awareness' is not directly identifiable within
boundaries or parameters of the Physical Universe ('Beta-Existence'); it simply operates
machinery there.

The Alpha-Spirit operates as an 'Awareness' independent of any body —even a 'spiritual' or
'etheric' one. Consideration for an 'energetic
body' has included many layers, levels or dimensions assumed during the experiences through
various "Universes"; and the more rigid, solid
and condensed the energy-matter (zero-continu-
ity) of a Universe, the more rigidly solid the
genetic vehicles for Life to communicate at
that level of Beta-Existence.

TECHNIQUES

  To get realizations that Self is apart
  from (and superior master of) a genetic
  vehicle ("body") a Seeker should focus
  Awareness through each part of the body:
  beginning with the feet and moving up into
  the head (and including the brain). In the
  past, mystics referred to these techniques
  as 'Activating the Light-Body' —but, in
  our Systemology we found it is the 'Awareness' itself that acts as "Light", not any
  "body".

  Begin with full directed attention (Awareness) on just the feet (even prior to
  treating the entire limb), or if that
  proves challenging at first, just one toe
  of one foot. Then concentrate that Awareness in that location and imagine that: if
  the feet were nonexistent, then Self would
  still continue to exist unchanged as the
  Alpha-Spirit. Next, consider that they are
  useful tools for communicating activity
  when operating a genetic vehicle in the
  Physical Universe, but they are not the
  "feet" of the Spirit; and Self is not dependent on feet of a "body" to act.

The intention of the exercise is not to lessen
or reject the genetic vehicle. An individual
not getting along well in this lifetime (or experiencing great pain) is already excessively
and **compulsively** 'out of communication' with

the "body." A genetic vehicle is exactly that:
a vehicle, instrument or tool treated like any
other 'possession' -but it should not be obsessively cared for or confused with the "Identity" of Self.

> The same exercise may be continued with
> the remainder of the body (the pelvic re-
> gion, sexual organs, digestive tract,
> chest, arms, neck, head, &tc.) —treating
> each with the same considerations, and
> moving off from each with the same realiz-
> ations, as with the feet. When this is ac-
> complished throughout the whole body, then
> the Seeker may look to consider the "body"
> as the whole of the genetic vehicle, an
> instrument useful for communication in the
> Physical Universe, biologically adapted to
> this Beta-Existence; but that 'Self' (I-
> AM) as 'Alpha-Spirit' is above and superi-
> or, independent and apart, from the genet-
> ic vehicle, with an actual existence 'ex-
> terior' to 'Beta', in an (Alpha)
> "Spiritual Universe."

APPLIED PHILOSOPHY
William Walker Atkinson (1862-1932), a founding
pioneer of American "New Thought", writes in
his esoteric library of arcane teachings:

> "Let the **Neophyte**, in imagination, leave
> the physical body and gaze upon the
> latter. A little mental practice will
> enable one to do this in imagination, thus
> bringing fully to mind the realization
> that it is possible for the Self to leave
> the body and dwell apart from it. When the
> mind has once grasped this possibility,
> the body will ever after be recognized as
> merely a physical machine, sheath or
> covering, of the Self—and one will never
> again commit the folly of identifying the
> 'I' with the physical body.

"Then let the Neophyte imagine themselves leaving behind their physical body, until, as Holmes says: '...thou at length are free, leaving thine outgrown shell by life's unresting sea.' Let them then consider themselves as occupying other and different bodies, one at a time, in different phases of life and condition, in different ages, &tc. This will bring about the realization that Self is something higher and independent of the particular physical shell or machine that it is now using, and which it may have at one time considered identical with itself. Then will the particular body occupied seem, in reality, to be 'my body' instead of 'I' or Me."

SYSTEMOLOGY TECHNIQUE 1-8-0, ISSUE-1
Elsewhere from Atkinson's arcane teachings:

"Let the Neophyte meditate upon the great 'Ocean of Life' in which the individual entities are but focal Centers of Consciousness and Force; see themselves, in imagination, as being an actual Center, with all the Universe revolving around them; see themselves as the pivot around which the Universe moves —the Central Sun around which the infinite world and planets circle in their cosmic flight. Let them feel themselves to be the focal Center of the Cosmos.

"And this is indeed, in accordance with the centuries old occult axiom, which informs us that 'the Cosmos is infinite; its circumference is nowhere and its center is everywhere.' Let the Neophyte lose all thought of the outside world in this meditation; let them regard it as totally unmanifest if they like, but see Self in Actual Existence and in Full Power. Let them realize 'I-AM' to the

fullest extent of their power of
imagination and conception."

[This procedure will require further revision
in future issues.]

APPROVAL FOR RELEASE:
LIMDIS-2018 (Arcane Teachings)
30, APR 2021 (Liber-3D)
Joshua Free, project director

Mardukite Babylon Site A, Research Facility, June 2017

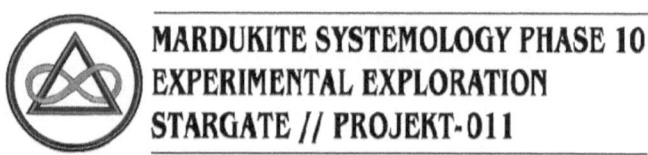

MARDUKITE SYSTEMOLOGY PHASE 10 EXPERIMENTAL EXPLORATION STARGATE // PROJEKT-011

MARDUKITE STARGATE PROJECT BULLETIN OF 20, JUNE 2017
BABYLON SITE, SAN LUIS VALLEY, COLORADO

TECH BRIEFING # B011-B [*Restricted (IV)*]

MARDUKITE PHASE-10 (SUMMER 2017)
Stargate Series – 6

SUMMARY

After ten years of developing a 'Mardukite Core' or underground foundation for continuing work, completion of that cycle and a transition toward 'Systemology' is the purpose of Phase-10. This purpose consists of an 'in-depth' exploration of the proverbial "Gates" -which is ironically the underlying theme behind every phase, level and gradient we have journeyed through to reach this point.

BACKGROUND

At the upper-end of the **spectrum** for potential work, we remain faced with a systematization of phenomenon cataloged as 'psychic' or 'psionic' in common-speak. Except to the effect that it might allow greater certainty on 'spiritual realizations', this work is classified as an upper-**end-point** because pursuit of these abilities directly does not seem to be a catalyst or route toward 'Ascension'. This makes them a 'byproduct' of the "Pathway" and not a means or **tier** by themselves. They are of greater common interest solely because they may be more easily 'capitalized on' or exploited for some other similar purpose.

INFRASTRUCTURE UPDATE

The inception of 'Operation-Eridu' has been

successful; the 'Babylon Site' serving functionally the past couple of months. All accumulated Mardukite resources are presently absorbed in the 'Babylon Site' and 'Stargate
Project'. We are virtually at a point of no return on this. We have also already attracted
attention of local law and code enforcement,
but it is being dealt with.

The structure used for upper-level experimental
research is 8-by-10 feet; with clearance for
the doors and a chair, 8-by-8 feet is prepared
for developmental work. The area is shielded
from radio-frequencies, microwaves and other
electromagnetic interference. Various experimental objects are often present, including a
seven-foot copper-framed pyramid large enough
for an individual to sit in. [We also have high
aspirations to similarly employ a 'Merkaba'
shape.]

CONCLUSION
In the plainest 'New Thought' terminology: we
are seeking a working knowledge of 'Human Consciousness' and command of the 'Human Condition' so that an individual might be 'free'
from the compulsive troubles and obsessive wor-
ries that accompany a spiritually, mentally and
emotionally fragmented existence and experience
of reality. It is critical that this work continues and that a firm foundation to support a
'Systemology Core' may be established.

APPROVAL FOR RELEASE:
31, OCT 2022 (Liber-011)
Joshua Free, project director

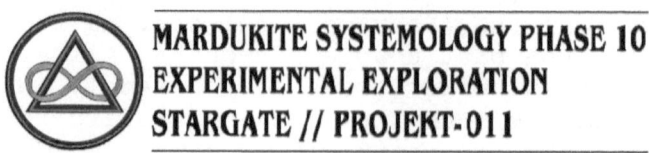

MARDUKITE SYSTEMOLOGY PHASE 10 EXPERIMENTAL EXPLORATION STARGATE // PROJEKT-011

MARDUKITE STARGATE PROJECT BULLETIN OF 5, JULY 2017
BABYLON SITE, SAN LUIS VALLEY, COLORADO

TECH SUMMARY # S011-D [*Confidential (VI)*]

SECRET DOCTRINES OF THE COSMOS (ARCANE TEACHINGS – PART 1)
Stargate Series – 7

SUMMARY
Principles of 'Hermetic Philosophy' frequently run parallel with Systemology, even if using different vocabulary than we do. Many years ago, the project director recovered a six-volume 'Esoteric Library of Arcane Teachings' (authored a century ago by W. W. Atkinson).

PROPOSAL
As the work seems wholly relevant to our efforts, we are preparing an annotated synthesis of this material for 'limited distribution' to Systemology Society members in 2018. Our edition of this library will be released in two volumes, each containing three of the six titles.

BACKGROUND (prepared by project director)
My personal experience with the "Arcane Teachings" began during my second year of initiation for this lifetime in the mid-1990's. I spent a phase of study and experimentation divided between: 'higher philosophies' of 'Hermetic Tradition', the Rosicrucians and other mystical 'Orders', much of which seemed too obscure in its communication relay to be practical; and also 'ritual magic' of modern 'New Age' tradi-

tions, most based on some 'higher law', but a direct relay of which was lost to an equally obscure array of culturally-colored labels, 'pantheistic' figures and 'esoteric' symbolism.Thus began my 'occult' quest to discover, as Arthur Edward Waite put it best: "the 'magic' behind the 'magic'" -and this is the sentiment I expressed blatantly at the end of the Mardukite 'cycle' of literary work in 2016 (the "Cybernomicon"), reviving Waite's words as a posthumous 'foreword' to the book:

"There is a door in the soul that opens to God —there's another door which opens to the recremental deeps and there is no doubt that the deeps come in when it is opened effectively...

"The mind is creative, but it must have a model on which to work. It must have thoughts to supply the power. Thought is energy, mental images are concentrated energy; and energy concentrated on any definite purpose becomes power.

"Every condition, every experience of life, is the result of our mental attitude. We can do only what we think we can do —have only what we think we can have — we can never express anything that we do not first hold in the mind.

"There arose the Substantial Creation [Primeval Dragon] which was first Nothing [the Abyss] and all that has followed in the past and continued is what defines our separateness. This state [of fragmentation and separation from the whole] is humanity's sickness and the Way of Return is our healing.

"There is a Magic which is behind the magic —the occult sanctuaries possess their secrets and mysteries. The written ceremonial is held by their self-imputed exponents to be either a debased and scandalous travesty or trivial and misconstrued application.

"A more inward purpose of Magic exists —
true and faithful investigations into the
ceremonial magic as it is found in the
grimoires gives the fullest evidence of
the futility of such rites.

"The True Path is a path of Undoing —
though it is at this point that so many
stand in fear of the irresistible consequences which follow from their own
teachings—the Returning of the Substantial
Creation into Nothing—it is an entrance
into the Darkness; an act of unknowing
wherein the soul is wholly stripped and
unclothed of all sensible realization of
itself."

REVELATIONS
These words are not revived from some obscure
teachings or secret level of curriculum; they
are from the introduction to the most popular
work circulated by Waite: his treatise on "Ceremonial Magic" —a complete compilation of all
the famous grimoire cycles: 'Key of Solomon',
'Goetia', 'Red Dragon of Honorius', 'Enchiridi-
on' &tc. —all of which are introduced with a
strict message from Waite that these grimoires
illustrate trivial exercises in demonstrating a
higher order of understanding. And we have
known this for over a century, yet we continue
to propagate such ridiculous methods of pseudo-
enlightenment in the 'New Age' today.

It is then quite clear why Waite left the 'magical' "Golden Dawn Order" to form a 'mystical'
one. It is true that the Magical Path may be
used as a bridge toward spiritual evolution for
the actual Self —'reprogramming' or 'defragmenting' a personal identity in times being
what they are at this point of humanity's development. But all "magic" is, by nature, an
external outer world demonstration of 'Cosmic
Law'; a communication out-flow of 'Cosmic Law'

using relative symbols and terms, relying on
what is often called 'Priest-craft'. This is
how the 'Arcane Teachings' or 'Secret Doctrine'
is recorded in "publicly-visible" publications
and traditions. This includes most related
books on the market today, leaving a host of
confusing and debatable 'esoteric symbolism'
waiting to be deciphered and misinterpreted
from the outside, without true initiation into
the **"Ancient Mystery School."**

There are certain individuals that will appreciate these sentiments after first having sin-
cerely played out the **exoteric** pursuit of 'ye
olde great magic games' and then, in reflection, having understood the insinuation that
there is some "Thing" behind all this and that
understanding this "Thing" is suddenly the most
important facet of our personal evolution —and
therefore survival. This "Thing", as put forth
in the 'Arcane Teachings', is THE LAW; just as
it appears in the related "Kybalion" text (by
the same author) as THE ALL; and in early "New
Thought" works as GOD (but not to be confused
with any relative theological concept of
"God").

CONCLUSION
Not all folk on the 'Magical Path' will reach
the same stage of spiritual evolution in this
lifetime. Some will remain transfixed by the
lights and glamour of that gradient of the
"First Gate" or "Moon-degree" often noted for
its 'Lunar Enchantment'. This is but the 'first
step' on the "Ladder" as we know from our ex-
plorations —and no matter how many times we may
'think' we have traversed "Seven Gates", so
long as it is experienced from the tier of the
'Magical Path', we have merely 'gleaned' "sev-
en" from the "first degree" of 'higher consciousness'.

At first it seems disheartening —all that we
have earned from the surface world and life-

128

long pursuits into the available published
texts is little more than an initiation to the
First Degree! And what's more, most individuals
will see this first tier as 'all' there is and
not a reflection of THE ALL. Therefore most in
the 'New Age' will not achieve the highest
realizations of the "Great Work" -the uncovering of the true 'Incommunicable Arcanum' —the
secrets revealed on the 'esoteric' Mystical
Path that are not 'communicable' without first
being realized. **Actualizing** this realization is
the quest we are now on.

APPROVAL FOR RELEASE:
LIMDIS-2018 (Arcane Teachings)
31, OCT 2022 (Liber-011)
Joshua Free, project director

Mardukite Babylon Site A, Research Facility, July 2017

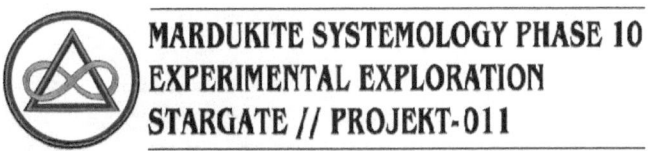

MARDUKITE SYSTEMOLOGY PHASE 10 EXPERIMENTAL EXPLORATION STARGATE // PROJEKT-011

MARDUKITE STARGATE PROJECT BULLETIN OF 10, JULY 2017
BABYLON SITE, SAN LUIS VALLEY, COLORADO

TECH BRIEFING # B011-C [*Restricted (IV)*]

HERMETIC PHILOSOPHY & W.W. ATKINSON (ARCANE TEACHINGS – PART 2)
Stargate Series – 8

SUMMARY
In 1908, in the midst of an era of practical magical revival, "The Kybalion" appeared; a unique metaphysical handbook styled in the 'Hermetic Tradition', and revealing the main 'esoteric' philosophical and spiritual tenets of the "Ancient Mystery Tradition."

Anonymously presented at first by "Three Initiates" and released by the 'Yogi Publication Society', later analysis of the 'Esoteric Library of Arcane Teachings' presented by William Walker Atkinson (1862-1932), showed all of the works to be of one and the same origin —from Atkinson, himself, an American pioneer of the 'New Thought' movement of the early 20th Century.

While the edition known as "The Kybalion" is perhaps his most famous book, Atkinson used the 'Arcane Scrolls' (part of what we refer to as the 'Arcane Tablets' in Systemology) as a basis to produce many volumes of material for his publishing company, under various pseudonyms including: 'Theron G. Dumont', 'Yogi Ramacharaka' and 'Magus Incognito'.

BACKGROUND
According to "The Kybalion", there are 'Seven
Primary Hermetic Principles'. Other traditions
have included them as the 'Seven Pillars', but
in the version of the 'Arcane Teachings' we are
presenting to the Systemology Society, Atkinson
refers to them as the 'Seven Cosmic Laws'.
These same principles are expounded upon
uniquely by each of the greatest teachers gone
past. They also form a foundation for any le-
gitimate modern 'mystical' revival or 'magick'
school.

The real value and purpose of the Mardukite
'Esoteric Library' selections, specifically the
"Arcane Teachings (Kybalion Unveiled)" series
of volumes presented to members of the Systemology Society (planned for 2018), is the ability
for the most profound and intricate Universal
lessons of the "Ancient Mystery School" to be
so purely and simply communicated in clear language.

APPROVAL FOR RELEASE:
LIMDIS2018 (Arcane Teachings)
31, OCT 2022 (Liber-011)
Joshua Free, project director

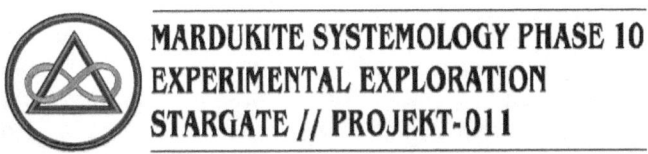

MARDUKITE SYSTEMOLOGY PHASE 10
EXPERIMENTAL EXPLORATION
STARGATE // PROJEKT-011

MARDUKITE STARGATE PROJECT BULLETIN OF
14, JULY 2017
BABYLON SITE, SAN LUIS VALLEY, COLORADO

TECH SUMMARY # S011-E [*Confidential* (*VI*)]

HERMETIC PRINCIPLES & COSMIC LAWS
(ARCANE TEACHINGS – PART 3)
Stargate Series – 9

DIRECTIONS
This bulletin is to be read in sequence with
other bulletins for 'Arcane Teachings' dated
July 2017.

THE SEVEN PRIMARY HERMETIC PRINCIPLES
The Seven 'Hermetic Principles' or 'Cosmic
Laws' are the entire subject of exploration in
our presentation of the 'Arcane Teachings' for
the Mardukite "Esoteric Library" (planned for
2018). They are demonstrated and described in
various ways throughout the material, but are
listed here for easy reference:

* I. The Principle of Mentalism.
  "The ALL is MIND; the Universe is Mental."

* II. The Principle of Correspondence.
  "As above, so below; as below, so above."

* III. The Principle of Vibration.
  "Nothing rests; everything moves; everything
vibrates."

* IV. The Principle of Polarity.
  "Everything is Dual; everything has poles;
everything has its pair of opposites; like and
unlike are the same; opposites are identical in
nature, but different in degree; extremes meet;
all truths are but half-truths; all paradoxes

may be reconciled."

   * V. The Principle of Rhythm.

   "Everything flows, out and in; everything has its tides; all things rise and fall; the pendulum-swing manifests in everything; the measure of the swing to the right is the measure of the swing to the left; rhythm compensates."

   * VI. The Principle of Cause and Effect.

   "Every Cause has its Effect; every Effect has its Cause; everything happens according to Cosmic Law; Chance is but a name for Law not recognized; there are many planes of **causation**, but nothing escapes the Law."

   * VII. The Principle of Gender.

   "Gender is in everything; everything has its Masculine and Feminine Principles; Gender manifests on all planes."

THE SEVEN COSMIC LAWS

The 'Arcane Teachings' have come down to the present age through the corridors of time, from the dim ages of past eras, races, and schools of thought. Even those highest in the councils of 'Custodians of The Scrolls', are unable to trace the 'Teaching', in an unbroken direct line, further back than the time of Pythagoras, and a little later in Ancient Greece; although they find many references to, and extracts from, the teachings of ancient Egypt and Babylon (Chaldea), which serve to show that Hermetic "Ancient Mystery Schools" were founded on occult instruction still more remote, re-ceived in a direct line of succession of teach-ers and pupils extending over thousands of years.

The 'Arcane Teachings' hold that the Cosmos is regulated by "Seven Laws", which are superim-posed by THE LAW upon 'Cosmic Will', and thus upon all that is manifested. These 'Seven Cos-mic Laws' are as follows:

* I. The Law of Orderly Trend.
"Under this law there is always manifested law and order in the Cosmos, from suns to atoms; from highest to lowest; matter, energy, and mind. There is no Disorder or Chance in the Cosmos."

* II. The Law of Analogy.
"Under this law, there is found a **correspondence** and agreement between all of the various forms of manifestation. What is true of the atom, is true of the sun. What is true of the amoeba is true of man, and beings above man. What is true of matter, is true of energy and mind. To know one is to know all. 'As above, so below,' as the Hermeticist expresses it."

* III. The Law of Sequence.
"Under this Law, there is included the activities of what is generally known as 'Cause and Effect.' Nothing happens by chance. Nothing happens without a **precedent** manifestation, and a subsequent manifestation. Nothing stands alone."

* IV. The Law of Rhythm.
"Under this law falls a variety of phenomena, among which is the important phenomenon of Vibration. Everything is in constant vibration—everything material, mental or of energy. Upon this fact depends the variety, degrees, states and conditions of the manifestations of the Cosmos. All is in vibration—physical, mental and spiritual. Vibration is the key of relative power, and relative activities. To control Vibration is to control all forces in the universe."

* V. The Law of Balance.
"Under this law there is to be found an explanation for the universal equilibrium, compensation and balance, observed in all of the manifestations of the Cosmos. One thing balances another, in the physical, mental and spiritual. Everything has something set opposite it, to balance it. Everything has its compensation.

Everything has its Cosmic price. In an understanding of the Law of Balance, there is to be
found the Secret of Power and Poise."

* VI. The Law of Cyclicity.
"Under this law is found the cyclic, or circular trend of all things, physical, mental and
spiritual. Everything moves in circles. The
wise and strong convert the circles into spirals. Instead of traveling around in an eternal
circle, the wise and strong rise in spirals to
attainment and advancement. Worlds and atoms;
Cosmos and Man; all are under this law, and
move in accordance therewith. To convert the
Circle into the Spiral, is one of the Arcane
Secrets, conveyed in its formulas."

* VII. The Law of Opposites.
"Under this law is to be found the explanation
of that wonderful fact in nature—the fact that
everything has its opposite; everything is, and
is not, at the same time; everything has its
other side; every truth is but a half-truth;
everything is a paradox; every thesis has its
anti-thesis; every truth contains a bit of untruth, and every untruth a bit of truth; every
male contains female—every female contains
male. Also the fact that opposite things are
alike, in the end; that extremes meet; the con-
tradictions may be reconciled."

APPROVAL FOR RELEASE:
LIMDIS2018 (Arcane Teachings)
31, OCT 2022 (Liber-011)
Joshua Free, project director

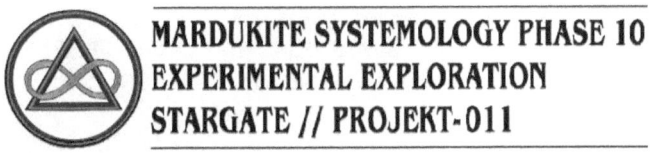

MARDUKITE SYSTEMOLOGY PHASE 10 EXPERIMENTAL EXPLORATION STARGATE // PROJEKT-011

MARDUKITE STARGATE PROJECT BULLETIN OF 19, JULY 2017 BABYLON SITE, SAN LUIS VALLEY, COLORADO

TECH SUMMARY # S011-F [*Confidential (VI)*]

SECRET FORMULAS OF THE COSMOS (ARCANE TEACHINGS – PART 4)

Stargate Series – 10

SUMMARY
Principles of 'Hermetic Philosophy' frequently run parallel with Systemology, even if using different vocabulary than we do. Many years ago, the project director recovered a six-volume 'Esoteric Library of Arcane Teachings' (authored a century ago by W. W. Atkinson).

PROPOSAL
As the work seems wholly relevant to our efforts, we are preparing an annotated synthesis of this material for 'limited distribution' to Systemology Society members in 2018. Our edition will be released in two volumes, "Secret Doctrines" and "Secret Formulas", each containing three of the six titles.

REFERENCES
"Secret Doctrines of the Cosmos" [05 JUL 17]
"Establishing The Self" [12 JUN 17]

BACKGROUND (prepared by project director)
In "Secret Doctrines of the Cosmos", I explain how my experience with the "Arcane Teachings" began during my second active year on the Pathway in this lifetime, during the mid-1990's, resulting from an esoteric pursuit of the

'higher law' of 'magic behind the magic'. This is to say, a more advanced 'Mystical Path' representing the true epitome of the 'Second Gate' (Mercury).

In "Secret Doctrines of the Cosmos" we are introduced to the 'Thing' behind all things —THE LAW, ALL or GOD. Traditional sources of 'exoteric' outer instruction only have faint understandings of this. The solution exists only in secret —hidden away in unseen 'esoteric' folds not concerned with general public opinions and not subject to the scrutiny of the masses. As John Toland expressed in his "Pantheisticon": 'Some things ought not be revealed to all people'. And even the writings themselves do not betray the true secrets, for there is 'a difference between knowing the Path and walking the Path'.

A 'SECRET FORMULAS' EXPERIMENTAL PROGRAM

* The first step is total realization of SELF-HOOD —the ability to assume full Awareness and knowingness, in "Self-Honesty," as SELF, "I" or "I AM" -meaning as the 'Alpha-Spirit'.

* The second focus is control of the vital energetic relationship between the "I" and the physical body —an energetic current that Atkinson has chosen to identify as 'VRIL' (of which is also a subject of great interest in the underground). [It is quite possible that 'Vril' is roughly equivalent to what we refer to as "ZU" in Systemology.]

* Thirdly, having mastered SELF and its command of the physical body, lessons conclude with examination of these applications in other outward expressions, such as 'personal magnetism' or 'mentalism' and the way in which we may influence others and protect from the influence of others.

* Additionally, we are interested in information regarding the 'Astral Plane', 'Spirit

Worlds', 'Spiritual Gateways' and the 'After-Life'.

NOTES: "Establishing The Self" [12 JUN 17] may
be inserted here in the 'Arcane Teachings'
series of bulletins as (Arcane Teachings – Part
4B).

APPROVAL FOR RELEASE:
LIMDIS2018 (Arcane Teachings)
31, OCT 2022 (Liber-011)
Joshua Free, project director

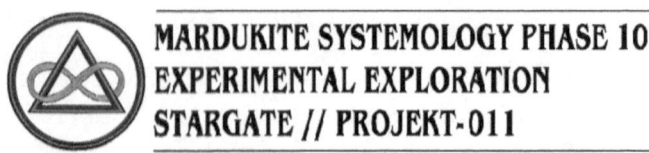

MARDUKITE SYSTEMOLOGY PHASE 10 EXPERIMENTAL EXPLORATION STARGATE // PROJEKT-011

MARDUKITE STARGATE PROJECT BULLETIN OF 27, JULY 2017
BABYLON SITE, SAN LUIS VALLEY, COLORADO

TECH REPORT # R011-B [*Top Secret* (*VII*)]

SYSTEMOLOGY TECHNIQUE 1-8-0, ISSUE 2
(ARCANE TEACHINGS – PART 5)

Stargate Series – 11

SUMMARY

The following techniques are derived from titles collected for our proposed edition of "Secret Formulas" ('Esoteric Library of Arcane Teachings' series) for members of the Systemology Society. These techniques should be experimented with further before considering them officially included in the "Technique-180" regimen that will open upper-level work. [This regimen will still require additional revision for future issues.]

REFERENCES

"Secret Formulas of the Cosmos" [19 JUL 17]
"Establishing The Self" [12 JUN 17]

BACKGROUND

The following exercises will assist to bring about increased realizations on the 'Mastery of Opposites'. It is adapted from an ancient formula; modern figures of speech being used here. [This tech report should be studied after the bulletin "Establishing The Self" (12 JUN 17).]

It should be understood that we have not diverted from the truths already established in "Systemology: The Original Thesis", however at each gradient-tier of work, we find ourselves refining our specific focus if we want to turn theory into practice and launch Systemology as an effective 'applied philosophy' toward 'Ascension'.

TECHNIQUES

The Neophyte is to place themselves in a condition and position of rest, calm and repose. Let them meditate upon the real nature of the "I" ("I-AM") and cast off the illusion of the personality-self, and its attributes. Then imagine rising above the lower planes of personality toward the higher planes of Self-Hood as in a balloon which is rising above the surface of the earth into the higher regions of purer, lofty, refined air.

Then throw all the likes and dislikes overboard from the mental balloon; loves and hates; prejudice considerations for and against anything and everything whatsoever, either good or bad in short the entire collection of inherited or acquired feelings and emotions which have formed the garment or body of personality for so long. As the mental balloon rises higher and higher throw off even the more subtle feelings and emotions, until finally divested of every iota of artificial character possessed, and SELF remains, naked as a new-born babe.

After a few trials of this exercise, the Neophyte will come to a new sense of power and understanding —a new realization of the real nature of Will -a realization that Pairs of Opposites (of the Personality) are but masks and clothing of the character he has been playing. Then the Neophyte may gradually return to the earth and resume the garments thrown off, but as a Master and Owner, not as a Slave to them as is standard-issue. This exercise quickens actualization of Self-Hood, and aids in Mastery of Opposites. The following exercise will also be found very useful in the same direction.

The Neophyte should place themselves in a position and condition of calm, restful repose, and then meditate upon the fact that contrasting and opposing feelings and emotions are in reality but the opposite poles of the same thing. In imagination, try the experiment of changing the polarity of some emotion —of inducing the state of love where hate has been dominant, or vice versa. Shift the polarity of feelings and emotions at will, backward and forward, alternating these considerations in practice. The realization attained is that feelings and emotions are far from being fixed and constant, as might be supposed, but are capable, if defragmented, of being shifted about fluidly at Will -and not as a 'stuck flow' of energy.

By shifting polarity an individual may change a painful feeling or emotion into its opposite. Distressing feelings may be changed in polarity, or balanced with their opposites. It is not always necessary to shift entirely to the opposite pole of the emotion or feeling; many adepts merely change to the opposite polarity in a sufficient degree to establish a balance and thus create a condition and state of poise and equilibrium. This results in peace of mind —which quiets the stormy sea of passion, emotion or feeling.

CONCLUSION
Concerning a Mastery of Pairs of Opposites: one finds a peace unknown to those who polarize in either extreme. A 'Master' is a Master of Opposites when they may shift polarity of considerations, emotion and feeling at Will. [There may be a connection between the 'Formula of Opposites' and the 'Middle Pillar Rite' employed in 'ceremonial magic', esp. 'Golden Dawn Tradition'; reference- Israel Regardie's "The Middle Pillar". (on file at the office-library).]

APPROVAL FOR RELEASE:
LIMDIS2018 (Arcane Teachings)
31, OCT 2022 (Liber-011)
Joshua Free, project director

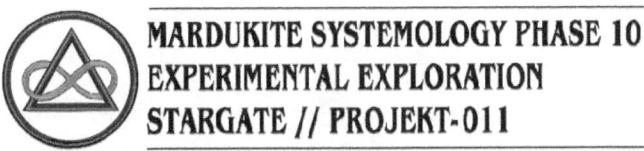

MARDUKITE SYSTEMOLOGY PHASE 10 EXPERIMENTAL EXPLORATION STARGATE // PROJEKT-011

MARDUKITE STARGATE PROJECT BULLETIN OF 04, AUGUST 2017 BABYLON SITE, SAN LUIS VALLEY, COLORADO

TECH BRIEFING # B011-D [*Restricted (III)*]

BASIC TRAINING REGIMEN (SUMMER 2017) (ARCANE TEACHINGS – PART 6)

Stargate Series – 12

SUMMARY
This bulletin includes 'basic' techniques intended for immediate release to limited access project members for experimentation and feedback. Although they seem "basic", it has been determined that certain "basic" effective rudiments are lacking in our development of a regimen for upper-level Systemology work.

CITATION
The following sections of "Secret Formulas" (Esoteric Library of Arcane Teachings, volume two) contain exercises derived from Atkinson's title "Mental Alchemy", chapter nine 'Mentalism in a Nutshell'.

REFERENCES
"Secret Formulas of the Cosmos" [19 JUL 17]

WILL AND ATMOSPHERE
The Neophyte should create a Positive Will Atmosphere, or Aura, for themselves, which will tend to serve as a protective armor, shielding him from adverse influences from outside, and also tending to render his positive power felt by those with whom he comes in contact.

The Positive Atmosphere is created by a pure

act of Will, aided by Visualization. A Neophyte should first realize that s/he 'is' Will itself; then visualize the Mind Stuff in the air of the immediate vicinity becoming charged with the positive power of their Will. It may aid to imagine being surrounded for a distance of about three feet with an 'egg-shaped aura' or atmosphere of highly charged Will, radiating outward and vibrating with an intense energy.

This phenomena is actually existent, although standard-issue senses cannot perceive the vibrations or aura. Treat yourself every day, or oftener, with the intent to increase the degree of your Positive Atmosphere. The more clearly you can visualize, or imagine, the existence of this aura or atmosphere, the greater will be your degree of positive personal atmosphere. Be not deceived in regarding Imagination as unreal or fanciful; it is a mental activity of amazing occult power.

PERSONAL POSITIVITY
A Neophyte may occasionally find they are in the presence of persons more 'positive' than themselves. In such cases they should at once determine that the other shall not 'overlap' them; but to at least meet the positive person 'edge to edge' if not further to 'overlap' the other. This is accomplished by immediately denying the positivity of the other person (silently and mentally) with an assertion: "I DENY YOUR POSITIVITY OVER ME." At the same time, focalize Will-Consciousness, seeing themselves as a focal center of Will, and having the Cosmic Will back of him. If a sense of negativity rises while mingling in a crowd, assert Self-Hood in the same way. Greater certainty and realization of one's SELF as a focal center of the Will, promotes a greater degree of 'Personal Positive Atmosphere' in manifestation.

VISUALIZATION AND IMAGINATION

Visualization is a personal creative process of manifesting 'Mental Image Pictures' on the 'Mental' and 'Material' Planes. Visualization consists in forming and holding a 'Mental Image' of things (conditions) as you wish them to be in actuality -as if it were actually extant in that moment. The 'Mental Image' tends to create a material (objective) form and existence; it is the 'mental pattern' around which the 'material conditions' tend to group themselves. It is the 'seed-form' of the thing itself. The circuits of a Visualization to observe (around which material realities form and crystallize) are:

(1) yourself as you wish to be.

(2) others as you wish them to be.

(3) conditions as you wish them to be.

STATEMENTS OF AFFIRMATION

Statements, 'postulates' (or 'affirmations' as some call them) are positive (or creative) assertions of the existence of the conditions you wish to bring about. These statements should be in present tense. Do not say to yourself, "Such and such a thing will be bye and bye," but boldly assert "Such and such a thing is existent and in actual being, now, this moment." The theory behind this is not necessary to discus in detail. Half-measure statements yield half-measure results. They tend to energize and vitalize practice with 'Mental Image Pictures' (or 'Imagination').

STATEMENTS OF DENIAL (this section requires additional systemological review)

'Mystic Denials' are a form of Statement. With an individual focalized in Will, they are able to exert much mystic power by boldly denying out of existence the obstacles and difficulties which beset their path. Obstructing things tend to disintegrate and disappear from one's mental world, which is followed later by a response of similar kind and degree in the material world. Do not be afraid to say: "I DENY this or that obstacle. It has no power over me. I deny it out of my world. For me it does not exist." Make your denials as positive as your statements. COMMAND, not beg or entreat.

MENTAL VIBRATION (FREQUENCY)
In all forms of 'Mentalism' there is evidence of Mental Vibration. Vibration is not confined to the gross material substance of the universe, but is equally in evidence in the 'Mind Stuff' that fills all space. When one thinks, feels, or wills, there is manifest vibration just as truly as in the vibration of the atom or tuning-forks. Each kind of thought, feeling or emotion has its own rate of vibration, or keynote.

When a certain rate of mental vibration is manifested it tends to reproduce similar vibrations, and consequent similar mental states in the minds of those coming within its field of induction. Just as a tuning-fork will cause similar vibrations in the objects in the room, so will a mind sending forth vibrations tend to reproduce those vibrations in other minds in its vicinity, or under certain circumstances, at long distances.

This being so, it follows that if an individual will carry in their mind a positive, persistent idea, backed up with an application of Will, they will be able to impress that idea upon others, with more or less effect. They may be aided in this by practice of Statements (postulates) and Visualization, for both practices tend to send forth mental vibrations of a high degree of strength and power.

THOUGHT-WAVES & MENTAL CURRENTS
There are waves and currents in the great ocean of 'Mind Stuff', just as there are waves and

currents in the ocean or in the air. Thoughts,
feelings and emotion tend to create waves or
currents in the 'Mind Stuff', which will flow
out in all directions influencing and affecting
others in their field of force, particularly if
those others happen to maintain a degree of
mental vibration corresponding to that of the
traveling wave or current. Every one sends
forth these thought waves or currents, usually
unconsciously and without direct intention, and
consequently with comparatively slight effect.
Those who understand 'Mentalism' are able to
consciously direct, concentrate and focus Will
upon who or what they wish to influence, and
consequently their thought waves and currents
travel direct to their mark, and create a much
greater effect.

THOUGHT-FORMS & WILL-INTENTION
Thought-forms are concentrated thought-waves or
thought-bodies usually projected from the mind
by concentrated thought and WILL, and which,
when coming in contact with others, have almost
as great an effect upon them as if the sender
were present in person exerting WILL upon the
person or persons. Masters that acquire concentration and focalization skills are often able
to send forth thought-forms of such high degree
of power and strength that they produce upon
others the mental impression that the sender,
himself, is actually present in person.

THE 'MAGIC LANTERN' TECHNIQUE
Fix your attention firmly on the symbol of the
'Magic Lantern', with its concentrated light of
WILL, and its painted 'slide' depicting the
chosen 'Mental Image Picture'. Regard the objective world, or persons, things, and circumstances, as the great plane surface upon which
you wish to throw or project your 'Mental Images' using the 'Lantern' so they may material-
ize objectively. Get this picture clearly in
mind. See your "I" as the Light in the Lantern

—its concentrated WILL focused directly upon the 'Mental Image slide' of the Lantern. Hold this consideration when practicing 'Mentalism' and always stand 'behind' your 'mental images', as the Light in the Lantern.

Having your 'Mental Image' impressed upon your imagined Lantern slide, direct and point your Lantern tube upon whatever object in the out- side world you wish. If you wish to impress a person with your thought, mentally direct and focus your mental Magic Lantern upon them (re- gardless of distance), just as you would upon a plane surface. The 'Mental Image Picture' is projected by means of the highly concentrated WILL.

If a number of persons are to be impressed, they may be considered as a 'group', or else the Lantern tube may be turned upon each in turn. If general conditions or environments are to be 'treated', imagine them as a whole, and focus your Lantern directly upon them, produ- cing a projection of gigantic proportions. These directions surely cover the whole pro- cess.

Places (present or absent) may be 'treated' in this way, in order to dispel undesirable condi- tions or change the vibrations. Conditions may be treated successfully by turning upon them a strong 'Mental Image' of the changed conditions you wish to bring about.

 * This formula may be applied across the boards and should not be immediately abandoned or disregarded in favor of some more complic- ated or metaphysically theoretical method until it is properly tested by individuals with acute concentration and focal skills.

APPROVAL FOR RELEASE:
LIMDIS2018 (Arcane Teachings)
31, OCT 2022 (Liber-011)
Joshua Free, project director

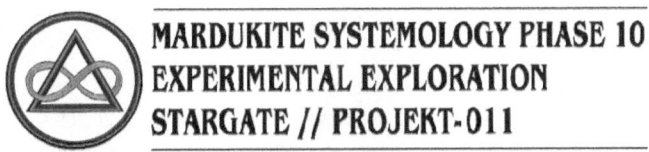

MARDUKITE SYSTEMOLOGY PHASE 10 EXPERIMENTAL EXPLORATION STARGATE // PROJEKT-011

MARDUKITE STARGATE PROJECT BULLETIN OF 16, AUGUST 2017
BABYLON SITE, SAN LUIS VALLEY, COLORADO

TECH SUMMARY # S011-G [*Confidential* (VI)]

ASTRAL PLANES & ASCENSION
(BASIC TRAINING – PART 2)
Stargate Series – 13

SYNOPSIS
This is a summary of "The Metaphysical Universe: Astral Planes" a paper written by W.W. Atkinson in the early 1900's. It will be included as an 'Appendix' to "Secret Formulas" (Esoteric Library of Arcane Teachings, volume two) planned for limited distribution to members of the Systemology Society in 2018-2019.

TECH SUMMARY
This bulletin draws upon the writings of 'New Thought' pioneer, W.W. Atkinson. This data is retained for future reference but does not necessarily reflect precise philosophic views or vocabulary of 'Mardukite Systemology' directly. It serves as a comparative study until such time that sufficient experimental research provides us with an 'official' definitive cosmology for our Systemology.

THE UNIVERSES OR PLANES
There are three great planes of manifestation in the Cosmos: the 'Material Plane'; the 'Astral Plane'; and the 'Spiritual Plane'. We use the term "plane" from necessity and in the absence of other words. Many mystics speak of each of these as a 'Plane of Thought', meaning

respectively thereby: (1) the plane of thought connected with sensations of the body, physical desires, &tc.; (2) the plane of intellect, reason, &tc.; and (3) the plane of higher mental activities and manifestations, familiarly known as the 'Spiritual Plane of Thought'.

A plane is not a place. A particular place may include several planes, and sub-planes; for the planes interpenetrate each other. A plane has no 'dimensions' in **space**, and rather more resembles a 'state' or 'condition'. It cannot be measured in the three dimensions, and yet it is capable of measurement by degrees in the 'Scale of Vibrations' (or frequency).

These states or degrees of vibration interpenetrate each other, without interference, but have correspondences or analogies in physical phenomena. The various planes of manifestation blend into each other, and each of the three planes has seven sub-planes, which are sub-divided into seven minor planes, and so on, until seven times seven acts of sub-division have been made as Gates.

On the 'Physical Plane' of the Cosmos occurs various manifestations of the physical world — the world of 'energy-matter'. It is the plane best known to us, for all of our physical activities are performed on some of its sub-planes. On these planes there are manifestations of matter of degrees unrecognized by standard-issue Human senses, as well as the familiar forms and degrees. Likewise there are forces and energies of which man of today is totally ignorant, with the exception of a few advanced souls who have risen above the ordinary race limitations. Our specific subject here, however, is the second plane of the Cosmos: the 'ASTRAL PLANE'.

THE ASTRAL PLANE
The term "ASTRAL" (from the Greek word meaning

"a star"*) regards 'regions' and 'beings' of a more ethereal and finer order and degree than our material world and its beings. It is believed that disembodied entities and supernatural beings abide in the 'Astral'.

Some schools use the term "Astral Plane" to designate only lower sub-planes of the Astral, using other terms to designate higher planes, which latter they often confuse with those of the 'Spiritual Plane'. Others include the entire series of 'above-the-Material planes' under the general term of "Astral Plane".

The 'Arcane Teachings' use the term "Astral Plane" to mean the **intermediate** plane of the Cosmos —the plane lying between the 'Physical' and the 'Spiritual', including, however, the higher as well as the lower Astral sub-planes.

There are many sub-planes on the 'Astral Plane', many of which bear close analogies to corresponding planes known to us on the 'Material Plane'. There are also sub-planes containing life activities, which are different from the more familiar ones, and which bear the same relationship to the latter that the 'black keys' on the piano-board bear to the 'white keys'.

On these "black-key" sub-planes dwell entities strange to human sight and thought, but which, nevertheless, form a part of the universal manifestation of life. These entities are non-human —never were human, and never will be human. Their evolution has been, and will continue, along totally different lines. Esoteric lore categorizes these entities under the general term of "elementaries" (or "elementals"), although their degrees and characteristics vary

---

* *Astral / Star* – we now know that the root for the terms *asterisk* and *astral*, &tc. predate the Greek language, emerging in Mesopotamia and the Akkadian *istra, istarte, ashtar,* &tc. relating to "gods" "stars" and "planets" and famously the Babylonian epithet ISHTAR for the **Sumerian** "*Inanna.*"

greatly, one from another.

THE LOWER ASTRAL PLANES
The sub-plane nearest the 'Physical' is the sub-plane in which 'Thought Currents' operate, 'Astral Bodies' are maintained, and 'Auric Colors' are visible. This sub-plane is often penetrated, unwittingly, by persons whose psychic faculties have become sharpened or more developed.

ASTRAL BODY
An 'Astral Body' has long been known in esoteric traditions by various names: "ethereal body", "fluidic body"; the "double" &tc. It is composed of Astral substance (matter). It bears the same relation to ordinary matter that steam does to ice. The 'Astral Body' goes exterior to the ordinary body of a person at its death. Under certain conditions it may leave the 'physical body' during waking hours, and project itself to distant points in space.

The 'Astral Body' is invisible to the ordinary physical senses, although those possessing Clairvoyant power, or well developed Astral Senses may detect it. Lore suggests that 'Astral Body' is composed of seven "sheaths" or "layers" of substance, the grosser of which disintegrate or 'sloughs off' when the entity rises to higher planes, and which must be again 'materialized' when it revisits the lower planes.

THE AURA
The 'Aura' and 'Auric Colors' of the 'Astral Body' are in the nature of emanations or radiations from the 'Astral Body', and which recent scientific investigation has proven conclusively, by means of photographs. The Physical Body, even, has its aura of vitality vibrations, or VRIL (ZU), which flow freely from it, particularly when vitality of the person is strong. This "VRIL" is the 'human magnetism' of

magnetic healers, and which serves to arouse strength and vigor to those to whom it is applied. The 'Astral Aura', on the contrary, is an emanation of mental states, feelings and emotions of the person's mind. It is egg-shaped, and extends on all sides of the person to a distance of about three feet. It manifests various colors, particularly around the head, the colors corresponding to the character of the mental states being manifested, or those habitual to the person. Persons in whom the faculty of 'Astral Sensing' is well developed may see these auric colors plainly:

* RED : animal passions, lust, anger, &tc;

* YELLOW : intellectuality in its various degrees and forms.

* GREEN : jealousy, but, in one of its deepest clearest shades, that which is generally called "tact," "agreeableness," "diplomacy," or in its lower forms, "deceit";

* BLUE : religious emotion, &tc. —light blue denoting what is generally called "spirituality," but which in reality is an ethereal, refined form of religious feeling. Spirituality is more a matter of knowledge and life development, rather than feeling or emotion;

* GRAY denotes selfishness;

* BLACK is the astral color of hate, malice and vengeful emotion.

THOUGHT-WAVES & THOUGHT-FORMS

Thoughts and mental states manifest in object-ive form. The person manifesting active thought or feeling, emanates waves and currents of thought-force which spread around him in constantly widening circles in every direction. In this way great thought-clouds are formed which hover over and around places to which they are attracted.

Thought-clouds of similar general character

tend to coalesce, mingle and blend with each
other, and to move toward persons, places and
localities in which similar thoughts or feelings are being manifested. The 'Law of Attraction' operates in this direction of drawing
thought influences toward those who are manifesting similar thought vibrations. Cities,
towns and smaller places (even places of business, office-buildings, houses, and rooms) have
their own particular thought atmosphere, which
may be felt by sensitives and by those possessing the faculty of 'Astral Sensing'.

Akin to these thought-clouds are thought-forms:
thought-clouds of great density and power of
cohesion. They are charged with strong Will or
ardent Desire of the persons emanating them —
and vitalized by the VRIL (ZU), or vitality of
the person infused into them. Such thought-
forms often exert nearly as great a psychic
power over those with whom they come in contact
as would the sender in person. They are akin to
'desire-elementals' (mentioned later).

Thought-clouds and thought-forms abide on the
Lower Astral Sub-planes until they finally disintegrate. They tend to coalesce and gather
around places in which vibrations are harmoni-
ous to their own. Some places have their mental
atmospheres of vice, others of greed, others of
industry, others of the reverse. In short
thought atmospheres exist everywhere on this
Lower Astral Sub-plane, just as does the material atmosphere exist everywhere on the material
plane.

LOWER ASTRAL SUB-PLANES
Those who are able to travel in the 'Astral
Body' find this thought atmospheric phenomena a
source of never failing interest, although at
times one is glad to will himself away from
some of the scenes, so gross and base are the
emotions and feelings manifesting in the dark,
heavy suffocating clouds of thought force —so

horrible some of the thought-forms. But even
these may be driven away by an exercise of
WILL, and thought-vibrations of contrary
natures tend to repel them and scatter them
away.

On a different class of sub-plane than above
are found manifestations of the 'scrap pile of
the Astral'. On this sub-plane are to be found
discarded Astral materials of 'Astral Bodies'
which have been 'sloughed off' by entities
which have discarded them as they have moved up
higher. Also, the disintegrating 'Astral Bodies' of entities which have failed to survive
and whose spirits have been resolved into their
original elements and become merged into the
general principle of Consciousness. 'Astral
Body' remnants discarded and disintegrating,
are not in any way related to the spirits which
formerly inhabited them. They are mere shells,
without soul or mind, and yet preserving a
slight degree of vitality.

Astral Corpses also become visible under certain conditions, often around graveyards,
battle-fields, &tc. -and are thought to be
ghosts, or 'spirits' of those who formerly inhabited them. They are, however, generally only
the grossest astral covering of the 'Astral
Body' —its 'shell' so to speak, and are no more
to be regarded as the deceased person himself
than is the physical body lying in the grave —
both are discarded coverings, or 'corpses'.

There are denizens of this loathsome place —inhabitants of this horrible abode. These entities, however, are not placed there for punishment. They are there because of their own
abnormal desires and tendencies, which unfit
them for the planes of even the lowest of disembodied human entities. They are unfit for association with the disembodied astral forms of
the beasts, which latter persist for a short
time after physical death.

Subject to the laws of humankind they are not
allowed the privilege of rapid annihilation bestowed upon the beasts —they must live out
their peculiar life to the end. They are the
pariahs, the ghoul-like scum of the human race,
who have removed themselves from the race and
have entailed upon themselves a **fate** of their
own. Their fate is a Living Death —a conscious
life in a corpse-like body, among corpses of
the Astral. They were the lowest of human
Satyrs. Nature finally casts over them the
spell of a deep sleep, from which they never
awaken, and from which they pass into disinteg-
ration and annihilation. They polluted the Sac-
red Altar. They stole the Divine Fire for dev-
ilish rites. They committed the Unpardonable
Sin. They removed themselves from the trend of
Cosmic Evolution. Their own Desire was their
Fate.

THE ASTRAL 'BLACK-KEYS'

The "Black-Keys" of the Astral scale include
sub-planes where non-human (or semi-human)
creatures dwell -those which are grouped together in occult classification under the general name of 'elementaries' or 'elementals'.
There may be found 'elementaries' of a scale of
life quite different from our own.

ELEMENTAL BEINGS

The 'elementaries' may be grouped into several
general classes, although the classification is
more or less imperfect. One of these classes
comprise "Nature Spirits", which, however, is
less accurate than poetical. These entities
have been known in legends by various names:
earth-spirits, gnomes; water-spirits, undines;
air-spirits, sylphs; fire-spirits, salamanders;
fairies; pixies; elves; brownies; djinns;
trolls; fauns; kobolds; imps; goblins; &tc.
Their forms are many and various, but most frequently human in shape.

The great majority of them prefer to avoid Humans altogether; humanity's habits and emanations distasteful to them, and the constant rush of astral currents set up by restless, ill-regulated desires, disturbs and annoys them. On the other hand, instances are not wanting in which nature-spirits have as it were made friends with human beings, and offered them such assistance as lay in their power. [Additional Ref: "Elvenomicon"]

Adepts know how to make use of the services of the 'nature spirits' at WILL, but the ordinary magician may obtain their assistance only by processes either of invocation or evocation; that is, either by attracting their attention as a suppliant and making some kind of bargain with them, or by endeavoring to set into motion influences which would compel their obedience. Both methods are extremely undesirable.

ARTIFICIAL ENTITIES
On other Lower Astral Planes there is another class of elementaries, which have been called 'artificial' or 'human-created entities'. This, the largest class of Astral entities. Being entirely humanity's own creation, they are interrelated with Humans by the closest bonds, and their action upon Humans is direct and incessant. The only division which can be usefully made is that which distinguishes between 'artificial elementals' made by the majority of mankind unconsciously, and those made by magicians with definite intent.

THOUGHT-FORCE ON EXISTENCE
The elemental essence which surrounds us on every side is susceptible to the influence of Human thought. It is affected when the Human 'mind' formulates a definite, purposeful thought. The effect produced is: the thought seizes upon the plastic essence, and molds it into a living being of an appropriate form —a

being which, once created, is in no way under the control of its creator, but lives out a life of its own, the length of which is proportionate to the intensity of the thoughts or wish which called it into existence. It lasts in fact just as long as the thought-force holds it together.

Most persons' thoughts are so fleeting that the elementals created by them last only a few minutes or a few hours, but an often-repeated thought or an earnest wish will form an elemental whose existence may extend to many days. Since the ordinary Human's thoughts refer very largely to himself, the elementals which they form remain hovering about, and constantly tend to provoke a repetition of the idea which they represent, since such repetitions, instead of forming new elementals, would strengthen the old one, and give it a fresh lease of life. An individual frequently dwelling upon one wish often forms a personal astral attendant which, fed constantly by fresh thought, may haunt them for years, ever gaining more and more strength and influence; and it will be easily seen that evil desire will affect moral nature disastrously.

Considering the amount of envy, hatred, malice and violence in the world, it will be readily understood that among the artificial elementals many terrible creatures are to be seen. A Human whose thoughts or desires are spiteful, brutal, sensual, &tc., moves through the world carrying with him everywhere a pestiferous atmosphere of his own, peopled with loathsome beings created to be companions; subjecting all who have the misfortune to come in contact with him to the risk of moral contagion from the influence of the abominations surrounding them.

Since such results have been achieved by the thought-force of men who were entirely in the dark as to what they were doing, it will readily be imagined that a Wizard who understands the subject, and can see exactly what effect he is producing, may wield immense power along these lines.

By advanced processes, artificial elementals of great power may be called into existence, and much evil has been worked in various ways by such entities. But it is true that if they are aimed at a person whom by reason of his purity of character they are unable to influence, they react with terrible force upon their creator; so that the medieval story of the magician being torn to pieces by the fiends he himself had raised, is no mere fable, but may well have had an awful foundation in fact.

THE HIGHER ASTRAL PLANES

We refer to 'higher' Astral Planes only by way of contrast with the Lower Astral Planes already mentioned -for some of these "higher" planes are quite low indeed as compared with the highest Astral Planes. Let us begin with the consideration of the lowest of these higher planes of the Astral, and then proceed to consider the planes higher in the scale.

In the first place, consider that the disembodied human spirit leaves the physical in a state or condition akin to sleep. It is carried by the attraction of its nature and character to the highest plane consistent with its nature — that is, to a plane corresponding with the highest qualities existent within itself. And upon that plane it gradually awakens into the 'Astral Life' of that particular plane.

Conditions of 'Astral Life' are so different from that of the 'Material Plane' that it is difficult to intelligently describe it. Each plane has planes higher and lower than itself, the above law being operative in all cases. The higher plane spirits have access to the lower, but the lower may not invade the higher. And this access is not in the nature of a physical

visit from the higher to the lower, but is in
the nature of a psychic consciousness, akin to
Clairvoyance, in which the spirit, while remaining on its own plane, still seems to have
traveled to the others, there to converse with
other spirits on these planes. The spirit itself, unless very advanced, does not realize
the true nature of the connection, but thinks
that it actually travels to the scene of the
lower planes.

EARTH-BOUND ENTITIES

On the very lowest of these 'higher' Astral
planes we find 'earth bound' entities of many
degrees. These are spirits of those who are so
material in their tastes, habits, trend of
thought and desires that they can never rise to
the higher states and conditions of the Astral.
They stay close to the earth, mingling unseen
in the scenes which they so loved during their
life in the body.

These entities are found in great numbers in
the 'astral atmosphere' where they poison the
'psychic atmosphere' to such an extent that
their presence may be felt, and often seen by
sensitive persons who happen to visit such
places. We may add as a caution to those who
are fond of dabbling in the psychic process of
Evocation, that it is largely from this class
of entities that many of the 'spirits' appear-
ing at seances are drawn. It is this class of
entities who so often impersonate disembodied
friends and relatives, and whose sneers are
scarcely concealed behind loving messages and
'spirit wisdom' they pass on to wondering mor-
tals.

THE PERSONAL UNIVERSE

Rising in the scale we find spirits who while
attached to material things nevertheless have
had ideals during their life —things for which
they had hoped, and dreamed, prayed and longed.

As the scale advances we find that the nature of the ideals advance from lower to higher —but the principle is the same. And for the lowest to the highest of these ideal degrees, the Astral Life contains that peculiar and wonderful condition or state known as the 'Idealistic State' or 'Personal Universe'.

This 'Idealistic State' is a real 'Astral Life' of the spirit, into which it enters after it has tired of the conditions it finds at first on the Astral 'Plane'. It is composed of a condition or state, or series of such conditions or states, in which it lives out in vivid imagination, or realistic dream-like states all of its unrealized personal ideals, hopes, expectations, desires, ambitions, aspirations, longings, and inclinations of its nature.

In this 'Idealistic State', the dreaming soul lives out countless lives, of infinite variety. To all intents and purposes, the soul or spirit (every Alpha-Spirit) lives an Eternity in the Idealistic State. Time is measured only by 'happenings' (events), and happenings of an Eternity may be crowded into a very short space of ordinary time, in the Idealistic State. Every possibility within its personality is lived out, outlived, and exhausted in interest, in this 'Idealistic State'.

'AFTER-LIFE' REPORTS
While in this 'Idealistic State', the spirit may be attracted by those on earth who are related to it by old ties or affection or interest, and in such case it may manifest by communications. But these communications contain only that which the spirit knows and experiences at the time. Thus the devout 'Christian soul' will report that it is dwelling in a Heaven of orthodox surroundings —the golden streets, harps, and milk and honey being described in detail. A good 'Catholic soul' will report a Catholic Heaven, with all the saints

present; and so forth. Each 'paints the Thing as they see it' and project it as the world of 'Things as They Are'. And each is telling the Truth from their own particular viewpoint. [Strange.]

The "Heaven" and "Hell" of the 'Idealistic State' is not a punishment or reward bestowed for good or evil deeds —it is but the working out of Cause and Effect —it is the fullest manifestation of Desire and one's Character. This 'Idealistic State' of the Astral Plane is not Fate, not Providence, not Destiny, not Reward and Punishment —it is but the operation of natural laws of Cause and Effect, Orderly Trend, and Logical Sequence, on the 'Astral Plane'. And "From one, know All."

SPIRITUAL ASCENSION

In the working out gradients of the 'Idealistic State', the most unpleasant experiences are lived through first, and then the higher ideals begin to manifest themselves —the soul rising to higher and still higher flights, until at last it reaches the highest degree possible to it by reason of its constitution, nature and character. And in that Life, if prepared, it may receive instruction from Beings higher in the scale, as well as from the more evolved souls of our own race who are attracted to it by reason of its desires and ideals.

Many spirits have received the help which led it to Ascension in this 'Idealistic State'. Also, many have received instruction which led to better conditions for growth in their next incarnation. "When the pupil is ready, the Master appears" on the 'Astral Plane' as on the 'Material Plane'. If you possess the seed of the ideal, the blossom and the fruit will surely be yours.

When impulses arising from personal desires, aspirations, and ideals of the spirit have expended themselves fully, and the 'alpha person-

ality' has been "lived out and outlived" in the
process —when there remain no further impulses
to exert themselves in the 'Idealistic State',
then the soul finds that it "has no further
game to live for" along the lines of personality. It feels aged, tired and weary, and the
desire for rest creeps over it, and it gradually sinks into a dreamless sleep, which ends
in the 'Death of the Personality'.

If "SELF-HOOD" ('Ascension') has not been attained by the soul, then it never awakens into
a new life, for Personality being all that it
possesses, and all personality being expended
and exhausted, then there is nothing left to
persist in new birth. But if 'Ascension' has
been attained, and the soul realizes that it is
more than the "Me" ("My") of itself, then when
the "Me" dies away, the "I" finds itself still
existent and filled with the impulse of the
Cosmic Will, which urges it forward to rebirth
in new bodies, to seek further and more advanced experience.

TOWARD INFINITY
There are 'Astral Planes' much higher than even
these here described, but communicating a description of them would be impossible at this
time. Some of these 'Higher Astral Planes'
transcend imaginations of the average person
leading a Earthly life today. And yet, over and
above the entire 'Astral Plane', there is the
great 'Spiritual Plane', which we would lack
words to even faintly designate. And yet, even
these exalted Planes await your coming, O Neophyte, whose feet are now well set upon The
Pathway!

APPROVAL FOR RELEASE:
LIMDIS2019 (Arcane Teachings)
31, OCT 2022 (Liber-011)
Joshua Free, project director

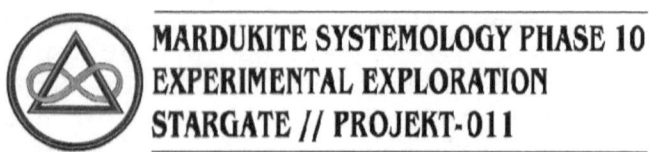

MARDUKITE SYSTEMOLOGY PHASE 10 EXPERIMENTAL EXPLORATION STARGATE // PROJEKT-011

MARDUKITE STARGATE PROJECT BULLETIN OF 01, SEPTEMBER 2017
BABYLON SITE, SAN LUIS VALLEY, COLORADO

TECH BRIEFING # B011-E [*Restricted (IV)*]

MARDUKITE PHASE-10 (AUTUMN 2017)

Stargate Series – 14

SUMMARY
This is a briefing to propose putting the 'Stargate Project' on hiatus and potentially decommissioning 'Babylon Site A' in San Luis Valley until further notice.

PROPOSAL
Intensive **logistical**, financial and legal complications have presented continuous challenges to maintaining a functional STARGATE program and keeping the BABYLON SITE operational for the 'Systemology Society'.

Limitations on the economic viability of this program and its research also continue to form a challenge as it will likely be many years before publications may be produced that directly support its funding.

No outside source of funding for STARGATE and the BABYLON SITE has been found that is not accompanied by 'grave' ulterior motivation and stipulation that the organization cannot afford to adhere to.

Numerous advancements in developmental research have taken place, therefore, in conclusion, the Council feels that this program requires additional review at a later date and should be continued.

IMPLEMENTATION

It is the opinion of this Council that off-site work toward a 'Systemology Core' should continue, but restrict itself to research and development of lower gradient-tier work that is more appropriate for immediately following the 'Mardukite Core' and 'Magic School'.

We will begin directing personnel away from posts at the BABYLON SITE and make arrangements for continuation of work elsewhere until such a time as STARGATE can recommence in San Luis Valley (at the BABYLON SITE or otherwise).

We will also begin relocating all materials and capital belonging to the BABYLON SITE to a remote storage facility in a nearby town (undisclosed) until such a time as a more permanent location is established to move such to.

APPROVAL FOR RELEASE:
31, OCT 2022 (Liber-011)
Joshua Free, project director

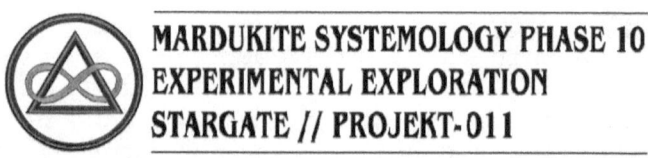

MARDUKITE SYSTEMOLOGY PHASE 10 EXPERIMENTAL EXPLORATION STARGATE // PROJEKT-011

MARDUKITE STARGATE PROJECT BULLETIN OF 13, OCTOBER 2020
BORSIPPA H.Q., SAN LUIS VALLEY, COLORADO

TECH BRIEFING # B011-F [*Restricted (IV)*]

MARDUKITE PHASE-10 RESTART
Projekt-011 Series – 1

SUMMARY
This is a briefing to propose a restart or re-instatement of efforts toward original 'Mardukite Phase-10' goals to develop a post-Mardukite (upper-grade) foundation for a 'Systemology Core'.

REFERENCES
All "STARGATE" files from 2017.

BACKGROUND
In the three years since the 'STARGATE'/'BABYLON SITE' project hiatus of September 2017, many developments for the 'Systemology Society' have ensued.

* A late-2019 public inception of the once underground 'applied philosophy' of our "Systemology" as 'Mardukite Grade-III' with:
  - a) "The Tablets of Destiny" (Liber-One)
  - b) "Crystal Clear" (Liber-2B)
  - c) "The Power of Zu" (Liber-S1Z)

* Publication of a complete 'Mardukite Grade-III' 'Master Edition' anthology, "The Systemology Handbook", which includes the above titles in addition to "Systemology: The Original Thesis" (Liber-S1X) and other bonus material.

* Development and publication of half of 'Me-

tahuman Systemology Grade-IV', collected and released as "Metahuman Destinations" from 'JFI Publications'.

* Establishment of a permanent base of operations in 'San Luis Valley' during the Summer 2020 that is approximately 10-11 miles from the original BABYLON SITE (2017). This new location will be called BORSIPPA H.Q. It will serve as a central base for 'Mardukite Research Org' (Systemology Society), 'Mardukite Academy' and 'Church of Mardukite Zuism' activities and global operations. A portion of this base is also designated for "JFI Publications".

PROPOSAL
Existing 'Grade-III' and 'Grade-IV' developments in Systemology offer a new practical approach to our 'applied philosophy' via "systematic processing" -a methodology of "piloted" mental exercises and spiritual techniques. This is something that we did not previously have worked out for STARGATE and could be the difference between success and failure if the project were reinstated. Given the completion of the "Mardukite Master Course" (Grade I-III), this Council believes the STARGATE project should be restarted. The proposed codename designated for this new endeavor is: "PROJEKT-011".

APPROVAL FOR RELEASE:
31, OCT 2022 (Liber-011)
Joshua Free, project director

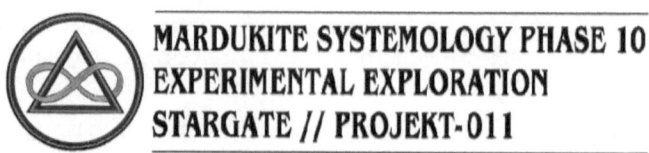

MARDUKITE SYSTEMOLOGY PHASE 10 EXPERIMENTAL EXPLORATION STARGATE // PROJEKT-011

MARDUKITE STARGATE PROJECT BULLETIN OF 20, OCTOBER 2020
BORSIPPA H.Q., SAN LUIS VALLEY, COLORADO

TECH REPORT # R011-C [*Top Secret (VII)*]

STARGATE TRAINING (AUTUMN 2020)
Projekt-011 Series – 2

SUMMARY

After three years of additional developmental research in Systemology (since the end of the original STARGATE series), we have established our first Ability Training Regimen for 'Wizard Level-0' (Grade-IV). It is expected that this cycle of work will reach the proposed goals of the Grade-IV tier -and be published in Spring 2021 as "Imaginomicon" (Liber-3D) from JFI Publications.

PURPOSE

This regimen was developed to assist 'Mardukite Systemology' Seekers (during "Wizard Level" Systemology grades) to develop 'Creative Ability', as maintained by an individual Alpha-Spirit, in its management of a 'genetic vehicle' (to experience beta-existence), and also while operating independently 'exterior' to reality agreements concerning the 'Human Condition' and 'Physical Universe'. This regimen is relatively subjective. It has no specific Processing End-Point and thus may be run virtually "infinitely" as an application. It requires no numeric assessment-value **evaluation.**

BACKGROUND

The project director accumulated a large collection of esoteric exercises and 'New Thought' techniques over a 25-year period. These were then tested by members of the Systemology Society and evaluated for their relevance to Grade-IV 'end-goals'. A precise study of 'background theory' is not necessary for the exercises to be effective.

DEVELOPMENTAL RESEARCH
After two years of intensive experimentation with innumerable "basic techniques" by many Seekers around the world reporting their results to the Systemology Society, surprisingly few exercises survived our rigorous testing and scrutiny for inclusion in this training primer. Some versions of these exercises have appeared in previous Mardukite and Systemology publications; others may bare striking resemblance to 'mystical' and/or 'occult' techniques found elsewhere among 6,000 years of esoteric lore.

APPLICATION
A Seeker will notice that as they develop greater degrees of Creative Ability, these 'exercises' may be repeated with cumulatively better results. These 'exercises' are approached on a gradient scale of 'success' that relatively extends to Infinity. An individual will get a 'sense' of their own present ability, which admittedly, can always be expressed 'stronger,' 'longer' or 'clearer' with additional practice.

RECORD-KEEPING
Recordable data (for training purposes) is virtually identical to traditional 'Systematic Processing Sessions', including: the session environment (location, weather, day of the week, &tc.); your apparent condition (a personal **Beta-Awareness** or Emotimeter evaluation)[*]

---

[*] See "*Crystal Clear: Handbook for Seekers*"; also available in the complete Grade-III 'Master Edition' anthology, "*The Systemology Handbook.*"

at the start and end; the specific exercises or techniques applied; the duration of time spent on each exercise and the entire testing session; energy handling (clarity of the operation, certainty of success, new realizations); the material objects encountered and other 'body phenomenon' (solid forms, imagery, physical/emotional reactions, discomfort or 'pings' sensed from the genetic vehicle).

COMPLETE INSTRUCTIONS
Even if an exercise seems 'familiar', pay particular attention to specific wording of directions for each application, treating each step in its own unit of time (separate from previous exercises). This regimen may be Self-Administered or 'Piloted'. In either case, to provide lasting 'gains', it is necessary to focus validation on what an individual is able to do, rather than 'exercising' in the direction of failure and shortcomings.

We have found it more effective for beginners to cycle through as many of the basic steps of each exercise as possible during a single 'creative training session' —because, when starting out, Seekers are likely to 'try' too intensely on particulars of an exercise, in exclusion to others, straining for a specific result or effect to occur. No effort should be applied; a Seeker should simply emphasize validating what they can do with each cycle.

Although relay of these 'exercises' is quite casual here (emphasizing light practice to encourage accumulating greater certainty), actual realizations and stable gains develop only by pushing through whatever fragmentation appears during practice —discomfort, **somatic** 'pings', intrusive thoughts, reactive images, various emotional responses. Only by working through these to the height of personal certainty and clarity are they useful tools for defragmenting such automatic (obsessive or compulsive) phenomenon.

At first, a Seeker may only be able to focus for a few minutes on the more basic steps of each exercise cycle, realizing it to the extent that present Actualized Awareness and attention allows —even if the extent of 'success' is a vague sense of certainty. As the individual continues their studies and practice (increasing their understanding, willingness and ability) the results become more vivid, certainty is stronger, greater realizations provide for higher 'ledges' of Actualization, and personal development relevant to approaching upper-level 'Gateways to Infinity' is demonstrably more apparent.

As an individual works toward Spiritual (or 'Alpha') Actualization (emphasized for 'Wizard-Level' Systemology) any one of these exercises produces increasingly better results the longer its clarity may be held. It is not unreasonable, as an individual advances, to eventually apply 30, 60 or even 120 continuous minutes (an entire two-hour **'creativeness** session') toward a single exercise with increasing cumulative results.

Each section represents a specialized cycle, building upon previous cycles. Even after greater certainty is established on a particular cycle: for each new creativeness session, an individual should start at the beginning ("#1") and move through each, however briefly, before going to the next.

There are no 'short cuts' to getting through and out from the trappings of this Beta-Existence; our Systemology is the most direct path we can access and best chance humanity has had toward its own Ascension, for at least 6,000 years.

ADDITIONAL NOTICES
Before proceeding take factual note that the

directives for this training regimen do not include personal intention (or commands) for a creation or image 'to persist'.

* Any 'masses' Imagined or Copied (and any Mental Images "manufactured") in these exercises and systematic processing should be handled by (**Alpha Thought**) consideration or command postulate, either: discarded, reduced down to a ball to toss away, dissolved to nothing, treated as being given away —or even pushed into the body from time to time to satisfy the illusion of replenishing energy (though all energy is actually manufactured by the 'Unlimited Self' when necessary).

The 'Alpha-Spirit' is a god-like artist with unlimited 'Creative Ability', access to limitless ink and pad of unending paper at their disposal. But over time, it became increasingly fixed on its one track of compulsive creation. Once we can rehabilitate SELF with certainty of its own 'Creative Ability' again —only then might an individual be convinced enough to finally tear off that top sheet of paper and regain the freedom of its true 'Spiritual Beingness'.

—#1—
PRESENCE: ENVIRONMENTAL SECURITY
• Look around your environment and spot objects that are acceptable—that you don't mind being present.
• Look around your environment and find objects that you wouldn't mind having.
• Look around your environment and spot locations where you are not.
• Look around your environment and notice persons that are not present; objects that are not present; animals that are not present; locations that are not present; times and incidents that are not happening.

—#2—

MENTAL IMAGERY: TURNING ON PICTURES

• Recall an actual event that has happened.
When was it? Where was it? Who was there? What
is its duration? Imagine the scenery. Notice as
many facets of perception as you can—time of
day, sensations, touch, weather, humidity, objects, brightness, smells, tastes, sounds, communications, dialogue, emotions of others, personal emotions, gestures, body positions,
external motion, personal movement, &tc.

• Repeat the above step several times (with
eyes closed if it is easier); recalling, imagining and looking at times/events which are
acceptable to view, noticing all the details
and facets—for example: when you saw something
beautiful; when you heard something you enjoyed; when you smelled something pleasant,
&tc.

• Continue until a clearer perception of Mental Imagery is realized.

:: Persistent Blackness/No Images—Imagine a
duplicate of the blackness in the same space as
the one you're looking at. Make a copy of it
beside it. Make another copy. And another. Several more. Push the copies together and compress into nothing. Make eight more copies;
then push them together and throw it away. Make
eight more copies; push them together and then
push them into the body. Continue this step until the compulsively generated blackness is under your control and you can perceive imagined
or recalled images.

—#3A—

PRESENCE: BETA-EXISTENCE SPACE-TIME

• Select two walls in a room with a clear path
to walk between them. Start in the center facing one wall and get the sense that you are
making the body perform these actions: Look at
that wall; Walk over to that wall; Touch that
wall; Turn around. Repeat the actions numerous
times between both walls, each time giving the

same attention to each action as if it's the
first time.

• For advanced practice, perform the previous
step as directed without moving the body from
the center of the room and with eyes closed.
Perform it again using Imagination and Self-
directed attention to alternate your Awareness
between the two walls and touch them (with your
Awareness). Then, repeat the actions, focusing
on getting an actual sense of the perception of
touching the wall. If this doesn't happen right
away, just imagine the feel of the wall.

—#3B—
PRESENCE: SPATIAL CORNER-POINTS
• Eyes closed, sitting near the center of a
room—Reach up with Awareness and locate an up-
per corner-point in back of the room. Then find
the second upper-corner. Focus all Awareness on
these back two corner-points without thinking
anything else. Keep all attention on these
corner-points.

• To take a step further as an advanced practice, during a separate creative session, perform the same procedure treating all four back
corner-points.

• This exercise can be extended to include all
eight corner-points defining a room. This
demonstrates basic principles behind the "imagined" or "spiritual" version of this exercise
called "Creation-of-Space."

—#4A—
FACSIMILE-COPIES: "WHAT'RE YOU LOOKING AT?"
• Eyes closed. What are you looking at? Imagine another copy just like it. Make another
copy next to it. And several more. Then compress them all together into a ball and discard
or toss away.

• Eyes open. Spot an object in the environment. Imagine a duplicate or copy of it right
beside it. Spot another object and repeat. Continue to do this with various objects.

• With eyes closed, get a sense of looking at the objects in the environment. Imagine a duplicate or copy beside each, one by one.

• With eyes closed, while indoors, get a sense of looking at objects outside the environment/room/building; and imagine a duplicate or copy beside each.

• Practice each of the above—but imagining a perfect duplicate of the object, making it in the same space, using the same energy-mass; then consider that the object is there again; then make a perfect duplicate; then consider the original object is there again. Alternate repeatedly between the original object and the duplicate.

:: Persistent Images/Imprints—Imagine a duplicate of the image in the same space as the one you're looking at. Make a copy of it beside it. Make another copy. And another. Several more. Jam the copies together into a ball and compress into nothing. Make eight more copies; then jam them together into a ball and toss it away. Make eight more copies; jam them together into a ball and push them into the body. Continue this step until the compulsively generated image is under your control.

—#4B—

FACSIMILE-COPIES: IDENTIFICATION & BODIES

• Eyes closed. Imagine a duplicate (identical copy) of your presently owned Human body out in front of you. Make a copy next to it. And another. And several more. When you have eight or so, push them together into a ball and collapse it into nothing. Imagine another duplicate. Make a copy next to it. And many more copies; then push them together into a ball and toss it away. Continue this step until you feel comfortable in creating bodies.

—Imagine a duplicate of your present body as ideal and healthy; then unmake it. Make it again; then unmake it. Alternate repeatedly.

—Looking into a mirror. Get the sense that

there is "something there"; then get the sense there is "nothing there." Alternate these considerations repeatedly.

• Eyes closed. Imagine a busy or crowded place, mall, depot or street corner. Place your point-of-view in a fixed location; then look around and spot objects, motions and people in this scenery. Practice this for multiple locations (preferably until an increase in actual perception).

–Choose the location you like best from the previous step to use for the remaining cycle of exercises; Imagine making a facsimile-copy of your present Human body to use as a point-of-view; then unmake the body and remain looking as an Awareness. Alternate repeatedly.

• Perform the previous step, but this time: Imagine an identical copy of the body out in front of you, using a point-of-view outside the body to look around the location; then use a point-of-view from inside the body to look around the location. Alternate viewpoints repeatedly.

–Perform the previous step, but this time adding: Get the sense of other persons acknowledging your presence when they are near or walking by (even if they don't look at the body).

• Select a basic solid object (pyramid, cone, cube, sphere, &tc.); Imagine using the "object" as your body to practice each previous step of this locational-cycle of exercises; making and unmaking, alternating viewpoints, spotting other objects, noticing motions and persons, and receiving acknowledgment ("hellos") for your presence. Now add to this cycle: unmaking the body and point-of-view in one spot, then making it again at other spots in the location. Get a sense of moving that body like a "playing piece."

–As before; Imagine using a duplicate copy of your present body.

–As before; Imagine use of an elderly body.

-As before; Imagine use of a child body.

-As before; Imagine using a body of a different gender.

-As before; Imagine using a body that appears strong.

-As before; Imagine using a body that appears wise.

-As before; Imagine using a sparkly cloud of silvery-white energy for a body with small golden balls for eyes.

-As before; using only the point-of-view as an Awareness with nothing added as a body.

—#4C—

FACSIMILE-COPIES: MACHINERY AND BODIES

• Select an object that has a basic mechanical function "to produce a flow." (This may be best practiced with a "sink" or "water-spigot" until there is an independent reality on electricity and basic motions.)

-With eyes open. Look at the mechanical-object in its "off" condition and imagine an identical duplicate beside it. Look between the two and spot any differences, adjusting your created duplicate to match the original. Continue until satisfied with the certainty of duplication.

-Turn the mechanical-object "on" and look at it in this condition, noting the motion and getting a sense of the energy-flow driving it. Adjust your imagined duplicate to match this in every way, noting the motion and getting a sense of the energy-flow involved.

• For advancing these steps, with eyes closed; use an object not present.

• Select a mechanical-object that has a basic "motor" function. (This may be best practiced with an "electric fan" until there is an independent reality on generators and engines.)

-Apply the previous basic steps for imagining duplicate machinery; this time giving particular attention to its internal mechanics: at basic, a circuit or energy flow that drives or propels the spinning motion of the blades and is started and stopped by a switch. As it runs (is "on") get a sense of the internal mechanics and match this energy and motion in your duplicate.

• For additional practice: use more complex machines; use machinery not present; use electronic devices. A basic study in physical mechanics on "how things work" is of benefit.

• Eyes closed. Imagine being a "motor-vehicle"; create the machine, the internal mechanics, and get the sense of identifying with it as a body. Establish a point-of-view from the car, while maintaining a sense of the energy and motion mechanically operating inside of it.

• For advancing this step further, move your point-of-view through each mechanical system of the vehicle as you imagine it running: steering, brakes, the engine, transmission, &tc. (to the best of your reality on these systems). Get a sense for how it operates from the inside.

• Apply basic directions for using a solid object in locational-cycle exercises (#4B), this time using a vehicle (such as a car) for a body. Run the whole cycle using the vehicle: everything from "making and unmaking" to considerations as a "playing piece."

• Imagine the creation and unmaking of various machinery, devices, motors, vehicles, engines, generators, and power plants. Imagine as much detail in your creations as you can.

   –Additionally; Imagine being various machinery. Alternate your point-of-view between inside and outside various vehicles and machines.

• Imagine the creation and unmaking of various personal "mental machinery": devices that inform you of things, so you don't have to know; devices that react for you, so you don't have to remember; devices that show impressions of what things are, so you don't have to look; devices that make your creations invisible as

soon as you imagine them; devices that turn
mental images into dark screens and black
clouds when you try to remember them; devices
that make mental images for you, so you don't
have to create. Consider other mental mechanism
that could be created.

   -Additionally; Imagine being various mental
machinery. Alternate your point-of-view between
inside and outside various mental machinery.

• Eyes open, outdoors, public area. Spot a
person that is standing or sitting for a while
(like at a bus-stop). Imagine the creation of
an identical duplicate copy beside them. As in
previous steps; look between the two and spot
any differences, adjusting your duplicate to
match.

   -Additionally; if the person leaves your view
during practice, simply select another. If they
change positions or spots in the area, adjust
your duplicate copy to match the motion. Practice this step with several persons.

• Once certainty is established with the previous step: use the step to duplicate a person;
this time giving particular attention to copying the internal parts of that body (bones, organs, muscle, &tc.) and get a sense of the **organic** systems functioning inside (as with the
previous exercise on machines).

   -Additionally; apply this step to duplicate a
moving person, copying the motion in your duplicate. Get a sense of how the internal organic machinery drive various motors and systems
during the motion. Practice this step with several persons. Practice this step repeatedly.

—#5A—
CONTROL: "WHAT IS THAT BODY DOING?"

• Get the sense of you making the body do
"what it's doing." Get the sense of making the
body sit in a chair. Get the sense that you're
making that body hold a book, &tc.

• Get the sense that you are behind the body,
controlling its movement by strings or beams.

Decide when to lift a finger of the body and
then do so, imagining its control by a string.
Decide when to lower it and then do so. Practice this on other movable parts of the body.
• Decide to conduct some activity (walk outdoors, &tc.) and focus Awareness behind the
body's head. Expand your POV to encompass the
entire space around the body. Move the body
around, still using its eyes, but imagine controlling the body from behind it.
• Perform the previous step, emphasizing attention on the presser (push) and tractor
(pull) energy beams directed to control movement of the body.
:: Compulsions/Ticks and Twitches—Consider a
behavior that the body does compulsively on its
own. Now decide to do this on your own determinism and you do so. Decide to stop and you do
so. Start it again and decide to increase/exag-
gerate the action; then you do so. Decide to
decrease the action and you do it. Decide to
stop again and do it. Repeated this cycle until
the behavior is under better control.

—#5B—
PRESENCE: DISTANCE & CONNECTEDNESS
• Eyes open. Spot two objects and notice the
differences between them; then note the distance between them. Then get a sense of the
space between them.
• With eyes closed, repeat the above step.
• Eyes open. Look around and spot an object
that you wouldn't mind connected to you. Get
the sense of making that object connect to you.
Then get the sense that it is separate from
you. Alternate. Determine how you could make it
connect. Then consider in what ways it is different from you.
• With eyes closed, repeat the above step.
• Eyes open. Spot an object. Decide that you
will walk over to the object and do so. Decide
that you will reach out and touch the object
and do so. Decide that you will let go of the

object and do so.
• With eyes closed, repeat the above step by extending your Awareness.
• Walking outdoors; get the sense of being stationary and moving space around you, then get the sense of moving through space.
• Eyes open, then eyes closed. Indoors and outdoors; spot two objects and notice the distances between the objects and you. Then get a sense of the space between them and you.
• Perform the above step using three objects.
• Look around and spot something that is still; then spot something that is in motion. Alternate repeatedly.
• Eyes closed, repeat the above step, using a point-of-view from spaces or locations where you are not.

—#6—
ALTERNATION: "BELL, BOOK & CANDLE"
• Select a small simple object (such as a "bell, book or candle") that is easily moved. Locate two spots. Move the object uniformly back and forth between these exact two spots at a consistent speed. Reach and let go for every spot change, leaving the object in precisely the same position at each spot for a moment.
• Select two small dissimilar objects (such as a "bell, book or candle") that are easily moved. Locate two spots (on a table). Place an object in each spot. Pick up "Object-1" and look at it. Notice its weight, its feel and its appearance. Get the sense of you making it more solid. Put it back in the same exact spot and position. Pick up "Object-2" and look at it. Notice its weight, its feel and its appearance. Get the sense of you making it more solid. Put it back in the same exact spot and position. Alternate this step between the two objects, each time treated as the first time.
• Continue the previous step until there is no compulsion toward automatic actions or responses, no fluctuation in attention and no de-

sire to "leave" the exercise.
• For advanced practice, perform the physical version of the previous step, then close your eyes and imagine six walls forming a room that is not located in the Physical Universe. Imagine two tables or pedestals in the room. Imagine "Object-1" is on one table; hold it still and make it more solid. Imagine "Object-2" is on the other table; hold it still and make it more solid. Imagine "Object-1" floating up in the air; get a sense of its weight, its feel and its appearance; then have it float back down. Imagine "Object-2" floating up in the air; get a sense of its weight, its feel and its appearance; then have it float back down. Alternate as described above.
• Continue the previous step until there is increased perception of actual solidity and weight (in addition to imagined).

—#7—
ALTERNATION (POV): AWARENESS OF SPOTS
• Eyes open. Locate a spot on the body, decide to reach out and touch it, then do so. Decide when to let go and do so. Find another spot on the body, and repeat the step. And again.
• With eyes closed, repeat the above step.
• Locate a spot in space, decide to move the body and touch it, then do so. Decide when to let go and do so. Find another spot in space, and repeat the step. And again.
• With eyes closed, repeat the above step.
• Locate a spot on the floor, decide to move the body over it, then do so. Find another spot on the floor, and repeat the step. And again.
• With eyes closed and without moving the body, repeat the above step.
• Locate two spots on the floor, decide to move the body over one, then walk toward it. Before reaching the spot, decide to change your mind and move the body over the other one instead. Find another two spots on the floor, and repeat the step. And again.

• With eyes closed and without moving the body, repeat the above step, relocating your Awareness-POV.

• Locate three points in the body; direct all attention on these three points in the body. Locate three points in space; direct all attention on these three points in space. Alternate these repeatedly—three points in the body; three points in space.

• With eyes closed, perform the above step; rapidly and repeatedly.

• Continue until there is perception separate from a body.

—#8—

PROCEDURE 1-8-0, ISSUE #4, ROUTE-8

• Eyes closed. Imagine you are extending your Awareness, reaching through the entire Physical Universe, as far as you can imagine. Now reach a little further beyond and outside of all dimensional space and find the Nothingness. Hold your point-of-view on the Nothingness, without thinking or imagining anything else.

  –Extend your reach out on the right side, getting a certainty of the Nothingness.

  –Extend your reach out on the left side, getting a certainty of the Nothingness.

  –Repeat the previous step for each other direction; reaching in front, reaching behind, reaching above, reaching below.

  –Extend your reach out to the right and left simultaneously, holding the perception of Nothingness in both directions.

  –Repeat the previous step for each direction-pair: in front of and behind you; then above and below you.

  –Extend your reach out on all six sides of you at once, maintaining a certainty of Nothingness in all directions.

• To take practice a step further, alternate between this point-of-view (on Nothingness) with eyes closed and the point-of-view toward the Physical Universe with eyes open. Look

182

around each time and orient Self to the environment.

• Alternate getting full perception of Nothingness and full perception of the Physical
Universe.

APPROVAL FOR RELEASE:APPROVAL FOR RELEASE:
30, APR 2021 (Liber-3D)
31, OCT 2022 (Liber-011)
Joshua Free, project director

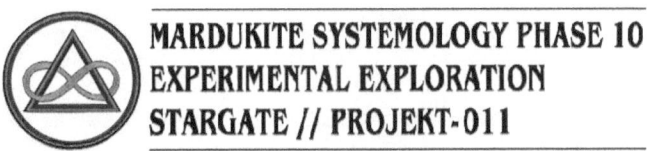

MARDUKITE SYSTEMOLOGY PHASE 10 EXPERIMENTAL EXPLORATION STARGATE // PROJEKT-011

MARDUKITE STARGATE PROJECT BULLETIN OF 17, NOVEMBER 2020 BORSIPPA H.Q., SAN LUIS VALLEY, COLORADO

TECH REPORT # R011-D [*Top Secret* (VII)]

IMAGINATION TECH (GRADE-IV) (STARGATE TRAINING – PART 2)*

Projekt-011 Series – 3

SUMMARY

'Imagination' is the primary subject of 'Systemology Grade-IV Wizard Level-0'. Our methodology emphasizes increased Self-directed 'control' (willingness, knowingness and ability) of communications and creation; the 'Alpha' condition of **'responsibility'** for cause and effect. This will be mainly taken up in the forthcoming publication: "Imaginomicon" (Liber-3D).

TECH SUMMARY

An 'Alpha-Spirit' occupying a point-of-view ("POV") in denser Universes along the 'Spiritual Timeline' progressively considers their own ability to have less direct effect on their environment —possibly fearing some "punishment" for this control and responsibility. But, this leads them to eventually stop knowingly create at all, putting these faculties on automatic — until finally forgetting their 'Creative Ability' altogether.

Use of 'Imagination' in 'systematic processing' allows Seekers to knowingly practice command of 'Creative Ability', the control and responsibility of being at 'Cause' —because they know

---

* This version is specially edited for "*Liber-011.*"

they are creating this illusion in their own 'Personal Universe' (where it is safe to do so). There is no kickback effect or consequence enforced by the 'Physical Universe' as a result.

The two Universes exist independent of each other. The more a Seeker is processed to realize this with certainty, the better their ability to handle existences of each Universe "As-It-Is" —not simply as they are "thought" to be, using some filter or circuit to receive fragmentary information. Only after the realization is present can a Seeker actually reassign their considerations.

'Mental Imagery' attached to an imprinted experience often carries an "energetic charge" of the original impression along with it. When stimulated as an automatic-response to something in the present environment, information from previous impressions (containing similar facets) is internally communicated as part of the reality experience.

DEFRAGMENTATION
In the beginning, the Alpha-Spirit used its Creative Ability for 'fun' - for 'art' - and its own personal amusement. Getting 'lost' and identified with the POV of its own Creations, 'not-knowing' the true nature of SELF as "I-AM", came later.

We can employ Imagination in systematic processing as a means of handling 'assignment of consideration' along a circuit or channel without restricting use only to **'activating-events'** which have both actually occurred and are within the scope of reality for a Seeker to effectively confront or recall (reach) directly (generally meaning, from 'this lifetime').

Most imprinting incidents become heavily charged as fragmentation only when an individu-

al is not willing to directly look, and therefore take control and responsibility for either
eliminating the creation or reassigning its
value, instead of relying on mental machinery
and other relays to handle perpetual creation
and interpretation of the reality experience.

An individual puts up so much resistance to a
reactive 'mental image', hoping to stop the motion it contains, meanwhile simultaneously and
compulsively creating it. The force applied
against it makes it more solid and thus perceived as stronger and more difficult to
handle. Then comes feelings of overwhelm as an
effect and abandonment of control and responsibility for treating its contents. If handled
directly with systematic processing, imprinted
information can be defragmented from the circuits; but this requires ability and willingness of the Seeker to actually 'look' at the
image they carry around from it.

DEFRAGMENTATION PROCESSING
Various training, exercises, techniques and
processes given in "Tablets of Destiny", "Crystal Clear" and "Metahuman Destinations" combine
to establish a systematic regimen for **'beta-defragmentation'**. We are now able to approach a
new level of 'beta-Actualization' by applying
'Imagination' and 'Creativeness Processing' to
our methodology. Material for this will be released in Liber-3D ("Imaginomicon") including
this updated tech report.

SYSTEMATIC PROCESSING SESSIONS
Systematic processing goals are achieved only
when a Seeker directs actual attention to the
exercises. This is referred to as 'presence' in
the outline for 'Grade-IV Standard Operating
Procedure' (given in "Metahuman Destinations").
The first steps begin with increasing Awareness
given to the present environment, especially
the session. Processing is directed toward
SELF, not one of the 'phases' or 'circuits' or

'imprints' created by SELF. Instructions are
referred to as "commands" because they intro-
duce Alpha-Thought considerations for a Seeker
to "run" on their own "operating system". "Processing Command Lines" (PCLs) are received from
a text or Pilot until an individual Self-de-
termines full control of command.

MENTAL MACHINERY & PRESENCE
A Seeker must actually be 'present' doing the
exercises. Most individuals operate on so much
automatic circuitry (looking through so many
filters) that very little 'Actualized Awareness' is present. At the start, before 'upper-level' considerations are treated in a session, we apply standardized systematic
processing methods. The assumption is that some
part of an individual's Awareness is compulsively fixed somewhere (or else too dispersed)
apart from their present environment.

OBJECTIVE PROCESSING & PRESENCE
When an individual stops looking, for whatever
reason, they use 'mental machinery' to do the
'looking' for them. Therefore, most 'objective
universe' processing methods to increase 'at-
tention-on-the-present' regard literally "looking" "contacting" and "communicating" with the
present environment. This demonstrates enough
certainty in the 'safety' of the environment
for SELF to actually apply its Awareness. Proper handling of various "Points-of-Views" (POV)
is an integral part of Grade-IV, because while
this 'crystal lens' remains fragmented about
'remote viewpoints', so too is the view taken
regarding 'Imagination' and 'Creative Ability'.

At the beginning of a session, a Seeker is directed to "look around" at their environment and
notice things, one to the next. The environment
may even appear to get 'brighter' as this happens. So much of what an individual really believes they are perceiving is actually fragmented by circuits and filters before the

information is even communicated to SELF.

This is better demonstrated, for example, when an individual enters a new environment: more attention is placed on what is around them. It does not take long for 'familiarity' to set in. Then 'scenery perception' is mostly created on automatic —not even really 'looked at' and sensed from an 'external' world anymore. The standard-issue individual is not educated to remain at "cause" over their own selective directed attention.

WIZARD GRADES
Techniques and training for 'Wizard Level-0' are intended to increase an individual's certainty toward operating as the Alpha-Spirit. This includes using "Zu-Vision" independent of a genetic vehicle or beta-existence. The most direct technique or PCL ("Be outside that body") is not necessarily the most effective if other strongly held reality agreements and fragmented considerations still impinge on an individual. Systemologist Seekers practice exercises to increase
the reach on knowing their own spiritual existence, rather than agreeing to carry a vague idea about it.

WIZARD LEVEL-0 (UPGRADING SESSIONS)
Practice while seated, with eyes closed (a blindfold may be used), using 'Imagination' (or **assumption** of a 'secondary POV') to treat the environment. An individual places full attention on the room (or object), closes their eyes and uses 'Imagination' to create a facsimile-copy of it. If an exercise requires contacting or moving an object in some way, then the Seeker is to remain in place and focus on a 'sense' of it actually happening in the 'Physical Universe' as fully as possible.

Other 'objective processes' practice Self-directing communication with objects, masses and

walls in the environment. A Seeker may be directed to pick a spot on an object and touch it;
and then they are directed to let go. When this
is carried through without lag, the Seeker is
to get a sense of making a decision of when to
touch and when to let go. For 'Wizard Level-0',
an additional step is added: to direct (or project) a "beam" (or 'Awareness') that is used to
touch and let go, rather than a hand. In the
exercise "Presence in Space-Time" (SOP-2C), the
Seeker contacts the walls while the body remains still, directing a POV (or 'Imagination')
to get the sense of moving back and forth
across the room.

WIZARD LEVEL-0 EMPHASIS
Systemology focuses on the Alpha-Spirit, the
actual SELF that controls a Mind-System and a
genetic vehicle. But what is actual for the Alpha-Spirit exists in a domain of Alpha-existence, not beta. When an individual is fragmented, their experience of 'thought' is
restricted to associative information kept in
circuits of the Mind-System connected to beta.
Beta-existence becomes superimposed over one's
own 'Personal Universe'. In our natural state,
the "I-AM"-SELF (Alpha-Spirit) can only have
its own abilities reduced as a result of its
own 'Alpha-Thought' —a high-level consideration
or command-level postulate on existence. We
have the ability to place our 'Awareness' at
'any' POV.

In the past, mystics and magicians emphasized
control of the body by operating from the Mind;
and their POV is very much entangled within the
Mind-System and the 'mental plane'. It is from
the 'mental plane' that an individual is very
Aware of 'mental fields' surrounding 'mental
bodies' and a whole vast network of circuits
and relays composing 'mental machinery'.

In most cases, 'New Age' practitioners remain
interior to the Mind-System. Of course, this is

a step above a fixation interior to a genetic
vehicle. However, it is not enough to access
the Higher Gates of Realization, which permit a
potential for direct experience of Higher Universes. Assuming an individual has successfully
defragmented emotional stores of reactivity,
this still leaves them somewhere around the
third (or fourth) "Gate" (or 'Veil') —still yet
to break totally free of the 'Mind'.

"SNAP-IN" & "SPIN-IN" EFFECTS
There are many instances when the POV of an Alpha-Spirit can be pulled-in or snapped-in on
the fields and mechanisms inherently part of a
'body'. This may take place during intense emotional stress or **trauma** when the perspective of
Self is fixedly tied in with (and distracted
by) sensations and 'pings' of a 'body'. This
strengthens circuitry for Identity, propagating
that SELF is located 'in' a body. This happens
much more often when an individual is already
suspended interior to a Mind-System, already
surrounded by the associative thought and **emo-
tional-encoding** circuits of the vehicle.

 * The Alpha-Spirit is capable of commanding a
genetic vehicle and its functions (mechanisms
and energetic fields) while retaining its original ('Zu-Vision') POV exterior and independent of the vehicle they are operating and Universe they operate it in.

'IMPLANT PLATFORMS'
Entrapment in a Mind-Body Identity is possible
and later cemented by 'Implants'. There are
many 'implant platforms' on which specific circuits operate. At this present level of work,
our concern is with a general realization that
they exist and that their installation has a
tremendous impact on the POV and considerations
remaining with an individual to knowingly
handle.

Many who already have a sense of their entry

into this 'Universe' and 'Human Condition' often liken it to 'falling into' or being 'sucked into', &tc. But in all cases where we have considered the action taking place to 'Implant' an individual with the 'Human Condition' in this Universe, the common theme suggests that: one is 'outside' and then one is suddenly 'inside' —and during the disorientation between, something happens.

PROCESSING INTERIORIZATION
Depending on whether a Seeker is working with this lifetime or has begun "Systemology Backtrack" work on the 'Spiritual Timeline', the same methodology is employed to start opening up these channels for exploration. Processing includes considerations (and sensations) attached to "going in" or "getting in" something or somewhere.

BRIDGE TO ADVANCED WORK
Significant 'energetic charge' is entangled with "Entry into Universes" or 'Implanting'. Much of this work is still under research and review at the Systemology Society for inclusion in higher Wizard Grades. You might wonder why we mention its background before closing out Grade-IV. We discovered (some might say 'by accident') that Tech applied for 'Wizard Level-0' can potentially trigger actual realizations of how a Seeker arrived 'here'. It is often reacted to without understanding and without realizing the nature of this phenomenon (ahead of time). Fragmented automatic-response circuits connected to these events add some difficulty in maintaining high enough Awareness to fully achieve goals set forth for Grade-IV.* By 'processing out' concepts of "moving inside" and "moving outside", a Seeker is less likely to handle such with automatic circuitry.

---

* Additional work to resolve this may be found in "*The Way of the Wizard: Utilitarian Systemology*" (*Liber-3E*) by Joshua Free.

"ZU-VISION" CONSIDERATIONS

Systematic processing (using Route-3 and/or Route-0)‡ is applied to defragment considerations for accessing "Zu-Vision," operating 'exterior' to the physical body, or even the handling of space and creation of a 'Personal Universe' -which are all the emphasis of Liber-3D ("Imaginomicon"). So long as a POV can be "snapped in" on the Mind-Body system outside of Self-Determination, the individual's Identity is still very much entangled and associated with those mechanisms. Areas to focus systematic processing include:

• Incidents when you wanted to get inside but can't
• Incidents when you were kicked out from where you wanted to be
• Being forced inside
• Incidents of being trapped inside
• Pulled in
• Pushed in
• The feeling or sense that you must get in
• The feeling or sense that you can't get in...

Such types of incidents potentially carry a heavily imprinted charge. This greatly reduces Self-Awareness and Self-Determination and therefore, presence, when left uncontrolled. You can use the above concepts for PCLs to treat circuits with "Recall"-style processing, or you can "Imagine" incidents and see what 'Mental Imagery' seems most appropriate. In either case, experiencing some release assists handling basics of upper-level work.

An Alpha-Spirit exists apart from thought and

---

‡ An individual may be trained in 'Professional Piloted Processing' using the materials contained in "*The Tablets of Destiny Revelation*" (*Liber-One*), "*Crystal Clear: Handbook for Seekers*" (*Liber-2B*), the "*Metahuman Destinations*" volumes, "*Imaginomicon*" (*Liber-3D*) and "*Way of the Wizard*" (*Liber-3E*); also available within two anthologies "*The Systemology Handbook*" and "*The Metahuman Systemology Handbook.*"

creation, but once it believes it is located among them, it is subject to its reality agreement with external conditions & environmental factors.

"UNIVERSE" CONSIDERATIONS
Another heavily-charged spiritual incident that may also be 'restimulated' and potentially detrimental to effective progress at 'Wizard Level-0' is "Collapse-of-Space" and "Collapse-of-Universes". This is something that all individuals have experienced intensely at some point on the 'Spiritual Timeline' at least once (with their 'Home Universe').

Just as there are experiences of one's own POV "snapping in" or "caving in" on a new plane of space or mass, so too are there times when the space and energy-matter (and the very corners of a Universe itself) "collapse in" on the individual. Heavy fragmentation charges on this experience can affect a Seeker's willingness to be responsible for "Creation-of-Space" as found in Grade-IV exercises.

The "hot buttons" treated in systematic processing for "Collapse-of-Universes" are quite similar to the "going in" and 'interior/exterior' buttons used previously. In this instance, rather than a POV being "snapped in" to some space or energy-matter, the reverse is treated:

• Incidents of space collapsing in on the POV
• The world closing in; the world folding up
• Energy imploding; energy collapsing in on the POV
• Corner-points collapsing; corner-points snapping in on the POV
• Sudden "uncreation" or "folding up" of all form
• The environment caving in on the POV
• Pulled backward from
• Falling away from
• Sense of everything suddenly becoming unreal...

As with the case of "POV snap-ins," these "creation cave-ins" may be encouraged or prompted by external sources and other-determined events —however, much like "invalidation" and other facets of personal degradation (that we choose to "accept" or agree to as "reality"), experience of any POV is still Self-Determined on some level; including "Entry into-" and "Collapse of-" Universes.

THE PERSONAL UNIVERSE

The 'Home Universe' of an Alpha-Spirit is created by (and subject to) the first Alpha-Thought: direct considerations and command postulates for any existence to be or not be. It is composed of that which an Alpha Spirit has created for and as their own consideration, when the "Home Universe" is the highest of 'Creative Universes'; not 'shared' in agreement with others; the truest form of Individuality in 'Spiritual (Alpha) Existence'.

An individual as Alpha-Spirit (true "I-AM"; highest POV) is still existentially 'occupying' as an 'Awareness' in their original Personal "Home Universe" foremost to any other Universe or POV. However, considerations and postulates for this Home Universe began to blur. Other reality agreements fix a POV in "shared universes", in which SELF could engage in 'creative display' and eventually 'games' with other 'Selves'. A reduction in Awareness and ability occurred when eventually Alpha-Spirits substituted considerations for the creation of their Home Universe by rigidly fixing reality agreements and POV in place with other Universes.

SHARED "GAMES" UNIVERSES

In a 'Personal Universe', the command postulates and considerations of creation and space require no energy or force in which to BE. Later agreements to use 'force—energy' (in Alpha-Existence) and 'effort' (in Beta-Existence) is a "game condition" only. At first, things could be brought into being for a Creative Universe by 'Alpha Thought' alone —and in many respects, the actual considerations and commands still originate at this level. However, with condensation of "Games Universes" and individuals considering energy-matter as more solid with each one, the 'actions' require applying a similar degree of energy. This further validates the substance and reality of a particular Universe.

ALPHA-COMMAND OF ENERGY-BEAMS

When POV is anchored to beta-existence, the Alpha-Spirit is still using energy-beams to control functions of a genetic vehicle. These are created and commanded at the Alpha-Thought level, but they are also directed by Will-Intention even when attention is focused on 'any' facet of beta-existence, such as a 'body' or the 'Physical Universe' in general.

An Alpha-Spirit uses energy beams for command of a Mind-Body system. These are treated lightly in other types of "energy work" regarding certain 'circuits' and 'flows' of the body —such as 'kundalini', 'yoga', 'chakras', &tc. But like other forms of mysticism, the practitioner has a tendency to remain quite fixed to the mental circuitry itself (rather than a perspective outside of it). One can use these methods and sometimes get lucky in managing some kind of repair of an existing state, but seldom does it permanently treat encoded and programmed conditions. This causes an individual to continuously require such corrective therapies. While the methods may produce an effect, they also validate operating reactively only, which puts the individual at effect. The effects of, for example, a "chakra-alignment" seldom last more than three days.

Handling 'energy beams' and 'flows' requires operating with clear channels from a point of direct consideration and command postulates in order to Will or Intend an energetic effect in beta-existence (or elsewhere). It requires no actual effort, because we are not using a physical means to affect physical mass. A Seeker may find working directly with energy is a bit above their "reality" to grasp at first. It is quite different from how they have agreed to consider standard operations and action in the 'Physical Universe'.

PERSONAL ENERGY SYSTEM
When controlling a genetic vehicle, the Alpha-Spirit will connect up circuitry and energy beams: running to the inside of the head, the back of the neck, all along the central nervous system or spine, the area called the Solar Plexus, and so forth. In the past these specific areas have been recognized and treated as 'energy centers' or 'light centers' that circulate specific types of energy. Yet most traditions just assume them to 'be', not realizing that SELF is not only operating them, but also responsible for agreeing to and maintaining their creation each step of the way.

There are evidently seven of these main 'centers' -and seven 'shells', 'bodies' or 'veils' that enshroud considerations of an individual when occupying their 'Beingness' in this 'Physical Universe'. In Systemology, we have been navigating our ascent up the "Ladder of Light" (Pathway) using calculable systematic correlations between these personal 'layers' that were added, and the cosmic "Gates" we descended.

HANDLING UNIVERSES & BODIES
Before heavy fragmentation occurs, an Alpha-Spirit is Aware that they are not actually located interior to any 'Creative Universe', but are instead "reaching inside" one to both operate and experience that operation. The individual (as an 'Awareness') is completely outside the boundaries of space, "looking in". [This applies to everyone, not only individuals

named Timothy Leary.] The Alpha-Spirit is actually already exterior to the entire Universe,
so the best "Secondary POV" (they think) is not
located behind the "body" it wants to operate
and experience, but from a POV that is inside
it. Which is, of course, how an individual gets
over-identified with (and can fixedly 'snap-in'
to) a "body" more permanently (as a consideration).

The more an individual associates their personal Identity (or Beingness) with the genetic
vehicle, the greater energy will be applied to
protect it and maintain its survival above all
other considerations. It is the "above all
else" to the detriment of Self-Awareness that
allows additional personal fragmentation.

When an Alpha-Spirit identifies with 'pain' (or
other sensations) of a physical body, additional circuitry is crystallized (or **calcified**) in
place, which we call "imprints". The 'shock'
snaps the POV into the body with force. The Alpha-Spirit now wants to protect itself and considers itself to share the same fate as the
body. It develops all manner of shields, filters, relays and other automatic mechanisms to
assist protecting the genetic vehicle. This
mode of action repeated numerous times through
many incarnations. The inherent sense of 'be-
trayal' inevitable down the line is sure to put
an individual out of communication with bodies
and spaces throughout this beta-existence altogether. The conclusion is another Universe collapse. Then, we'll find considerations for the
next shared-agreement Universe to sink one
notch lower as a common denominator.

The Alpha-Spirit too often maintains an interi-
or POV for the genetic vehicle, but realizing
it is not always a 'safe' place to be, sets up
additional 'points' to view from just outside
of it. This is the area that Awareness will
suddenly move to, using Self-generated respon-

se-mechanisms, during severe accidents. These incidents of 'unconsciousness' are actually times when the POV has been spontaneously expelled from ("forced out" of) the genetic vehicle. It is also from this point that Awareness will suddenly "snap-in" on the body again. The very fact that these incidents result in sudden shifts of interior and exterior and interior (again) POV, outside of one's direct Self-determinism, contributes to the ongoing difficulty one has in "getting out" as a stable condition and resuming control of a body knowingly and willingly from outside, as opposed to being "stuck" inside of one.

CONCLUSION

Proper handling of these fundamentals lends greater understanding on primary areas of 'energetic charge' on a case, and ability to target channels and terminals associated with these turbulent incidents -and process them out. This package (described in this bulletin) is what led a Seeker to the point they are now. A Professional Pilot gains the training, skills and certainty necessary to effectively assist others to redirect their course, expand their considerations and increase their reach, so as to fly out and beyond the boundaries of beta-existence.

APPROVAL FOR RELEASE:
30, APR 2021 (Liber-3D)
31, OCT 2022 (Liber-011)
Joshua Free, project director

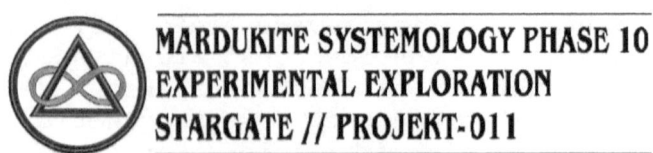

MARDUKITE SYSTEMOLOGY PHASE 10 EXPERIMENTAL EXPLORATION STARGATE // PROJEKT-011

MARDUKITE STARGATE PROJECT BULLETIN OF 15, DECEMBER 2020 BORSIPPA H.Q., SAN LUIS VALLEY, COLORADO

TECH SUMMARY # S011-H [*Confidential (VI)*]

REMOTE VIEWING TRAINING EXAMPLE (RV CASE STUDY #0)

Projekt-011 Series – 4

SUMMARY
The name "Russell Targ" (b. 1934) shows up frequently in the original SRI work for Stanford and the 1970's/1980's "Stargate Project" documents and other work connected to 'Remote Viewing', particularly in regards to 'Ingo Swann', 'Pat Price' and 'Harold "Hal" Puthoff'.

REFERENCES
All "STARGATE" files from 2017.
All "PROJEKT-011" files from 2020.

TECH REVIEW
The "New Realities" channel on YouTube, launched by interviewer Alan Steinfeld on 24, July 2006, includes an interview with Russell Targ concerning 'Remote Viewing', titled: "Russell Targ teaches Remote Viewing in one simple lesson" (and the video runs for approximately five minutes).

TECH SUMMARY
The following tech summary is based on a video and transcript of the interview and demonstration.

BACKGROUND
Russell Targ assisted in developing a 'remote

viewing' program at Stanford Research Institute (SRI) in the early 1970's that was eventually sponsored by various "Intelligence Companies" (IC) over the decades.

The video is clearly an excerpt of a longer interview. Alan Steinfeld begins by saying: "Let's go into how easy it is to do this". The only tools given to him by Targ are a 'pad of paper' and a 'pen' (and the instruction which follows).

INSTRUCTION
Targ explains: "The way this works is that I have an object that I've brought here for you that you've never seen. It's an interesting unusual object that I have in my pocket. What you want to do is close your eyes and describe the fragmentary pictures that come to view; what surprising thing pops into mind."

ADDITIONAL GUIDELINES
"Usually the first impressions are golden. It's as though you've just 'reached' out and dipped into the psychic signal. It doesn't make any sense. A person says they're 'looking at this thing and it doesn't make any sense at all'. It's as though you've drawn that first outline and the CIA says it looks like you're at the right place. What else can you tell me? What else is happening when I hand you this object; what additional interesting thing comes to view?"

RESPONSE (RESULTS)
Steinfeld responds: "So, I'm picturing you handing me an object..."
Targ: "Yeah. Or the object is in your hand. You can see this thing in your hand..."
Steinfeld: "Okay, what comes to view..."
Targ: "They say, 'yeah, this first sketch is not bad'; we say 'you contacted the object'. I'm not gonna give you any clues..."

Steinfeld: "Okay..."

Targ: "All I'm allowed to say is 'tell me more'."

Targ looks over at what Steinfeld has doodled on the page.

Targ: "Maybe you got... over there on the left, that's very..."

Steinfeld: "This is kind of like a little plant image that I thought of. I mean, it just came to me, the idea that that would be sort of... I don't know, the image just sort of arrived..."

Targ: "Delightful. So a 'Judge' would already be able to match up my object with your drawing."

Steinfeld: "Oh, really?"

Targ: "So, if you said 'I gotta go now, that's all I have', and I pulled out six possible objects from the closet along with my object, a 'Judge' would already be able to match... and I realize you're struggling all the way, that as you say 'this isn't it, this reminds me of something, this isn't it'... but you've already described my object."

Steinfeld: "I have?"

Targ: "Isn't that interesting?"

Steinfeld: "It is to me. Okay..."

Targ: "Would you like to see what I have?"

Steinfeld: "Yeah, I would."

Targ removes what appears to be an 'apple slicer' from his pocket that has an 'eight-rayed star' pattern very similar to Steinfeld's doodle.

CONCLUSION

Targ explains: "What it proves is that, even an interviewer on camera can expand his awareness to be in contact with something besides his physical body. So, it shows that there's more to us than just being a physical body. We 'inhabit' physical bodies; it's no doubt wise to take care of them –but there is more to us and more to our awareness and more experiences available to us than what you would think if you just think that you're made of meat and potatoes, and that kind of expanded awareness can lead you to learn to 'quiet your mind', reside in that 'loving space' that the Mystics have taught about for thousands of years. And that 'space' is available without having to be-lieve anything silly. It is a gift that's available to expanded awareness."

APPROVAL FOR RELEASE:
31, OCT 2022 (Liber-011)
Joshua Free, project director

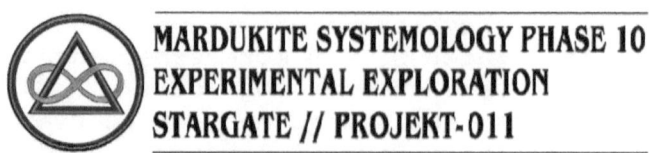

MARDUKITE SYSTEMOLOGY PHASE 10 EXPERIMENTAL EXPLORATION STARGATE // PROJEKT-011

MARDUKITE STARGATE PROJECT BULLETIN OF 09, JANUARY 2021 BORSIPPA H.Q., SAN LUIS VALLEY, COLORADO

TECH BRIEFING # B011-G [*Restricted (IV)*]

"ZU-VISION" ACADEMY LECTURE (ABRIDGED) (GRADE-IV, WIZARD LEVEL-0) BY JOSHUA FREE

Projekt-011 Series – 5

SUMMARY
The project director presents a briefing sum-
mary on "ZU-Vision" to the Mardukite Academy of
Systemology.

DEFINITIONS

ZU-VISION: the true and basic (Alpha)
Point-of-View (POV, perspective) maintained by 'Self' as 'Alpha-Spirit' outside
the boundaries or considerations of the
Human Condition (Mind-Systems) and 'exterior' to beta-existence reality agreements
with the 'Physical Universe'; A POV of
Self as 'a unit of Spiritual Awareness'
that exists independent of a 'body';
'Spirit Vision' in its truest sense.

ACADEMY LECTURE
With the continuation of "STARGATE 2017" as
"PROJEKT-011", and the upcoming 'Liber-3D' release as "IMAGINOMICON", you're going to be
hearing a lot about "ZU-Vision" and "remote
POVs" (or "remote viewpoints") and "remote
viewing" more frequently. This direction of
pursuit is of high-interest to the upper-grade
work. And this is a matter that requires some

clarification because we have a lot of 'mystic-ally-minded' individuals in the Systemology So-ciety and at the Academy that have already had a lot of experiences, or read books about, the whole idea of 'Astral Projection' -and there is likely going to be some confusion about all of this.

Systemology recognizes three main parts to the individual having a human experience here on Earth: the 'Alpha-Spirit', the 'Mind-System' and a 'genetic vehicle' or 'body'. I think we can establish that, even if 6,000 years of spirituality, mysticism, religion and philo-sophy has not provided intellectual satisfac-tion of these facts, the 'Master Grade' work of the Mardukite Academy should have -or at the very least, 'Grade-III Systemology' has already provided a Seeker with greater certainty in this direction.

We have these three parts then: a unit of 'Awareness' as an 'entity' or 'being' that we consider the individual or "I-AM", the 'Self' or 'Alpha-Spirit' as we call it; the "Mind-Sys-tem" is some kind of energetic construct that the Spirit has either inherited somehow, or else it is the composite solidification of the cross-circuitry developed after trillions of years, relatively speaking, of making 'postu-lates' as a 'Spiritual Being' (we aren't sure on that yet); and finally, this 'Spirit' is us-ing a 'Mind-System' for this business he's got-ten wrapped up in called 'control of a body'. And it seems this Alpha-Spirit has gotten into a bit of a mess with this whole ordeal; because at the point or level of this version of 'beta-existence' we got down here, the poor chap is pretty 'spun-in' on the idea that "I-AM" and the "body" are the same identity.

Our experimental research demonstrates that a Seeker should undergo the entire regimen of 'Beta-Defragmentation', using all the available

Grade-III and Grade-IV material on 'systematic processing', before making "ZU-Vision" a focus. But, given the type of work introduced in 'Liber-3D', it is likely that a Pilot will encounter this phenomenon at some point -just by the nature of the type of work we are doing and the effects that some 'systematic processing' can have. In either case, it is something that needs to be understood for all Pilots -and it is particularly critical for continuing success and upward reach of "PROJEKT-011".

Throughout history, individuals have sought out Nature, been involved with some type of aesthetics (such as the arts or music), sought religious experience or meditation, all as a means of getting in touch with, or having a glimpse of, this other natural state of the Spirit. By this, we of course mean a state or experience that is 'outside of' or 'exterior to' this 'beta-existence'. This is the 'effort' or 'intent' to "escape from" that is inherent to all individuals occupying a POV or existence in this 'prison universe'.

All of the 'objective processing' in our Systemology, and just about every technique in our "Stargate Training, 2020 Issue", may not only assist in developing "ZU-Vision" skills, but may even trigger an experience unexpectedly. And of course, this is something that every Systemology Pilot or Mardukite Minister should be prepared for if they are going to use our methods for counseling or spiritual advisement. The tech report on "Imagination Tech" from November 2021 is also critical knowledge for handling "ZU-Vision".

Although the phenomenon is not necessarily unique to Systemology, the semantics for "ZU-Vision" has a short cute back-story. Of course, the concept of "ZU" has been with us a while, since the development of the 'Mardukite Core' over a decade ago; but the term "ZU-Vision" is a relatively recent addition to our vocabulary and it works just fine; but it has a somewhat unlikely origin.

In the 1990's there was a table-top occult role-playing game system published called "Nephilim" -and in it, a player was this eternal spirit that would inhabit various bodies on Earth throughout time, chasing a mystery or fighting against world domination by some secret society. The point being, the individual would accumulate experience as a spiritual being that would control a human body at various points throughout history -none of which were the actual being themselves, of course. The bodies were referred to as **'simulacrum'**. But now in this game manual we read:

> "KA is the vital energy of the Nephilim. It is the measure of the Nephilim's wisdom. It shows its growing comprehension of the universe and measures its progression on the pathway to Agartha. Nephilim must raise their dominant KA to 90 points in order to reach Agartha. Thus a Nephilim's spiritual progress is measured by its KA."

More to the point: one of the techniques an individual can **enact** in the game is called "KA-Vision", which is described as: "a magical sight unconnected to any normal senses. KA-Vision reveals magic fields which surround and permeate all things." And of course, that isn't precisely how we're defining it. But, the subject of "KA" came up during "The Power of Zu" lecture series a year ago in late 2019, and when we wanted to distinguish our application of "Spirit Vision" from what is found elsewhere in esoteric lore and mysticism, "ZU-Vision" stuck.

I have frequently joked about operating the body like a marionette doll or puppet. It's not really a joke. This is what is actually happening. Except, and here we are again, we are treating things in Systemology -spiritual phenomenon or abilities that are inherent to the Alpha-Spirit, that they are actually doing on automatic. The Alpha-Spirit is already operating the body in this way, with energy beams for strings, but this is done so compulsively that the Knowingness has gone away.

What are we doing when we treat the body as a marionette? We are rehabilitating the individual with the Knowingness of what is already happening on automatic, with whatever energy-machines and mechanisms are set up to accomplish this apart from the 'Awareness' of the individual doing it. This is something that 'Liber-3D' treats, but will only go as far as is necessary to establish solidity for the gradient-tier criteria of Grade-IV.

Cumulative application of this work is what will get an individual 'out of the body' -and all other 'systematic processing' is supplemental to this. The other techniques we have that precede this are all cumulatively establishing the certainty and horsepower an individual requires to achieve these newer heights as stable progress and not just fall down afterward. As I've said before, we may be operating in mirror of the "Gates" represented by the 'Tower of Babylon' but we are not 'leaning our ladders against the sky'.

One of the issues with presenting 'Self-determined' "ZU-Vision" prematurely is that it, by itself, does not necessarily provide solid gains toward 'Ascension' without the type of processing found in "Crystal Clear" or "Metahuman Destinations" -or what we intend to present as 'Liber-3D' this Spring. So, when you have a Seeker that is not so bad off as to 'snap-in' on the body again right away, but not defragmented enough to appreciate the spiritual experience, you've just given someone another means of illusory escapism.

Because in addition to the cases of "compulsive 'can't get out' from the Human Condition", you will find the case of "obsessive 'must get out' from" -and this individual is having a hard time of it, because they aren't playing the 'Game' at all; their entire occupation of attention in Life is on withdrawal, escape, retreat and such. Where Life is a 'Game', the whole game-time is spent 'avoiding' the "Game". And this is one of those widely-circulated commonly-used go-nowhere 'Eastern'-style practices of pseudo-enlightenment that have already been played out and tested; and you find out you have increased your tolerance to sit still up on some mountainside somewhere for thirty years and don't really get much else accomplished. It's already been done. No one got to 'Nirvana' that way.

In your more typical case, you have the Seeker that is 'compulsively' "stuck-in" and "spun-in" and they "can't get out" -and that is part of the 'implant' or 'imprinting' that is on the circuit too. Their consideration is one regarding 'loss'. The idea of 'loss' of a 'body' is too great; or the consideration that the body 'needs' them, and such. There are a lot of considerations on these lines that keeps an individual engaged with, and manifesting, a "stuck flow" of one direction or another. And of course, the standard-issue Human has a lot of attachment to the sensations and gravity of the 'Physical Universe'.

There have been a lot of mystical attempts in the past -there have been efforts made by 'New Thought' organizations during the mid-1950's that we tend not to talk about -there has been a lot of recent interest in this idea of being "stuck in 'The Matrix'" and such. Most standard-issue Humans, as entrapped as they may be, still have an innate sense that there is more to existence than what they are sensing with the faculties of a 'genetic vehicle' and that they, themselves, are to some degree aware that they are a 'spiritual being' having a 'human experience' -I know this is a cliché statement these days.

But, if nothing else, that statement is the basic common denominator of all religion and spirituality if you strip away all of the other **'dogma'** and suppositions about 'Divinity' or 'Heaven'. But even this realization is only perhaps given a brief amount of attention for a little while on Sundays, or maybe just every Christmas, or something like that -and the individual goes about the rest of their lives completely **immersed** in experiencing the trappings of the Human Condition. This is one of the things that exercises in "ZU-Vision" may perhaps provide some relief in. And an advanced version of "Stargate Training" could be run in "ZU-Vision" -even though there are advanced suggestions throughout it, the whole thing can be run that way.

The emphasis of 'systematic processing' in the forthcoming "IMAGINOMICON" or 'Liber-3D' is actually more directly regarding 'Imagination' and 'Creative Ability' than blatantly "ZU-Vision" -although it is certainly embedded within the same cycle of work. However, it is critical for a Seeker to gain certainty over their own ability to 'Create' and manage a 'Personal Universe' before a Pilot starts 'ejecting' them from this one and too much "Sys-180 Nothingness" is processed. Because what an Alpha-Spirit seems to dislike more than anything else, apparently, is to confront Nothingness. So, you have to make sure to rehabilitate the ability to handle 'Mental Image Pictures' and 'Imaginative Creativeness' before pushing the "ZU-Vision" button hard -and for this reason much of this material will really be treated as 'upper-level' work rather than for a basic 'Beta-De fragmentation' regimen.

As an individual frees up more of their considerations, more becomes possible. It's as simple
as that. It only seems like it should be more
complicated; and there have certainly been
enough people that **insist** that it should be.
But, for example, how much more complicated
should it be to "change your mind" than to
simply 'change' your 'mind'. Seriously. And
this is one of the most difficult things for
some individuals to do -especially when their
own point-of-view is rigidly and compulsively
fixed "inside of" the 'Mind', or worse, the
'Body'.

You've probably already experienced the type of
standard-issue experiences that most significantly validate what we mean by "ZU-Vision" at
least once during the present lifetime or incarnation. These might occur right before falling asleep, when intensely ill, during a serious accident and especially at the death of a
body. These incidents are what store up as the
experiences of being "outside of" the body -and
unfortunately, they are all situations that
place the individual at 'Effect', meaning that
the resulting "leaving" is 'other-determined'
and not 'Self-determined'. This also makes "ZU-
Vision" seem like an undesirable state to some
fragmented individuals -and so a Pilot sometimes finds strong resistance from the Seeker
on this right from the start.

Our original experimental research involved
very direct processing commands to "be outside
the body" -or rather, "be outside that body".
This worked for some individuals, but we spent
the past several months of "PROJEKT-011" looking through various 'New Thought' techniques of
the past century and we're going to continue
doing that. We've been doing that since the inception of Systemology -but really, ever since
the launch of "STARGATE 2017" we've been very

intensely exploring many of this older 'New Thought' research from the early and mid-1900's that has essentially been forgotten or dismissed for one reason or another -particularly among the contemporary 'New Age' scene.

During the past year of intensive experimental research on the application of 'systematic processing', one of the key factors we learned from many hours of practice is that a Seeker should be processed on considerations using alternation of those considerations. For example: "Get the idea that you can operate that body from outside of it"; "Get the idea that you can't operate that body from outside of it". Spending some time on these fluid considerations actually frees up the flows on that circuit; and you are left with a greater determinism on the power of that choice. When an individual is obsessively or compulsively performing any action or pattern of thought, just how much power of choice are they actually enacting in their Life?

It is important to note that we are processing a Seeker toward the direction of increased 'Self-determinism' and 'Power of Choice' -not 'Freedom'. By applying 'Self-determined Power of Choice', an individual is actually 'playing' a "Game". When the Alpha-Spirit had unlimited freedom, infinite space and no barriers or forms or others to communicate with, they were not very happy -they would rather be playing a "Game".

Now, essentially, there is nothing wrong with willingly and knowingly playing the 'Physical Universe Game on Earth' in itself -but the standard-issue individual does not even know that they 'are' playing a "Game"; and likewise cannot leave the "Game" at will. With those two conditions in mind, an individual can have a very difficult time getting along down here. For one, they will have an insatiable drive to 'find something' -because apparently part of their 'Game Conditions' is a "not-knowing". So, now you have a lot of people down here that are trying to 'figure something out' that doesn't even matter; but they know they just 'have to figure' whatever it is out. Somehow that 'thing' is the 'Key' -but, of course, it never is and they've just more or less spent a life making the 'Physical Universe' a little bit more solid by their participation.

An Alpha-Spirit has the 'Creative Ability' to manufacture a 'Personal Universe'. It might be more correct to say that to do so is a basic function, because this is already happening. But, eventually this individual 'Universe' is merged with, or **invested** in, some kind of 'Beta-Existence' and so the make-up of the 'Personal Universe' is added to the melting pot of a 'Shared Universe' -but the Alpha-Spirit is still creating and occupying the 'Personal Universe'; and it is only by personal consideration and agreement (as reality) that a 'blurring of the boundaries' ensues. And eventually these 'thresholds' or 'boundaries' manifest more solidly as "Gates". But the point is that this 'fragmentation' is essentially an accumulated confusion of displacing or **misappropriating** 'Physical Universe' agreements on one's own 'Personal Universe'.

Whether an individual realizes what they are doing or not, all the true mystical phenomenon and spiritual experience originates from the individual's existence as a 'spiritual being' in a 'Spiritual' or 'Alpha' state. By rehabilitating an individual's ability to operate from the higher ideal states of Knowingness and Beingness, we are able to 'swing wide the gates' on what is potentially possible to experience during the course of one's spiritual lifetime. Rather than agreeing to lower and lower considerations for the 'Universe', an individual can be brought up to their once-forgotten heights

of existence and participate in the creation of
a new and better 'Universe' for all those in
agreement. Together, we can shape the world as
is fitting to be inhabited by the metahumans
that continue to wake up to themselves every
day. Thank you.

APPROVAL FOR RELEASE:
31, OCT 2022 (Liber-011)
Joshua Free, project director

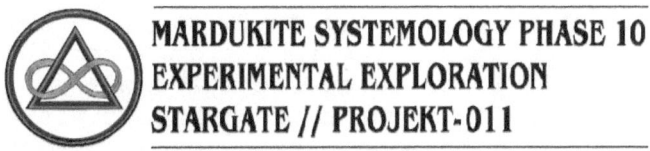

MARDUKITE SYSTEMOLOGY PHASE 10 EXPERIMENTAL EXPLORATION STARGATE // PROJEKT-011

MARDUKITE STARGATE PROJECT BULLETIN OF 18, MARCH 2021 BORSIPPA H.Q., SAN LUIS VALLEY, COLORADO

TECH REPORT # R011-E [*Top Secret* (VII)]

SPIRITUAL ENTITIES & FRAGMENTS
(CLASS-6 PILOTING)
Projekt-011 Series – 6

SUMMARY

The Alpha-Spirit is able to 'BE' in many places at once, because it is a non-local unit of 'Awareness' (not actually locatable in any space) -and thus is also able to operate relatively from many places at once.

CONFIDENTIALITY

Although developed as part of Grade-IV (Wizard Level-0) work for 'Liber-3D', this is a "PROJEKT-011" report pertaining to "Alpha-Defragmentation" theory -which is really appropriated to higher gradients of Systemology work, such as 'Class-6 Pilot Training'. This material should be disclosed to a Seeker (or Pilot) only after the "Beta-Defragmentation" systematic processing regimen (of Grade-III and Grade-IV).

BACKGROUND

As a 'unit' of 'Spiritual Awareness', the Alpha-Spirit does not actually have a mass or wavelength and is a 'static' relative to the 'Physical Universe' ('Beta-Existence'). The ability to be 'located' in space-time is a result of personal considerations and agreements -particularly concerning the viewpoint (point-of-view, POV) taken up. Where attention is

placed, where intention is directed, wherever
the individual is perceiving from, from the POV
that an individual is operating from -this is
what locates 'Self'; and these viewpoints are
not fixed or entrapped, again, except by consideration. The Alpha-Spirit can actually 'locate' itself anywhere in the Universe (or Universes).

ADVANCED PREMISE
It is established within our Systemology that
the Alpha-Spirit, during the time spent with
the Human Condition (and prior), has at various
times and for equally various reasons, fragmented "Self" by leaving 'pieces' of 'Awareness'
behind. These fragmented parts act like "entities"; they are 'automatic circuits' left created in perpetuity and apart from 'Self-Determinism' thereafter. In essence, this is the
upper-level understanding of "fragmentation".
Part of what takes place during "Beta-Defragmentation" (systematic processing regimen) is
the reclaiming of 'lost' "Attention-Units" (or
'Awareness') from the "Backtrack".

TECH SUMMARY
Rather than maintaining a fluid ability to
knowingly operate (a POV, &tc.) from a location
(or source-point) and withdraw from it at will,
the standard-issue human being generally has
allowed their attentions to get fixed or entrapped -particularly involving the 'Physical
Universe' and a 'genetic vehicle'.

An individual actively participates with creation of reality by their attention ('Awareness'). Although there are waveforms and cues
and signals that we receive from the external
world and others, the translation of these frequencies into the comprehensible world we actually experience as reality around us (and its
perceivable solidity) is entirely generated
from 'within'.

As an individual goes about their life (or many lifetimes), small bits of 'Awareness' are distributed or projected throughout space-time by thought and attention. This energy is what we refer to as "ZU" although it has had many names at varying points of understanding throughout history. This energy is exchanged as a communication between the Alpha-Spirit and a Universe, as well as with other "game-players" also occupying attentions in that Universe.

The reason we apply the term "ZU" is because the 'Spiritual Life Force Energy' and the 'Awareness' of the individual that is often 'abandoned in place' rather than dissolved, are the same energy (ZU).

PROCESSING (AND PILOTING)
A Seeker (or Pilot) may successfully process a 'split-fragment' directly by handling the exact moment (incident or event) at which "Self" (the Alpha-Spirit) 'split-off' or 'divided'. In the more advanced "A.T." (Ascension Tech) for upper-level Systemology 'Wizard Grades', this would be handled by 'processing the fragment' itself; and such seems quite 'esoteric' at the present knowledge-tier.

There is a drawback to the direct approach, and it is the reason why 'Beta-Defragmentation' processing toward "Self-Honesty" (particularly when only treating 'this' lifetime) does not equal the attainment of "Ascension" in the way that upper-level 'Alpha-Defragmentation' is intended to. But a Seeker first needs to actually 'get into the building', 'check in' and 'orient themselves' as a presence before they take a walk 'upstairs'. To ensure this, we have a systematic sequence of exercises and progressive techniques that we apply as 'Beta-Defragmentation'.

Drawbacks to the direct approach arise when the Alpha-Spirit not only fragments itself, but those fragments potentially continue to fragment -just as the individual themselves has (most likely) continued to fragment elsewhere since the target incident. In energetic terms, forcing the reconnection prematurely can essentially 'short-circuit' personal flows (and produce a wide variety of physical illness and 'pings') because there are also other missing fragments 'in between'.

An individual may also find that "ZU-fragments" from other people also get 'stuck' to them. In many ways, these are the energy-circuits that act as individual entities or 'spirits' that can affect a person's life. One of the other issues with presenting this work too early in the progress is that, much like the case of "Backtrack" or 'past lives', an individual is naturally inclined (by standard-issue) to rely on these 'other entities' and 'past life imprints' to be the total justification for creations, actions and 'Self-determination' in 'this' lifetime. Grade-III and Grade-IV methodology increases the Seeker's personal horsepower on "responsibility" prior to introducing these other factors.

APPROVAL FOR RELEASE:
31, OCT 2022 (Liber-011)
Joshua Free, project director

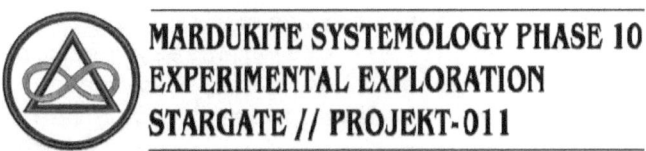

MARDUKITE SYSTEMOLOGY PHASE 10 EXPERIMENTAL EXPLORATION STARGATE // PROJEKT-011

MARDUKITE STARGATE PROJECT BULLETIN OF 30, APRIL 2021
BORSIPPA H.Q., SAN LUIS VALLEY, COLORADO

TECH BRIEFING # B011-H [*Restricted (IV)*]
(REVISED 30, APRIL 2022)

BETA-DEFRAGMENTATION SCHEDULE (VERSION 1.3)
Projekt-011 Series – 7

SUMMARY
This is the primary outline for Class-3E Piloted "Beta-Defragmentation" Systemology Operating Procedure as of 30, April 2022.

TRAINING MATERIALS (REQUIRED)
GRADE-III: "The Systemology Handbook"
         -or-
         "Systemology: The Original Thesis"
         "The Tablets of Destiny" ('One')
         "Crystal Clear" ('2B') and
         "The Power of Zu" ('S1Z')
GRADE-IV: "Metahuman Systemology Handbook"
         -or-
         "Metahuman Destinations" ('Two')
         "Imaginomicon" ('3D') and
         "The Way of the Wizard" ('3E')
    *Liber designations in ('parenthesis')

OPERATING PROCEDURES
Once a Seeker has completely worked through
Grade-III, and the hot-buttons and circuits of
Grade-IV, all remaining 'Beta-Defragmentation'
is primarily accomplished with 'systematic cre-
ativeness processing' (see "Imaginomicon").
This also requires imagining the creation and

218

handling of various 'terminals' -possibly hundreds of different objects, masses, persons, and incidents -those that carry 'emotional encoding' (or 'associative imprinting') restricting "free" consideration (or fixing 'Awareness' outside 'Self-determination'). Each 'Mental Image Picture' representing a 'terminal' is systematically handled in one's 'Personal Universe' until the 'creation', 'protection' (preservation), and inevitable 'destruction' of it is freely treated, and comfortably acceptable, on all of its channel 'circuits'.

Then, a Seeker cycles through all former work, but applying 'Imagination' ("IMAGINE") to the 'Processing Command Line' (PCL) -adjusting all processing so as not to invoke any 'physical actions' (during 'objective processing') or 'recall' pertaining to experience of 'Beta-Existence' (in this lifetime). Therefore, the final cycle through all 'Beta-Defragmentation' processes is 'Imagined' (or operated with "ZU-Vision"). A final checkout for "Self-Honesty" is handled with Route-3E processing as given in "The Way of the Wizard" (Liber-3E).

When an individual is clear of compulsive and unknowing tendencies to 'create', has fully rehabilitated 'creative faculties' of a 'Personal Universe', and regained a commanding viewpoint as the Alpha-Spirit 'exterior' to any considerations for the 'Physical Universe', we consider that individual defragmented or 'Actualized' up to a 'beta-state' of "Self-Honesty" -a basic stable point, just outside the 'Mind-System', from which to knowingly continue the human experience -and if so inclined, pursue a higher echelon of spiritual ability with the Mardukite 'Wizard Grades' of 'Metahuman Systemology' and beyond to "Ascension".

APPROVAL FOR RELEASE:
31, OCT 2022 (Liber-011)
Joshua Free, project director

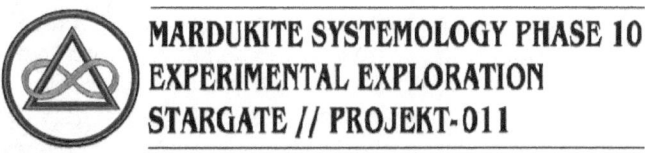

MARDUKITE SYSTEMOLOGY PHASE 10 EXPERIMENTAL EXPLORATION STARGATE // PROJEKT-011

MARDUKITE STARGATE PROJECT BULLETIN OF 01, MAY 2022 BORSIPPA H.Q., SAN LUIS VALLEY, COLORADO

TECH SUMMARY # S011-J [*Confidential (VI)*]

MARDUKITE PHASE-10 // "PROJEKT-011" (CLASS-6)

Projekt-011 Series – 8

SUMMARY
'Mardukite Phase-10' or "STARGATE 2017" resumed in October 2020 as "PROJEKT-011" during the "Imaginomicon" (Liber-3D) R&D period until April 2021. Attention remained on the 'Freedom From', 'Metahuman Ethics' and 'Personal Integrity' serials from Summer 2021 until Spring 2022 for the publication of "The Way of the Wizard" (Liber-3E) in order to end cycle on Grade-IV material and bridge to Grade-V.

PROPOSAL
In addition to planned developmental research and Grade-V experimental programs at the 'Mardukite Academy', it is the decision of this Council that exploratory work resume on "PRO-JEKT-011". Since the caliber of this work is considered Grade-VI or Grade-VII (according to the 'new' Standard Grading System established in 2019), "PROJEKT-011" is approved to continue on the basis of speculative experimental research only -and only by individuals assigned to this limited access project.

LIMITED ACCESS
An individual 'cleared' for participation in "PROJEKT-011" (in 2022) would have completed a

220

basic 'Beta-Defragmentation' program. This is
not necessarily a requirement depending on what
outside assistance may be required for this
project. However, any 'outsiders' solicited to
assist must be 'cleared' for involvement using
basic Class-3E protocols for 'Ethics' and 'Personal Integrity' (which in this case, becomes
'personnel integrity' checks).

CODENAME BACKGROUND
This part of the long-standing "STARGATE" program of 'Mardukite Phase-10' is titled "PRO-
JEKT-011" after a character from the TV-Show
"Stranger Things" named 'Eleven' (often designated as "011"). On the show, the girl 'Eleven'
is a subject of the CIA 'MK-Ultra/Stargate'
projects emphasizing 'remote viewing' and
'telekinesis' (or psychokinesis, "PK"). There
are so many parallels between the full run of
past Mardukite (and future Systemology) work,
and the show (including 'gateways to other
worlds' and 'Lovecraftian horror'), that a book
could be dedicated to that subject alone. [hint
hint]

ENERGY HANDLING
Direct processes incorporating 'direct handling
of energy-beams' are restricted from use in the
Master Grades (Grades I-III) and, to some extent, in Grade-IV. In basic 'Beta-Defragmentation' processing, 'TERMINALS' are treated directly by consideration with little attention
given to corresponding energy-flows that result
on a circuit. Prior to that, earlier 'Grades'
demonstrate how "magick" and "religio-spiritu-
ality" rely heavily on treating '**SYMBOLS**' for
effective connectedness.

There is some confusion on 'why' we would restrict energy-handling when it seems coun-
ter-intuitive to what we are doing in Systemology.

The truth is that we do not actually restrict

energy-handling as an 'absolute'; we simply focus on other aspects for 'systematic processing' instead. Our standard regimen of
'Beta-Defragmentation' actually increases a
Seeker's certainty on ability to confront and
handle 'ENERGY-BEAMS' and 'ENERGY-FLOWS' directly -especially after they are already
skilled in handling the same via 'consideration'. However, any practice directing 'energy-
beams' with certainty with 'Alpha-Thought'
(postulates) is another matter, because energy-
beams do not generally get the type of 'Physical Universe' response we would like to see
manifested for our own validation.

DEVELOPMENT PROPOSAL
At lower-grades, a Seeker is still very much
"in their head". Management of 'energy' generally involves a lot of 'Thinkingness' at that
level -but really 'energy' should be handled
via 'Alpha-Thought'. This requires operating
apart from, or 'exterior to', the 'Mind-System'
and not from 'inside' of it -otherwise an individual gets too wrapped up in considering the
'mechanics' as they might apply to 'Beta-Existence'.

As with any type of 'systematic processing', a
Pilot should validate what a Seeker 'can' do
-what is within their reach or ability or ac-
ceptability level. The main issue with handling
'energy-beams' is that an individual has a
tendency to invalidate their intentions when
attempting to work with them at first, because
the 'Physical Universe' does not react accordingly. Essentially, at lower-grades, the Seeker
is still invested in too much 'reality-agree-
ment' with the 'Physical Universe'. Therefore
upper-level work should emphasize the ability
to break these 'reality-agreements'.

PRACTICE WITH 'ENERGY-BEAMS'
Rather than practice 'imagining visible energy-

streams', a Seeker should at first practice with 'energy-beams' as they actually are in the 'Physical Universe' (and often elsewhere), which is 'invisible'. Even on the material level, we do not say that energies around us do not exist simply because we do not readily 'see' them as they are -but we say that they are 'invisible', or else not perceptible without specifically tuned receptors for those wave-forms or frequencies. For example, consider the "cellular waves" that crisscross so abundantly through our civilization today.

When an individual first begins working with 'energy-beams' they should imagine it invisibly suspended in the air. The 'energy-beam' does not itself radiate energy; it is a "standing-wave" or "wave-function" of energy (ZU) flowing as itself. This would be the same type of "pressers" and "tractors" used to 'push' and 'pull' at things -similar to the strings on a marionette puppet-doll. That is not, however, what this present bulletin will be introducing.

In this practice, begin with an 'energy-beam' that is approximately three feet long. This can be run using 'conceptual' and/or 'creativeness' systematic processing protocols. For example, if necessary, the Seeker should just "get the idea" that the 'energy-beam' is there. Get certainty on this before proceeding.

Then practice alternating the size of the 'energy-beam', stretching it from three feet up to ten feet and then compressing it back down to three feet. The value in this exercise is in the actual 'stretching' by intention; a Seeker should not simply imagine that the beam is suddenly each length. After a while of this practice, the 'energy-beam' may have a tendency to 'snap' into one position or the other -but it is the Seeker's creation and they are to maintain 'Self-determinism' of its creation.

Similar to other "Stargate Training" this

should be practiced incrementally over a period of time rather than Seeking an 'ultimate' end-point in one "creativeness session". The "reality" an individual has on this process will increase over time.

APPROVAL FOR RELEASE:
31, OCT 2022 (Liber-011)
Joshua Free, project director

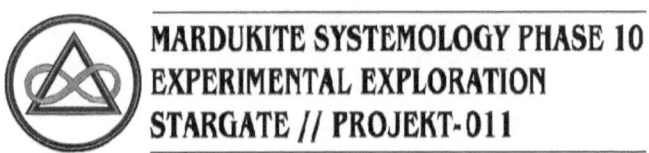

MARDUKITE SYSTEMOLOGY PHASE 10 EXPERIMENTAL EXPLORATION STARGATE // PROJEKT-011

MARDUKITE STARGATE PROJECT BULLETIN OF 06, JUNE 2022
BORSIPPA H.Q., SAN LUIS VALLEY, COLORADO

TECH REPORT # R011-F [*Top Secret (VII)*]

"PROJEKT-011" & PSYCHOKINESIS (PK)
(REVIEWS & UPDATES - SUMMER 2022)
Projekt-011 Series - 9

SUMMARY
A subset of Mardukite Systemology Phase-10
"STARGATE//PROJEKT-011" concerns itself with
two 'by-products' of upper-level Systemology
'Wizard Grades', most specifically, 'remote
viewing' and 'telekinesis' (or 'levitation',
&tc). At our present stage of developmental research for the "Pathway", we are most concerned
with what, if any, practical experiments might
be drawn for this and what the potential for
'Piloting' such ability-sessions would actually
be -although most upper-level A.T. Systemology
work is flown 'solo'.

[This bulletin will focus on what is referred
to as "PK" or "psychokinesis" -which for our
purposes is functionally identical to "telekinesis".]

BACKGROUND
The basic theory behind 'telekinesis', 'levitation' or 'psychokinesis' (all of which we will
generalize as "PK" for our short-hand) is relatively mystical and esoteric -mostly involving
'energy-beams' and high-level communication
maintained between an operator and their target. And of course, we do not necessarily mean
the "talking" kind of communication.

Although it is not frequently discussed socially, many individuals have had isolated experiences where the seemingly "supernatural"
occurs -and by this we mean the intention to
move an 'object' and having it happen without
physically touching it. Other times it seems to
occur unintended altogether, but accompanying
intense emotional states. This would indicate
that potential for "PK" is highest when the
'game condition' that an individual is "not
supposed to" is not present in mind, and they
simply 'do' it.

Therefore, since the phenomenon is obviously
'possible' in theory, there must be systematic
methods for generating it at Will -or rehabilitating the basic faculties of the ability.

TECH SUMMARY
The primary concern with "PK" (or any
'psychic'/'psionic' ability) is the matter of
personal considerations and postulates (or 'Alpha-Thought'). One of the difficulties in employing 'traditional' mysticism, 'self-help'
techniques and any variety of general 'positive
thinking' is that the individual is actually
fighting against themselves and previously made
reality-agreements, whether or not these are
recognized and even remembered. A small wisp of
momentary 'positive thinking' does not sweep
away mounds of entangled personal energy-masses
and imprints.

Of course, the most direct method of 'systematic processing' toward these ends is spotting
and handling the exact moment (or incident)
when agreements (considerations) were actually
made and held on to. Of course, for many individuals, this chain of implanting most likely
goes back much further than just 'this' lifetime. Thus, it is a limited technique at lower-
tiers of application.

ARCHAIC ESOTERICISM

The original source material for 'psychic' ('parapsychological' or 'metapsychological') research is now a minimum of over 60 years old. It does not speak much of what we refer to in "PK" except in regards to "Spiritualism". By the term "Spiritualism" we mean specifically the intentional practice of 'psychic medium- ship'; thus a practitioner is a "Spiritualist". And while this was once much more visible in popular culture, the appearance of too many fraudulent charlatans (and increased display of "stage magic") in the past forced this element of society underground.

Esoterically speaking, nearly all effective methods of "divination" involve some element of "PK". For example, a "planchette" moving across a 'talking board' is not much different than "table-tipping". Both involve 'levitation' to a certain degree. Minute muscle-responses that reflect answers with a "pendulum" or a "dowsing rod"; the proper shuffle and selection of "cards"; or the drawing of "runes" or "ogham sticks" from a bag -all are considered 'random events' in material science -all could be equally treated by 'quantum physics' or 'meta- physics' as having various 'Observer-effects' in probability or else a 'perturbation' from sources 'exterior to' this 'Physical Universe'.

Our concern, from a systemological perspective on traditional "PK" (or any similar 'psychic' phenomenon) in regards to 'mediumship', 'chan- neling' or other "Spiritualism", is the depend- ency on an 'outside' source other than the Seeker/individual ("Self") for effect. In fact, the Seeker is the 'effect-point' in this commu- nication. Even if we were to assume that it is a part of the Alpha-Spirit themselves that is influencing the results of some phenomenon, the fact that it is originated unknowingly and that the 'source-point' is misidentified just sets the individual up for additional fragmented considerations.

ARCHAIC CASE-REVIEW: TABLE-TIPPING

In view of the facts given in the last paragraph, the phenomenon of "Table-Tipping" is
probably one of the easiest examples to reference and an easy starting place for our investigations. Of course, our last paragraph raises
the issue that the activity evokes assistance
(communication) of some foreign 'spiritual entity' as opposed to placing the individual conducting the operation at Cause. The practice
itself is in some ways similar to the child's
game of "light as a feather; stiff as a board"
except that it does not employ a physical
'group-lift' effect in any way. In this instance, participants place their hands on top
of the table -not underneath it, as we might
expect.

ADDITIONAL ESOTERIC REFERENCE

Potential future considerations about the "Magic Carpet".

CITATION

As suggested in Raymond Buckland's "Book of
Spirit Communication" (2004); first published
as "Doors to Other Worlds" (1993):

> "...persons participating should sit
> evenly spaced around the table. Everyone
> should start this with feet flat on the
> floor, hands loosely in their laps (you
> will put your hands on the table after
> this preliminary exercise). Breathe
> deeply; calm yourself. Then, as you
> breathe, imagine you are breathing in the
> soft, positive, white or blue light of
> protection. Feel it filling your body,
> driving out any negativity as you breathe
> out. See it expanding to fill the circle
> of friends about the table. Continue to
> breathe deeply until light expands to fill
> the whole room..."

"...all should lay their hands on the
table, palms down, along the edge. Initially it's a good idea to make an unbroken circle of the hands. Touch your two
thumbs together, spread your fingers and
have your little fingers touching the
little fingers of the people on either
side. If there are not enough people to go
all around the table this way, then separate your own hands but [still] touch the
little fingers to those of your neighbors.
[Then]...ask aloud 'Is there anybody
there?' Repeat this a few times. You can
add, 'If there's anybody there, would you
please communicate by moving the table?'
You should shortly feel the table start to
move..."

SUPPLEMENTAL CASE-REVIEW
Many years prior to our 'Mardukite Phase-10'
efforts, one of our esteemed colleagues repor-
ted experiences from their teens:

"...Table-Tipping seances that my family
used to do at home. In this, a crowd sits
around a table (usually a light card
table) chanting 'Table up!' for many, many
hours until the table floats up. I even
tried it once with two other kids to make
sure the adults weren't fooling us. It can
be done consistently if you persist long
enough (but it truly is a long time). We
never knew if we were pulling in some
spirit or just getting an unknowing group
effect..."

"...there would not be a single twitch
(nothing encouraging whatsoever) for most
of the time spent chanting ...we would be
90% there and nothing would be happening.
Once we got the first twitch, there would
be only a few minutes of twitching and
then the table would rise cleanly into the
air in a very precise manner. If anyon

raised a finger off the table, it would drop like a stone. Sometimes one of us would be around but not in the seance. In that case, we would often have them go over and try to push down on the table. When I tried this, it felt like pushing down on a float in the water. It took considerable force to get it down by an inch or two..."

THEORIES ON ARCHAIC CASES

Based on what we know of both 'physics' and 'metaphysics', there are really only two basic energetic theories behind the aforementioned 'levitation' phenomenon:

a) 'energy-beams' (currents, force &tc.); or

b) 'energy-fields' (frequency of the mass).

There is also a third possibility that it involves both of the above. Whether or not these considerations are relevant (or necessary to know) as superior to the basic consideration that such is even possible -such would require more experimental research and evaluation.

We are not entirely left in the dark at this juncture of the journey, however; those that have tread some of this terrain before us leave breadcrumbs of their suppositions -as we read further in Buckland's "Book of Spirit Communication":

"The actual force that initially moves the table is the force of the combined muscle power of the sitters. By that I don't mean that the sitters are consciously making the table rock. It's the spirit who makes use of that muscle power to do the physical moving but then directs it to provide the intelligence..."

"...Colin Brookes-Smith developed and set up electronic apparatus to determine the source of the 'lift'. ...his research indicates that in fact the lift comes from

above the table! ...may be some correlation [to] the venturi effect in aircraft
whereby the airplane is lifted by the air
passing over the top of the wing, not that
flowing underneath it."

Our esteemed colleague from the 'Supplemental
Case-Review' continues:

"...an oddness to the feel of the energy,
and the feel of the table, and the way it
moved. It did not seem at all like someone
invisible was lifting it or like it was
being moved by mechanical means. It didn't
have the snap of a strong magnetic field,
but it did have some similarities to motions induced by electrostatic charges...
Since nobody's hair stood on end, it would
not actually have been electrostatic, but
the similarity implies an energy field of
some sort."

"My impression is that a field permeated
the table and moved it rather than some
beam coming down and pulling it up. One
could feel a faint energy flow through
one's hands to the table and a bit of attraction between the table and the hands
(and you had to forcefully pull your hand
off to break contact). [Given your original question,] I would conclude that although it might be possible to 'lift' an
ashtray with an energy-beam, it might be
easier to 'permeate' the ashtray and move
it upwards that way."

PROJEKT-011: 'REMOTE-POV' (UPDATE)
References: Preliminary details concerning "Re-
mote-POV" and "ZU-Vision" appear in 'Liber-3D'
("Imaginomicon").

Handling "Remote-POV" and "ZU-Vision" concerns
'space', 'universes' and 'Games' and is therefore more appropriately handled in Grade-VI
('Wizard Level-2') rather than emphasized

strongly in lower-gradients. But the fact remains that 'remote viewing' and 'telekinesis' are "hot" subjects these days -and they are colorful "metahuman" ideals that inspire many to originally pursue the 'Pathway', even though it is not officially a public 'selling point' for Systemology or Mardukite work.

Unless a systemologist understands that they are handling 'space' when they are handling "ZU-Vision", there is little rehabilitation value in its practice. By handling 'space', we are again back to the idea of handling 'Universes' -and this is the upper-level goal behind "ZU-Vision". When you have 'space' you have 'freedom'; but you also have 'distance', which can act as a 'barrier'. Then there is 'energy-mass' and the things you 'have' -and these represent 'terminals' for communication across distance, because you have an apparent 'thing' there now. Even if its some kind of 'corner-point' or some 'spot' in space, you have some 'thing' by which to define some parameter of 'dimension'.

Then, there is this matter of "Remote-POV" -and this needs to be clarified very understandably (although we have said these words before). The systemological message concerning this is not only a semantic cleanup, it is the key to the whole thing -and that is: the individual, their actual "Self", is already in a "remote" location from the body. It is merely fixated on the POV of the body and via a whole process over misidentification of the "Self" for the "body", thereafter restricts its viewpoint from the body's eyes. When we speak of a "Remote-POV" (or elsewhere as 'remote viewing') we mean specifically 'remote' from the 'body', or else 'remote' from where the individual has located its primary consideration of Beingness. Elsewhere, these "Remote-POV" are also called "secondary POV" (such as in 'Liber-3D').

One of the techniques is to put (or imagine) a
little gold disc, about an inch or two in dia-
meter, out to anywhere we wish to view -simply
by using intentionally directed 'Awareness' -no
effort involved. The disc is used to receive
the same type of perceivable waves of existence
as the faculties of the 'genetic vehicle'. Even
if an individual does not receive full perception, they are often able to get some sense of
a 'scene' by the end of Grade-IV. This does not
mean that the scene is accurate for the present
space-time of the 'Universe' -or even apply to
'this' Universe. Thus, no results or 'wins' of
any kind should be invalidated; the techniques
like this can be 'imagined' until intended effects are considered 'actual'.

The techniques of "Stargate Training 2020"
['Stargate//Projekt-011' bulletin of 20, October 2020] are just as relevant now as they were
nearly two years ago -they haven't changed. The
most basic method for developing "Remote-POV"
is to alternate flows of attention ('interior'
and 'exterior'): 'spotting' (with eyes open or
closed) three points in the body and then three
spots in the room (repeating for as long as desired).

PROJEKT-011: 'SENSORY DEPRIVATION' (UPDATE)
The TV-Show "Stranger Things" depicts use of
'Sensory Deprivation Chambers' for both 'sensitivity training' and practice of 'Remote Viewing' (relatively similar operations to our pursuit of "ZU-Vision" in Systemology).

Even when not employing the large 'full-body
submersion' model at "Hawkins National Laboratory", there are many instances throughout the
series when the character "Eleven" accomplishes
achieving these 'perceptual isolation' states
on her own, using only a blindfold and a silent
environment or in combination with a 'pool' or
'tub' of water mixed with an excessive amount
of salt. In this wise, the functional goal is

not submersion, but the ability to 'float' in suspension on the surface.

The 'Sensory Deprivation Tanks' used in most publicly accessible facilities are a combination of the two extremes displayed on "Stranger Things". On the one hand, they are exceptionally large 'tubs' that allow an individual to be stretched out flat on the horizontal surface of the water; on the other, they are generally large 'shells' that can be enclosed to shut out all outside light. Often they have internal colored-lighting options, sometimes referred to as "chakra-lights". One of our members considers use of lighting as "dirtying the float" -the term "float spa" being the semantics typically used.

Not surprisingly, 'Sensory Deprivation' was intensely studied by military forces around the world -and even employed as an interrogation tactic (which the European Court of Human Rights has deemed 'inhuman and degrading'). Although many 'therapies' are developed using short-term applications, long-term (or enforced) application of 'perceptual isolation' can actually trigger extreme anxiety, hallucination and depression -particularly among those highly fragmented individuals.

But even among the less esoterically-inclined, the "general population most likely goes to ['float spas'] for the relaxation benefits, and maybe the light psychedelic effects that can occur during a float". For example, the "Sage Float Spa" (in Santa Cruz, California) hails itself (on its website) as:

"...your go-to place to relax in a distraction-free setting that provides the opportunity to internally tackle whatever challenges you may be facing. Conquer stress, anxiety and depression, sleep better, jump-start creativity and connect with your intuition. Commit to self-care, unplug and realign..."

Another clinical expression for this activity is dubbed "REST" -'Restricted Environmental Stimulation Therapy'. The typical liquid solution for 'Floatation REST' (as you find at most 'float spas') is body temperature water supersaturated with enough 'epsom salt' to allow the individual to float. The standard sized 'chamber' or 'tub' filled with approximately a foot of water requires around 1000 pounds of 'epsom salt' -with most 'float spas' utilizing magnesium-rich varieties of the salt.

There is, at this time, no official advisement or protocols for usage in combination with "PROJEKT-011" -but this subject is something to be reviewed at a future date.

APPROVAL FOR RELEASE:
31, OCT 2022 (Liber-011)
Joshua Free, project director

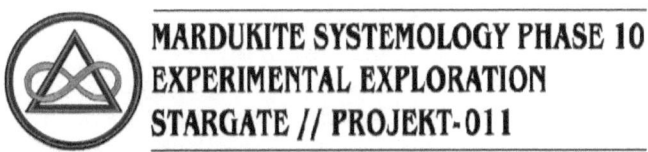

MARDUKITE SYSTEMOLOGY PHASE 10
EXPERIMENTAL EXPLORATION
STARGATE // PROJEKT-011

MARDUKITE STARGATE PROJECT BULLETIN OF 08, JULY 2022
BORSIPPA H.Q., SAN LUIS VALLEY, COLORADO

TECH REPORT # R011-G [*Top Secret (VIII)*]

PROCESSING TOWARD PSYCHOKINESIS (PK)
(A 'CLASS-6' EXPERIMENTAL EXPLORATION)
Projekt-011 Series – 10

SUMMARY
The subject of 'psychokinesis' (PK), 'telekinesis' or 'levitation' is one primary facet of exploration for "PROJEKT-011" Grade-VII research. It is treated as a 'by-product' of ascending the "Pathway" in Systemology; the demonstration of this ability is not an actual grade-goal.

REFERENCES
All "STARGATE 2017" files; and all "STARGATE//PROJEKT-011" files.

BACKGROUND
The systematic methodology developed for metaphysical or personal defragmentation in 2019 and 2020 does not specifically pertain to 'levitation'-type development techniques -even when we consider the 'objective exercises'. Among these, the closest we probably have within the standard regimen is **"Bell, Book & Candle"** from the 'Metahuman Destinations Cycle' in 2020 -specifically the more advanced 'mental' or "ZU-Vision" version of it.

SYSTEMATIC PROCESSING PROTOCOLS
All "PK" experiments are probably best operated from "ZU-Vision" -of course, this limits the

access most Seekers would have to this work.
Since it is classified as Grade-VII, a serious
issue is not foreseen in this area. It is important that the bulk of this work remain classified so as not to invalidate the Seeker's
'gains' and 'wins' as they progress on the
"Pathway".

THE 'HIDDEN STANDARD'
The general public ought not to know about upper-level A.T. Wizard-Grade work, so that Systemology is not branded as offering "supernatural abilities." Such might cause individuals
to carry a 'hidden standard' regarding processing. At any gradient of the "Pathway", a
Seeker should be checked out (preferably on a
GSR-Meter) to see if "Psychic abilities" are a
'hidden standard' for Systemology work (or the
"Pathway"). The term 'hidden standard' implies
that effectiveness of all systematic techniques
will be gauged by whether or not an individual
believes themselves closer to achieving that
'standard'.

NOTES: SUCCESS, PATH-GAIN & 'WINS'
This work is classified as Grade-VII (Class-6)
because it represents some of the most upper-level 'by-products' (we dare not say
'goals') of the 'Pathway to Ascension'. It is
not placed lower on the 'Ladder' because an emphasis or focus in this direction is not a
'route' or 'means' toward accelerating progress
on the 'Pathway'. This does not mean that there
is not some merit to its pursuit (at higher
Grades) or that it is not without 'common interest' by the community at large. But, in any
case, it is treated 'supplemental' to the Pathway and not as a 'required integral' -at least
at this point in its development.

Another concern is 'invalidation' of results
-mainly, the Seeker 'invalidating' their own
'wins' and 'gains' if expected manifestations
do not occur. There are techniques that get

around this. [This is explained in the next section on 'Ashtrays'.] But the fact remains that our studies demonstrate that there is no observable validation for an individual until ability is at least 90% 'there'. This means that for the majority of the time an individual is practicing their 'telekinesis' or 'levitation' directly, the results are not sensed and there is no feedback from, for example, energy-matter in the 'Physical Universe'.

This hypothetical 90%+ is the quotient of "ZU" or "Actualized Awareness" directed as attention by the Seeker as 'Cause'. It is, in essence, a "Causation Quotient" ("CQ") -a term we can coin for our NewSpeak. Material science seems to have some inkling that this phenomenon is the case, but they usually always liken it back to material terms, such as the 'percentage of the brain utilized' or something of that nature.

The issue arises when a Seeker starts at, let us say 10% "CQ", and then does some intensive 'systematic processing' sessions toward changing considerations and then is able to apply 30% to their next 'objective exercise', there still is no 'visible' change in the 'Physical Universe' to validate the 'gains' -and an individual is likely to invalidate the whole thing and drops back down to 10%. For this reason, if such a tier of 'Systemology Work' were to be introduced to a Seeker too early on the "Pathway" it could prove detrimental to the stability of all the progress they had made thus far.

Our colleague contributing anonymously to 'Stargate Project Bulletin of 06, June 2022' goes on to explain:

"I don't think the weight or the size of the object makes any difference unless you pick something bigger than you can move with your hands (which brings in additional considerations of inability). I think that when you are at the 20% level, you

238

are at 'cause' over 20% of the 'IS-ness'
factor of a 'match' or an 'ashtray' or a
'20-pound weight'. Therefore, it doesn't
help to use a lighter object -in fact, it
might be harder if the object is too
light. I also don't think you'll see any
effects on a weighing scale until you are
up at the 90%+ level, because the object
is in a 'Physical Universe' frame of reference and agreeing with that and behaving
properly until you are at so much 'cause'
over it that you can override that."

SUPPLEMENTAL ARCHAIC CASE BACKGROUND
Of the nearly twenty popular 'psychic development' programs or workbooks explored by the
Project Director specifically regarding
'telekinesis' (&tc.), about a dozen of them
used an "ashtray" for their instruction, demonstration or practice object. Upon discovery of
this fact, it seemed like something beyond coincidence was taking place -and suggested a
common source behind the type of 'psychokinetic' development programs (secret or otherwise)
starting up during the early 1970's -and prin-
ted materials of the era related to the same.

As a supportive example, the motion picture
"Vibes" (1988, starring Jeff Goldblum, Cyndi
Lauper, Peter Falk and even the proverbial
'warlock' himself, Julian Sands) briefly depicts activities of a professional 'psychic research' program where one participant is attempting to 'move an ashtray' out from the
circle that has been drawn around it on the
table. After several hours of intensive concentration, the ashtray finally slides an inch
across the table surface out of the circle.
"You did it!" the researchers exclaim. "Yes,"
the man responds, looking down in his lap,
"I've also 'wet' myself."

A second common component of the 'ashtray example', and several others not using an 'ash-

tray', also seemed to be related. In this practice, the individual is 'physically' moving the
'ashtray' with each command of it -thereby getting objective wins on the line of 'causation'.
The individual 'commands' the motion by 'postulate' ('Alpha-Thought') and then sees the ac-
tion-cycle through by actually manipulating an
objective change in the 'Physical Universe'.
This is far superior practical logic for development compared to most of the preexisting archaic examples that we could find.

Tracing these two practices back prior to the
1970's took a bit of time, but our office did
accomplish this. We were able to independently
identify the origins of the 'moving an ashtray'
routine to the mid-1950's -to a "training
routine" demonstrated at a 'self-help' confer-
ence (called the "Freedom Congress") held on 04
July 1957 at the 'Shoreham Hotel' in Washington
D.C., hosted by none other than the 'New
Thought Master of Ceremonies' for that era, Lafayette R. Hubbard.

The exercise is referred to as "TR-8" ('Training Routine #8') in the 1957 "Training Course
Manual" and the instructions also appeared in
the now-out-of print 1975 edition of "Dianetics
Today". The actual title of the technique is
'Tone-40 on an Object'. "Tone-40" is defined in
Mr. Hubbard's "Technical Dictionary" as: "giving a command and just knowing that it will be
executed despite any contrary appearances" or
"a positive postulate with no counter-thought
expected, anticipated or anything else". Apparently this is indicating a direct-command 'postulate' -similar to what we deal with in Systemology in regards to 'Alpha-Thought'. His
concept of 'tone' is roughly equivalent to our
idea of "Beta-Awareness".

According to the research of the Project Director: the purpose of the exercise is not necessarily to actually move the object, but to

practice and perfect putting intention into communication. These "TRs" are instructed and practiced at the most basic levels of their organization -with versions included in their entry-level "Communication Course".

SUPPLEMENTAL ARCHAIC CASE REVIEW
While we are not necessarily officially implementing any version of 'Tone-40 on an Object' for our own Systemology regimen, it is an interesting archaic case study to review; and it has no doubt been usurped (or bastardized) into many other 'traditional' and contemporary 'psychic development' programs. It does, however, provide an exercise that is simple to practice -and may be useful for development in related subject areas of focus for "PROJEKT-011". We also know, with certainty, that in the cases of Ingo Swann, Hal Puthoff and Pat Price: all of them 'drilled' intensely, using the original "TR" versions prior to their involvement with SRI and 'Project Stargate' in the early 1970's.

The first version of the 'training drills' appear in the 1957 "Training Course Manual" compiled by L. Ron Hubbard Jr., and John W. Galusha. It includes details no longer provided in supplements for the current Compact Disc version of the "Freedom Congress" released in 2005 (ISBN: 9781403118189; 1403118183). To determine when this change occurred during the 50 years (1957-2005) would require another full investigation, for which this Office does not presently have time or resources for. While both versions refer to the drill as "TR-8", utilize an ashtray, and agree that the basic commands communicated are: "Stand up"; "Thank You"; "Sit down"; "Thank You"; there are actually several differences between the original and current issues of this exercise.

In the original 1957 version, the student is sitting in a chair, facing a chair, which has

an ashtray on it. In fact, the image of an am-
ber-colored glass ashtray on a red velvet chair
(or floating slightly above it) is the iconic
representation of the "Freedom Congress" (and
the '18th American Advanced Course' that sub-
sequently followed it, also in 1957). In the
present (revised) version, the student is
"standing beside a table holding ashtray".

Both versions prompt the student to manually
make the object ('ashtray') comply with the intention directed (or 'commanded'). The stated
purpose of the exercise is also promising (from
a systemological perspective): "To clarify intentions as different from words. To start student on the road to handling objects and people
with postulates. To obtain obedience not wholly
based on spoken commands."

ARCHAIC CASE REVIEW (INSTRUCTIONAL)
Each of the "TRs" includes, what is referred to
as, a 'training stress'. This is meant to be
understood as the "various ways and means of
getting the student to achieve the goals of (a)
training step" -or else the particular 'significance' that is "stressed" each step of the
way. The 'training stress' (or instructions)
indicated in the revised 2005 version are relatively lackluster when compared to the original, indicating simply to:

"...have the student give orders for a
while alone. Then begin to nag him to get
them up to 'Tone-40' commands. Have the
student silently permeate the object with
the command and an expectancy that it will
do it. When student can 'see' his intentions going in accurately, when he wonders
why object doesn't instantly obey, when he
is not stumbling through energy or depending on his voice, the training process is
flat..."

The original 1957 "Training Manual" version
(that also appears in the 1975 edition of "Dia-

netics Today") provides much greater detail for the exercise and its instruction. For example, differing greatly from above, the 'training stress' is 'coached' as instructed here:

"...during the early part of this drill, say in the first coaching session, the student should be coached in the basic parts of the drill, one at a time. First, 'locate the space', which includes himself and the ashtray but not much more... Second, have him 'locate the object in that space'. Third, have him 'command the object in the loudest possible voice' he can muster. ...when shouting is completed, have student use a normal tone of voice ...attention on ...getting the intention into the object. Now have student do the drill using the wrong commands... Next, have the student do the drill silently... Next..."

The original version also details some helpful coaching dialogue examples that could (theoretically) be converted to Piloted 'processing commands' (PCLs) for experimental research. For example: "Are you willing to be in that ashtray?" And then: "Are you willing for a thought to be there instead of you?" Elsewhere it suggests the coaching command: "Think the thought __"; then, "Imagine that thought being in that astray". In this wise, it is clear that an 'ashtray' is a suitable object, because as a bowl-like vessel it is easy to imagine 'filling' it with an intention.

SYSTEMATIC PROCESSING TOWARD "PK"
Up until this point in "PROJEKT-011", we have operated on the theory that the most appropriate application of 'systematic processing' is directed toward the 'considerations' (and 'postulates'/'Alpha-Thought') maintained concerning one or another 'spiritual ability', e.g. "levitation". In fact, the various methods of 'sys-

tematic processing' accumulated in our core materials for Systemology (published 2019-2021) could all be used as a 'regimen' or 'rundown' toward one particular 'concept', e.g. "levitation" -just as much as they can be used to process considerations on a specific 'channel' toward a specific 'terminal' (energy-mass). For this reason, all available materials should be reviewed for this application.

SYSTEMATIC PROCESSING TOWARD "PK" (PROTOCOL)
Although some coaching/instruction might be warranted, the bulk of Systemology A.T. (upper-level Wizard-Grade) work is most effectively "flown solo" by a Seeker that has already completed the basic 'Beta-Defragmentation' regimen. While directing attention for "Remote-POV" (RV) can be more easily 'Piloted', the updated protocols for 'Piloting' direct "PK" experimental research (beyond the 'considerations' handled with other processes) are still under review and will require additional development within "PROJEKT-011" for future issues.

SYSTEMATIC "PK" PROCESSING (EXPERIMENTAL)
The following are just a few examples of 'systematic processing' drawn from our existing materials, but which is written to apply directly to the subject or concept of "levitation".

These suggestions simply provide the basic start for a skeletal-outline of a 'systematic processing' regimen that could target any concept. Traditionally we target 'terminals' and not 'concepts', which is another reason this is considered more 'advanced' work within our Systemology -and requires additional review for future issues.

EXAMPLE#011.PK.1 (Ref: Liber-2B,Two,3D)
  (SERIES-A)
   Circuit-1: "Recall/Imagine a time when you enjoyed 'levitating' something."

244

Circuit-2: "Recall/Imagine a time when you enjoyed someone else 'levitating something."

Circuit-3: "Recall/Imagine a time when someone enjoyed another 'levitating' something."

(SERIES-B)

Circuit-1: "Recall/Imagine a time when you disliked 'levitating' something."

Circuit-2: "Recall/Imagine a time when you disliked someone else 'levitating' something."

Circuit-3: "Recall/Imagine a time when someone disliked another 'levitating' something."

(SERIES-C)

Circuit-1: "Recall/Imagine a time when you could 'levitate' something and chose not to."

Circuit-2: "Recall/Imagine a time when someone else could 'levitate' something and chose not to."

Circuit-3: "Recall/Imagine a time others could 'levitate' something and chose not to."

EXAMPLE#011.PK.2 (Ref: Liber-Two,3D,3E)

("HELP" – The 'hot-button' that restrains an individual from using abilities because they believe they are helping others by holding them back.)

(SERIES-A)

Circuit-1: "How could you help another by not 'levitating'?"

Circuit-2: "How could another help you by not 'levitating'?"

Circuit-3a: "How could another help others by not 'levitating'?"

Circuit-3b: "How could another help themselves by not 'levitating'?"

Circuit-0: "How could you help yourself by not 'levitating'?"

245

(SERIES-B)

Circuit-1: "How could you help another by 'levitating'?"

Circuit-2: "How could another help you by 'levitating'?"

Circuit-3a: "How could another help others by 'levitating'?"

Circuit-3b: "How could another help themselves by 'levitating'?"

Circuit-0: "How could you help yourself by 'levitating'?"

EXAMPLE#011.PK.3 (Ref: Liber-2B,Two,3D,3E)

("PROBLEMS" – The 'hot-button' that restrains an individual from using abilities because they believe they are solving a problem.)

(SERIES-A)

Circuit-1: "What problem could you solve by not 'levitating'?"
   \ "Consider how that would be a solution."

Circuit-2: "What problem could another solve by not 'levitating'?"
   \ "Consider how that would be a solution."

Circuit-3: "What problem could you solve by preventing others from 'levitating'?"
   \ "Consider how that would be a solution."

(SERIES-B)

Circuit-1: "What problem could you solve by 'levitating'?"
   \ "Consider how that would be a solution."

Circuit-2: "What problem could another solve by 'levitating'?"
   \ "Consider how that would be a solution."

Circuit-3: "What problem could you solve by permitting others to 'levitate'?"
   \ "Consider how that would be a solution."

EXAMPLE#011.PK.4 (Ref: Liber-2B,Two,3D,3E)

("INVALIDATION" – The 'hot-button' for 'imprinting' that restrains an individual from using abilities because they believe they cannot. This is run on a 'GSR-Meter' if possible (which is what they are worded for). The incidents are dated and located; similar previous incidents on any 'chain' or 'circuit' are dated and located -and the whole 'channel' is defragmented or processed-out.)

(SERIES)

Circuit-1: "On 'levitation', has another invalidated you?"

\ Recall. Confront. Analyze. Look for similar previous. Repeat. (Do this for each circuit.)

Circuit-2: "On 'levitation', have you invalidated another?"

Circuit-3a: "On 'levitation', has another invalidated others?"

Circuit-3b: "On 'levitation', has another invalidated themselves?"

Circuit-0: "On 'levitation', have you invalidated yourself?"

APPROVAL FOR RELEASE:
31, OCT 2022 (Liber-011)
Joshua Free, project director

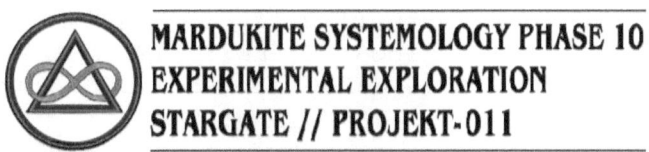

MARDUKITE SYSTEMOLOGY PHASE 10 EXPERIMENTAL EXPLORATION STARGATE // PROJEKT-011

MARDUKITE STARGATE PROJECT BULLETIN OF 01, AUGUST 2022 BORSIPPA H.Q., SAN LUIS VALLEY, COLORADO

TECH BRIEFING # B011-J [*Restricted (IV)*]

PROPOSAL FOR "LIBER-011" AUTHORIZED ('THE METAPHYSICS OF STRANGER THINGS')

Projekt-011 Series – 11

SUMMARY

'Mardukite Phase-10' has been in continuous effect (in one subset program or another) and
supporting ongoing development of the Mardukite
and Systemology movement for over half of a
decade. The integrity of "STARGATE//PROJEKT-
011" has remained undisturbed during that time.

The plan to continue in this direction has not
been altered in any way -except that present
emphasis of the 'Mardukite Academy' and Research Org. ('Systemology Society') is
presently the solidification of Grade-V; and
the primary focus of "STARGATE//PROJEKT-011"
significantly overshoots current goals.

PROPOSAL

In view of the accumulated files and materials
for "STARGATE//PROJEKT-011" and the present-
time pop-culture interests of society, the
Council approved the Project Director's proposal for an 'early experimental exploration' edition of Grade-VI/VII "Liber-011" as 'an unofficial fan guide' to the TV show "Stranger
Things".

TITLE

The complete title for 'Mardukite Esoteric Lib-

rary Catalogue No. 011' will be: "THE METAPHYS-
ICS OF STRANGER THINGS: TELEKINESIS, TELEPATHY
& SYSTEMOLOGY (AN UNOFFICIAL FAN GUIDE)" by
Joshua Free.

PUBLICATION SCHEDULE
The title ('Liber-011') is to be prepared from
existing files and supplemental articles (supplied by the Project Director) during the
months of August and September 2022. Print
setups must be completed within the first third
of the month of October for the start of our
announcements between mid-October and the end
of October (Samhain, Halloween). The projected
release date of the debut edition is 23, November 2022.

APPROVAL FOR RELEASE:
31, OCT 2022 (Liber-011)
Joshua Free, project director

REFERENCE SECTION

STRANGER
APPENDIX

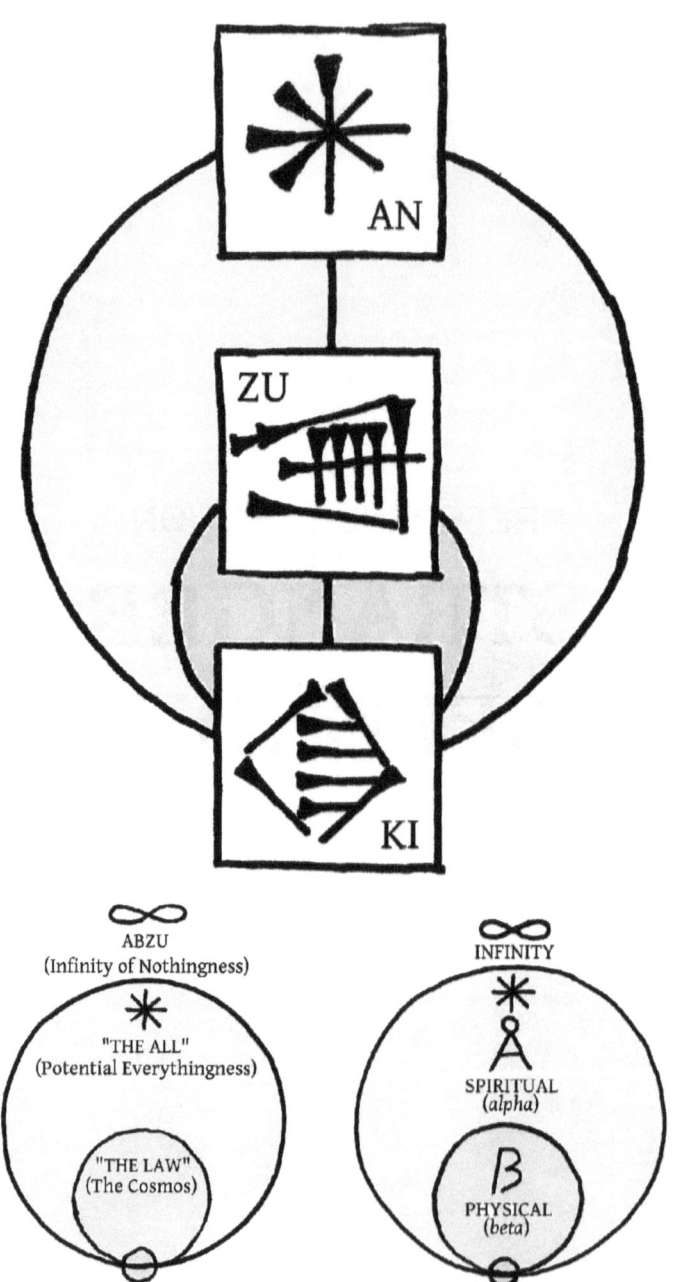

AN

ZU

KI

∞
ABZU
(Infinity of Nothingness)

✳
"THE ALL"
(Potential Everythingness)

"THE LAW"
(The Cosmos)

∞
INFINITY

✳
Å
SPIRITUAL
(alpha)

β
PHYSICAL
(beta)

:: APPENDIX A ::
—Mardukite Zuism: A Brief Introduction—

According to the most ancient historical records written at the birth of our modern civilization...

432,000 years ago, a small population of advanced beings—called the ANUNNAKI—began developing the planet Earth for their purposes. These elite Self-Actualized spiritual beings resided on Earth in physical bodies, but found their forms inadequate for the physical labors required. Enter: the "Human Condition." Ancient "cuneiform" tablet writings from Sumerians and Babylonians of Mesopotamia are clear regarding the original creation and systematic programming of Humanity.

> CUNEIFORM is the oldest known writing system used by scribes of ancient Babylon to record their wisdom and the history of humanity on clay tablets.

"Cuneiform" is named for its style of wedge-shaped script formed by a reed pen called a "stylus." Rather than an alphabet of letters, cuneiform writing is a system of "signs" representing "things" and "ideas." These may even be combined to represent even more complex "signs."

Many concepts adopted for modern "Mardukite Zuism" and its "Systemology" are derived from cuneiform tablets.

The ANUNNAKI introduced complex writing systems in order to program civilization and all parameters of Reality for the Human Condition. Legendary "Tablets of Destiny" (Divine Truth, supreme knowledge and cosmic power of the "gods") were first introduced to Humanity in the Babylonian narrative known best as the "Epic of Creation.

Ancient Babylonians used the *Tablets of Destiny* & *Creation Epic* to systematize all cosmic knowledge into a workable paradigm called "Mardukite Zuism"—a systemology received directly from the ANUNNAKI.

> PARADIGM : all-encompassing standard or religion used to view the world and communicate reality.

SYSTEMOLOGY : applied philosophies (of *Mardukite Zuism*) combined with personal spiritual techniques and technology (*"Tech"*) effectively demonstrating systematic principles of a "paradigm."

THE SYSTEMOLOGY OF LIFE, UNIVERSES & EVERYTHING.

The *Arcane Tablets* describe the division of the ALL by the LAW, outside of which is but INFINITY. The *Epic of Creation* describes these activities as "mythology." The "Standard Model of Systemology" that is applied to *Mardukite Zuism* uses the same information to demonstrate...

that ALL ("AN-KI") envelops both:
the Spiritual Existences ("AN")
and the Physical Existences ("KI")
divided by Cosmic Law and
connected by Life-Awareness ("ZU")
and beyond which is only the Abyss,
an Infinity of Nothingness ("ABZU")

MARDUKITE ZUISM DEFINITIONS FOR STANDARD MODEL OF SYSTEMOLOGY.

ABZU = the Abyss; Infinity; Infinity of Nothingness; that which extends, is exterior to and beyond of, all spiritual and physical existence.

ANKI : the ALL; All Existences; Everything that is AN and KI; Everything that is conceivable; represented by the "Standard Model of Systemology."

AN : the "Spiritual Universe" or "Heavenly Zone" comprised of spiritual energy-matter, in the direction of Infinity—the "Alpha" existence independent of, and superior to, the physical, *beta* or KI.

KI : the "Physical Universe" or "Earthly Zone" comprised of physical energy-matter in action across physical Space and observed as Time in the direction of Physical Continuity—"beta" existence condensed from, and subordinate to, the spiritual, *Alpha* or AN.

ZU L "to know"; "knowingness"; "Awareness" or "conscious-ness"; spiritual energy-matter of AN observed as "Lifeforce" in KI; "Spiritual Life Energy"; the actual personal spiritual beingness or "Awareness" of Self as the Alpha-Spirit which extends along a "line" from the Spiritual (AN) to the Physical (KI).

THE TABLETS OF DESTINY &
BABYLONIAN CREATION EPIC.

Seven cuneiform tablets compose the ancient *Babylonian Epic of Creation*, named the *Enuma Eliš* by scholars after its opening lines. These seven tablets are the basis for what later traditions refer to as the *"Seven Days of Creation."* The *Epic of Creation* tablets describe development of all existences with a Divine artistic perfection. The *Enuma Eliš* is the core example of religious literature from Babylon, which served as the basis for ancient *"Mardukite Zuism"*—the first true systematized religion in history.

The Absolute *behind* and *back of* ALL Existence is referred to on the *Tablets of Destiny* as the INFINITY OF NOTHINGNESS; a constant static latent unmanifest potentiality of ALL and Everythingness.

The LAW—Cosmic Law—is defined as the Cosmic Dragon—TIAMAT—on *"Epic of Creation"* Tablets. She is the First Cause or movement across a "Sea of Infinity." Later, the LAW becomes a division between Spiritual Existence (AN) and any Physical Universe (KI). The LAW—*Tiamat*—permeating ALL, uses the *Tablets of Destiny* and then fixes the systems of finite potential:

The Systems of Manifestation—

Substance, Motion and Awareness.

"Before 'Heaven' or 'Earth' were named," a formation and interaction of active existences—"substances" and "bodies" and "Life" and "gods"—creates turbulence and waves of action through space.

The governing system of Cosmic Law—*Tiamat*—responds accordingly. She fixes the *Tablets of Destiny* to her "deputy"—a messenger wave action of the LAW named *"Kingu"* and sends him rippling out to "meet" the *Anunnaki* "gods."

The *Anunnaki Assembly* of "gods" prepare to battle The LAW.

When none among them comes forth to engage, the *Anunnaki* "god" MARDUK volunteers as hero to confront *Kingu* and *Tiamat*—but with a condition that the *Anunnaki Assembly* recognize him as "Chief of the Gods" upon his success.

When *Marduk* approaches *Tiamat* (LAW) directly, he is flanked by *Kingu* and the "army of Ancient Ones." *Marduk* relinquishes the *Tablets of Destiny* from *Kingu*. With the *Tablets of Destiny*, *Marduk* successfully conquers the true understanding of "Cosmic Law" and thereby conquers *Tiamat*.

Marduk uses the Tablets of Destiny to discover "Self-Honesty" and Divine Knowledge governing "Cosmic Ordering"—systems dividing the "Spiritual Universe" (AN) from a "Physical Universe" (KI).

The two Universe types are connected only by a stream of Spiritual Awareness (*Lifeforce*) that Sumerians called ZU.

Wisdom of the Arcane Tablets is later passed down to and concealed by an ancient esoteric secret society in Babylon: the Scribe-Magicians, High Priests and Priestesses of *Mardukite Zuism*.

Self-Honesty is a term describing an original "Alpha" state of clear knowingness and Self-directed beingness. "Self-Honesty" is the most basic and true expression of Self as "I-AM"—free of artificial attachments; reactive-response conditioning; and imposed or enforced programming as Reality for the Human Condition. Spiritual development in modern *Mardukite Zuism* is referred to as the "Pathway to Self-Honesty" and the "Gateway to Infinity." It is modeled directly from the Ancient Mystery Tradition as observed at the original Temples of Babylon.

THE ANUNNAKI LADDER OF LIGHTS & BABYLONIAN GATEWAYS TO INFINITY.

ZIGGURAT TEMPLES in Babylonia—and throughout Mesopotamia—served to remind populations of the "bond" or ZU connecting "Heaven" and "Earth." Seven-stepped "levels" of the physical *Ziggurat Temples* of Babylonia—and seven corresponding Gates—represent spiritual levels of actualized Awareness; states of Self-purification (or "spiritual defragmentation") as they ascend in the direction of AN toward Infinity of Supreme Beingness—the Pathway of Self-Honesty—in imitation of the footsteps of the gods during their descent through the "spheres" or "Gates."

COSMOLOGY AND METAPHYSICS.

All Things in the Physical Universe are in motion—wave motions of "energy and matter in space measured as-and-across time." Continuity of the Physical Universe (KI) is divided by LAW and encompassed by the ALL (ANKI). The direction of AN extends toward ABZU, an Infinity of Nothingness beyond effective existence.

The Alpha Self or Alpha Spirit is the true source—the "spiritual cause" of "physical effects." It engages Self-determined WILL from its "spiritual" Alpha existence as an Actualized Awareness impinging on "physical" Beta existence and experienced as "Life."

Communication of clear wisdom and true knowledge from Arcane Tablets is distorted as it passes through time and geography, diverse languages and authoritarian cultures using the "Power" to program the masses and fragment the Human Condition away from Self-Honesty.

Use of this ancient wisdom reveals the Keys to "Cosmic Ordering"—applying the highest understanding of "cause-and-effect" sequences to all action in the Physical Universe, and to all *Self-directed* applications of WILL-Intention and Effort.

MARDUKITE ZUISM, SYSTEMOLOGY & SPIRITUALITY.

The Spiritual Universe (AN)—of metaphysical or spiritual energy and metaphysical or spiritual matter is not dependent on the Physical Universe (KI) to exist; the two are existentially independent of each other, maintaining a single channel, conduit or connection, which is Alpha Spirit "Awareness" as Spiritual Life or ZU.

The Alpha Spirit engages a ZU-line, a spiritual lifeline of ZU energy to a genetic vehicle or organic body to experience physical beta existence.

ALPHA SPIRIT : a Spiritual *life-form*; the True Self or "I-AM"; a unit of *Awareness;* a *Spiritual Beingness* that controls a physical body or "genetic vehicle" using a Lifeline or continuum of spiritual "ZU" energy.

ASCENSION : actualized Awareness elevated to (AN) spiritual existence that is exterior to beta-existence; the ability to *Self-direct* from *Spirit* as *Self* in existence independent of any "body."

256

BETA-EXISTENCE : manifestation of a Physical Universe (KI); conditions of energy-matter manifested in a state of condensed existence matching frequencies specific to space in the Physical Universe.

FRAGMENTATION : breaking apart; scattering the pieces; fractioning wholeness; fracture of holism; discontinuity; a separation of totality; anything outside or apart from original clarity (or *Self-Honesty*).

GENETIC VEHICLE : Physical *life-form*; physical (*beta*) body controlled by an Alpha Spirit using a continuous Lifeline of ZU energy; an organic catalyst for a Spirit to operate causes and observe effects (in *beta*).

HUMAN CONDITION : a standard issue default programmed state of Human experience; receptacle for Alpha Spirit Awareness that is generally accepted to be the extent of its potential identity (*Beingness*).

ZU-LINE : Spiritual Life-Energy (ZU) continuum; an energetic channel or Identity-Continuum connecting Alpha Spirit Awareness from Infinity-to-Infinity including the full Physical or *beta* range of existence.

The true Destiny of Humanity is to achieve spiritual Self-Actualization; the reunion of Self with the Infinite.

Attaining Self-Honesty in this Life is the most important step a person can take toward achieving their highest ideals, goals and realizations as a Spiritual Being.

The Highest form of "True Worship" begins with the Spirit—the true Self—and all external practices, rituals, ceremonies and historical examples are but outer reflections of this ideal. The Highest form of "Sin" is against the Spirit—against the Self—and its ability to maintain Self-Honesty.

There are modes of thought, action and Self-direction of effort that will contribute toward Ascension; and modes that lead away from that.

Beta experiences of "Sin"—pain, fear, guilt, anger—are all related to personal fragmentation; and emotional turbulence from all of these may be released—and intention energy redirected—because:

We all co-create the reality we experience in this lifetime!

SPHERES OF EXISTENCE AND INFLUENCE & A UTILITARIAN SYSTEMOLOGY OF ETHICS.

The prime directive of all beta existence is: *to exist.* The continuation of existence is the purpose behind all existence. Between realization of Self and Infinity, there are many spheres of existence that we may influence.

All of the spheres are interconnected. There is nothing in existence that is in absolute exclusion to all existence. Each sphere of existence supports subsequent existences and assists reaches toward higher spheres of influence.

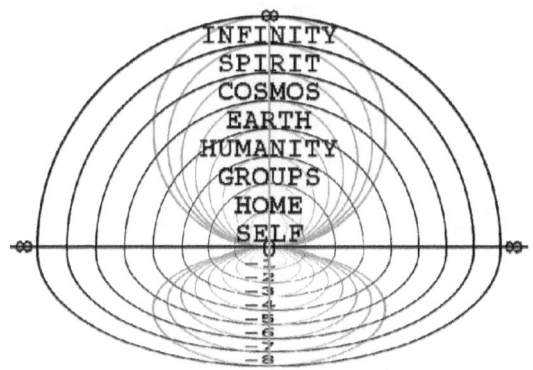

The greatest good contributes to the greatest continuation of optimum existence and survival for the greatest sphere of inclusion. Degrees of rightness and wrongness are determined by Cosmic Law and are reflected in the quality and continuation of optimal existence at the highest sphere of existence. Individual happiness is attained via the channel to the highest sphere. Unhappiness is a result of "selfishness," lack of "Spiritual Self-Actualization" and/or reach of "Actualized Awareness" beyond *Self* as identified to a *body*.

GOALS & IDEALS OF MARDUKITE ZUISM.

The word "ZU" meant "knowing" in original Sumerian cuneiform script. Goals and ideals of Zuism reflect this. *Mardukite Zuism & Systemology* seeks to assist an individual in reclaiming a total realization of the True Self or "I-AM" knowingly as the Immortal Alpha Spirit, in line with a most ancient directive: to "Know Thyself."

In view of the fact that all modern humans are subjected to technologies depriving them of their freedoms to *be, think, know* and pursue truth: goals and ideals of *Mardukite Zuism & Systemology* are to effectively repair abilities and elevate certainty of an Individual to increase and direct "Actualized Awareness" toward Higher Gateways of Spiritual Ascension.

History demonstrates how dangerous, troublesome and easily misused the concept of "RELGION" is; so, for purposes of incorporating *Mardukite Zuism* and its *Systemology* as a contemporary standard, the idea is treated here as defined.

RELIGION : a concise spiritual paradigm, fixed set of beliefs and practices, regarding Divinity, Infinite Beingness—or else "God."

—*Mardukite Zuism* operates under a premise of very specific beliefs and "systemology" of "applied spiritual technology."

—*Mardukite Zuist Religious Doctrine* fundamentally relays the previously described "Highest forms" of Worship, Cosmic Law, and Ethics.

Mardukite Zuist Spiritual Doctrines and its *Systemology* successfully meet modern "religious" criteria for:

a) A Description of Cosmic Creation;

b) Belief in a Supreme Infinite Being;

c) Ethics Leading to Human Ascension;

d) Ethics of Conduct Toward all Life and Existence;

e) Immortality of the Human Spirit;

f) A Published Library of Religious Literature;

g) Traditions of Practice and Application; and

h) A Spiritual Advisement Methodology.

Spiritual Philosophy of *Mardukite Zuism* is systematized by a Standard Model of Systemology. It demonstrates Absolute Supreme Beingness associated with the Highest realization of "God" as INFINITY. No thing is Higher or Absolute than the *Infinity of Nothingness*—and reducing Supreme Beingness to any finite personality or character trait is to limit and defile what is herewith represented, but with lesser "words" and mundane sentiments or semantics.

The Highest Name of God cannot be conceived
—hence our symbolic use of the Infinity Sign:

...or Sumerian cuneiform word-sign: "ABZU"—
"The Infinite Nothingness and Source of All ZU."

—The Spiritual Universe (AN) is *All-as-One* because it exists as an infinite singularity or stasis: infinite potential with no gradient or observed motion; which is its own continuity.

—The Physical Universe (KI) is *All-as-One* because it is in continuous motion, with all manifest parts working systematically as the condensed solid continuity of beta-existence.

—A "spiritual continuum" or "conduit channel" of ZU (or a "*Zu-line*") from a Spiritual Universe (AN)—links our Awareness levels of "I-AM," "True Self" or Spirit ("Alpha Spirit") with varying potential "Point-of-View" and degrees of motion experienced in the Physical Universe.

—The Alpha Spirit or "Soul" is the true Awareness, "I" or "Self" connected to the operation and control of the physical body.

THE BASIC CONCEPT OF THE HUMAN SPIRIT & SYSTEMOLOGY OF SPIRITUAL ADVISEMENT

The true Self is the "I" or "I-AM" or "Spirit"
regardless of its *perceived* position in spaces,
Point-of-View, degree or level of Awareness.
Spirit remains at its original fixed true point.

Whatever "spiritual energy-matter" (*if any*) that may compose the Alpha Spirit or makeup of "soul"—it must occupy this "other space" with its spiritual existence and then project its Awareness and Will onto the Physical Universe (KI) in order to experience the *Game* we call "*Life.*"

This "*Spiritual Life Energy*" or *Awareness* of a *Spiritual Being* is treated as a "Lifeforce" and "Consciousness" and goes by many names throughout the history of language, mysticism and spirituality—but we find the idea first treated as ZU on cuneiform tablets of Mesopotamia.

On an Identity-lifeline or continuum of ZU energy, an Alpha Spirits is operating from a Spiritual Universe to experience in *beta-existence*. We refer to this concept as the *"ZU-line"* on the Standard Model of Systemology to illustrate the projected Awareness from Spirit (as an epicenter or fixed point) to any other *Point-of-view* (POV) anywhere in existence.

ZU is the name given to the spiritual beingness or essence of all Life in existence—and Self is a concentrated center or focal point that projects Awareness on a ZU-continuum or Zu-line toward a point of artificial Identity separate from Self.

The True Self of an Individual Human is a "spiritual universe cause" of "physical universe effects"—engaging as an immortal Alpha Spirit with a Self-determined Will actualized as an Awareness along a ZU-continuum (or *"Zu-line"*), extending from Infinity-to-Infinity, through every possible frequency and vibration along the total spectrum of physical and metaphysical existence.

The Mardukite Chamberlains, an underground research organization established in 2009, dedicated itself to recovery and consolidation of relevant historical, scriptural & ritual records of ancient Mardukite Babylon in Mesopotamia, following up the founding of Mardukite Ministries (Mardukite Zuism) by Joshua Free the previous year, in 2008.

By 2011, a Mardukite Alumni faction (International Systemology Society) began research and development into new methods of:

applying ancient wisdom as a futurist spiritual technology
that effectively awakens, unlocks and fully actualizes
spiritual potential of the Human Condition.

A systematic and logical approach to spirituality is visibly demonstrable on the Standard Model of Systemology, where ZU-line frequencies are represented at various degrees:

• "zero-point" body death;
• cellular life and sensory perceptions of a genetic body;
• bio-chemicals induced by emotion;
• thoughts and intention transmitted between our Alpha Spirit and the "genetic vehicle"—
• all the way "up" the scale to a perfected clarity of Self-Actualized Awareness of I-AM as our true "Alpha" state, just below Infinity and Absolute Beingness.

Full potential of ZU in is only altered from its natural state as a result of personal fragmentation of the Human Condition. This may be restored by systematic spiritual practices.

The *Pathway to Self-Honesty* is a personal journey and spiritual adventure marked by progressive clearing of personal energy channels fragmented by emotional imprinting and programming-data accumulated from "experiences" in the environment—the "debris" that fragments the total actualized experience of Self in Awareness as the Alpha Spirit.

The first and most important step—Before an individual can actualize potentials of the Spirit as Self, they must fully realize:

> The *I-AM Self* and the *Alpha Spirit* are One and the same.
> This state of Knowingness is a primary intention of basic
> spiritual practices of Mardukite Zuism & Systemology.

Mardukite Zuism is a religious philosophy; *Mardukite Systemology* is an applied spiritual philosophy, of which is adopted by *Mardukite Zuism*, but is not dependent on it as a belief system. *Mardukite Zuism* materials, *Systemology* books and advanced training courses are also available to Mardukite Ministers seeking qualification as specialized Clergy, Priests, Priestess, and Professional Pilots of systematic processing.

:: APPENDIX B ::
—Systemology Glossary for Liber-θ11—

A-for-A (one-to-one) : an expression meaning that what we say, write, represent, think or symbolize is a direct and perfect reflection or duplication of the actual aspect or thing—that "A" is for, means and is equivalent to "A" and not "a" or "q" or "!"; in the relay of communication, the message or particle is sent and perfectly duplicated in form and meaning when received.

acknowledgment : a response-communication establishing that an immediately former communication was properly received, duplicated and understood; the formal acceptance and/or recognition of a communication or presence.

activating event : an incident or occurrence that automatically stimulates a conscious or unrecognized reminder or 'ping' from an earlier *imprinting incident* recorded on one's own personal timeline as an emotionally charged and encoded memory; an incident or instance when thought systems are activated to determine the consequence or significance of an activity, motion or event—often demonstrated as *Activating Event → Belief Systems → Consideration*.

actualization : to make actual, not just potential; to bring into full solid Reality; to realize fully in *Awareness* as a "thing."

affinity : the apparent and energetic *relationship* between substances or bodies; the degree of *attraction* or repulsion between things based on natural forces; the *similitude* of frequencies or waveforms; the degree of *interconnection* between systems.

agreement (reality) : unanimity of opinion of what is "thought" to be known; an accepted arrangement of how things are; things we consider as "real" or as an "is" of "reality"; a consensus of what is real as made by standard-issue (common) participants; what an individual contributes to or accepts as "real"; in *NexGen Systemology*, a synonym for *"reality."*

allegorical : a representation of the abstract, metaphysical or "spiritual" using physical or concrete forms.

alpha : the first, primary, basic, superior or beginning of some form; in *NexGen Systemology*, referring to the state of existence operating on spiritual archetypes and postulates, will and intention "exterior" to the low-level condensation and solidarity of energy and matter as the 'physical universe'.

alpha-spirit : a "spiritual" *Life*-form; the "true" *Self* or I-AM; the *individual*; the spiritual (*alpha*) *Self* that is animating the (*beta*) physical body or "*genetic vehicle*" using a continuous *Lifeline* of spiritual ("*ZU*") energy; an individual spiritual (*alpha*) entity possessing no physical mass or measurable waveform (motion) in the Physical Universe as itself, so it animates the (*beta*) physical body or "*genetic vehicle*" as a catalyst to experience *Self*-determined causality in effect within the *Physical Universe*; a singular unit or point of *Spiritual Awareness* that is *Aware* that it is *Aware*.

alpha thought : the highest spiritual *Self-determination* over creation and existence exercised by an Alpha-Spirit; the Alpha range of pure *Creative Ability* based on direct postulates and considerations of *Beingness*; spiritual qualities comparable to "thought" but originating in Alpha-existence (at "6.0") independently superior to a *beta-anchored* Mind-System, although an Alpha-Spirit may use Will ("5.0") to carry the intentions of a postulate or consideration ("6.0") to the Master Control Center ("4.0").

AN : an ancient "Sumerian" cuneiform sign for Heaven or "God"; in *Mardukite Zuism and Systemology* designating the *'spiritual zone'* (or *'Alpha Existence'*); the *Spiritual Universe*—comprised of spiritual matter and spiritual energy; a direction of motion toward spiritual *Infinity*, away from or superior to the physical (*'KI'*); the spiritual condition of existence providing for our primary *Alpha* state as an individual *Identity* or *I-AM-Self* which interacts and experiences *Awareness* of a *beta* state in the *Physical Universe* (*'KI'*) as *Life*.

anchor (conceptual) : a stable point in space; a fixed point used to hold or stabilize a spatial existence of other points; a spatial point that fixes the parameters of dimensional orientation, such as the corner-points of a solid object in relation to other points in space; in *NexGen Systemology*, "beta-anchored" is an expression used to describe the fixed orientation of a viewpoint from Self in relation to all possible spatial points in *beta-existence* ("physical universe"), or else the existential points that fix the operation of the "body" within the space-time of *beta-existence*.

Ancient Mystery School : the original arcane source of all esoteric knowledge on Earth, concentrated between the Middle East and modern-day Turkey and Transylvania c. 6000 B.C. and then dispersing south (Mesopotamia), west (Europe) and east (Asia) from that location.

apparent : visibly exposed to sight; evident rather than actual, as presumed by Observation; readily perceived, especially by the senses.

archetype : a "first form" or ideal conceptual model of some aspect; the ultimate prototype of a form on which all other conceptions are based.

ascension : actualized *Awareness* elevated to the point of true "spiritual existence" exterior to *beta existence*. An "Ascended Master" is one who has returned to an incarnation on Earth as an inherently *Enlightened One*, demonstrable in their actions—they have the ability to *Self-direct* the "Spirit" as *Self*, just as we are treating the "Mind" and "Body" at this current grade of instruction; previously treated in *Moroii ad Vitam* as a state of Beingness after *First Death*, experienced by an *etheric body*, which is able to maintain consciousness as a personal identity continuum with the same *Self-directed* control and communication of Will-Intention that is exercised, actualized and developed deliberately during one's present incarnation.

assessment : an analysis or synthesis of collected information, usually about a person or group, in relation to an *assessment scale*.

assessment scale : an official assignment of graded/gradient numeric values correlated to specific tiers with individual preassigned meanings.

associative knowledge : significance or meaning of a facet or aspect assigned to (or considered to have) a direct relationship with another facet; to connect or relate ideas or facets of existence with one another; a reactive-response image, emotion or conception that is suggested by (or directly accompanies) something other than itself; in traditional systems logic, an equivalency of significance or meaning between facets or sets that are grouped together, such as in $(a + b) + c = a + (b + c)$; in NexGen Systemology, erroneous associative knowledge is assignment of the same value to all facets or parts considered as related (even when they are not actually so), such as in $a = a$, $b = a$, $c = a$ and so forth without distinction.

assumption : the act of taking or gathering to one's Self; taking possession of, receive or behold.

attenergy : *NexGen Systemological NewSpeak* for "attention energies"; the flow of consciousness "energy" that is directed as "attention"; semantic recognition of an axiom from the *Arcane Tablets* that states: "energy flows where attention goes."

attention : active use of *Awareness* toward a specific aspect or thing; the act of "attending" with the presence of *Self*; a direction of focus or concentration of *Awareness* along a particular channel or conduit or toward a particular terminal node or communication termination point; the Self-directed concentration of personal energy as a combination of observation, thought-waves and consideration; focused application of *Self-Directed Awareness*.

authoritarian : knowledge as truth, boundaries and freedoms dictated to an individual by a perceived, regulated or enforced "authority."

awareness : the highest sense of-and-as Self in knowing and being as I-AM (the *Alpha-Spirit*); the extent of beingness directed as a POV experienced by Self as knowingness.

axiom : a fundamental truism of a knowledge system, esp. *logic*; all *maxims* are also *axioms*; knowledge statements that require no proof because their truth is self-evident; an established law or systematic principle used as a *premise* on which to base greater conclusions of truth.

Babylonian : the ancient Mesopotamian civilization that evolved from *Sumer*; inception point for systematization of civic society and religion.

Backtrack : to retrace one's steps or go back to an early point in a sequence; an applied spiritual philosophy within *Metahuman Systemology "Wizard Grades"* regarding continuous existence of an individual's *"Spiritual Timeline"* through all lifetime-incarnations; the course that is already laid behind us; a methodology of systematic processing methods developed to assist in revealing "hidden" *Mental Images* and *Imprints* from one's past and reclaim attention-energies "left behind" with them by increasing ability to manage and control personal energy mechanisms fixed to their continuous automated creation.

band : a division or group; in *NexGen Systemology*, a division or set of frequencies on the ZU-line that are tuned closely together and referred to as a group.

BAT (Beta-Awareness Test) : a method of *psychometric evaluation* developed for *Mardukite Systemology* to determine a "basic" or "average" state of personal *beta-Awareness*; first developed for the text *"Crystal Clear."*

"bell, book & candle" : three dissimilar objects that are kept accessible during a processing session (the book is often a copy of *The Systemology Handbook* or a hardcover copy of *The Tablets of Destiny* with the dust-jacket removed if it is less distracting that way); a term meant to indicate a Pilot's "objective processing kit" of objects generally present in the session room (accessible on a shelf, table or pedestal stands); in *NexGen Systemology,* the name of an objective processing philosophy pertaining to command of personal reality; historically, a formal ritual used by the Roman Catholic church to ceremonially declare an individual "guilty of the most heinous sins" as "excommunicated (to hold no further communications with) by anathema"—whereby a *bell* is rung, a *holy book* is closed and all *candles* are snuffed out—thus we therapeutically use the same symbolism historically representing religious fragmentation for modern systematic defragmentation purposes.

beta (awareness) : all consciousness activity (*"Awareness"*) in the "Physical Universe" (KI) or else *beta-existence*; *Awareness* within the range of the *genetic-body*, including material thoughts, emotional responses and physical motors; personal *Awareness* of physical energy and physical matter moving through physical space and experienced as "time"; the *Awareness* held by *Self* that is restricted to a physical organic *Lifeform* or *"genetic vehicle"* in which it experiences causality in the *Physical Universe*.

beta (existence) : all manifestation in the "Physical Universe" (KI); the "Physical" state of existence consisting of vibrations of physical energy and physical matter moving through physical space and experienced as "time"; the conditions of *Awareness* for the *Alpha-spirit (Self)* as a physical organic *Lifeform* or *"genetic vehicle"* in which it experiences causality in the *Physical Universe*.

beta-defragmentation : toward a state of *Self-Honesty* in regards to handling experience of the "Physical Universe" (*beta-existence*); an applied spiritual philosophy (or technology) of

Self-Actualization originally described in the text *"Crystal Clear"* (*Liber-2B*), building upon theories from *"Systemology: The Original Thesis."*

biological unconsciousness : the organism independent of the sentient *Awareness* of the *Self* to direct it; states induced by severe injury and anesthesia.

biomagnetic/biofeedback : a measurable effect, such as a change in electrical resistance, that is produced by thoughts, emotions and physical behaviors which generate specific 'neuro-transmitters' and biochemical reactions in the brain, body and across the skin surface.

cacophony : dissonant, turbulent, harsh and/or discordant sound or noise.

calcified : in nature, to calcify is to harden like stone from calcium and lime deposits; in philosophic applications, refers to a state of hardened fixed bone-like inflexibility; a condition change to rigidly solid.

capable : the actual capacity for potential ability.

CAT / "Creative Ability Test" : a method of increasing personal freedom and unlimited creative potential of the Alpha-Spirit (Self) independent and exterior to conditions and reality agreements with beta-existence; a Wizard-Level training regimen first developed for the Grade-IV text *"Imaginomicon"* (*Liber-3D*).

catalog / catalogue : a systematic list of knowledge or record of data.

catalyst : something that causes action between two systems or aspects, but which itself is unaffected as a variable of this energy communication; a medium or intermediary channel.

causative / causation : as being the cause; to be at cause.

chakra : an archaic Sanskrit term for "wheel" or "spinning circle" used in *Eastern* wisdom traditions, spiritual systems and mysticism; a concept retained in NexGen Systemology to indicate etheric concentrations of energy into wheel-mechanisms that process *ZU* energy at specific frequencies along the *ZU-line*, of which the *Human Condition* is reportedly attached *seven* at various degrees as connected to the Gate symbolism.

channel : a specific stream, course, current, direction or route; to form or cut a groove or ridge or otherwise guide along a specific course; a direct path; an artificial aqueduct created to connect two water bodies or water or make travel possible.

charge : to fill or furnish with a quality; to supply with energy; to lay a command upon; in *NexGen Systemology*—to imbue with intention; to overspread with emotion; application of *Self-directed (WILL)* "intention" toward an emotional manifestation in beta-existence; personal energy stores and significances entwined as fragmentation in mental images, reactive-response encoding and intellectual (and/or) programmed beliefs; in traditional mysticism, to intentionally fix an energetic resonance to meet some degree, or to bring a specific concentration of energy that is transferred to a focal point, such as an object or space.

circuit : a circular path or loop; a closed-path within a system that allows a flow; a pattern or action or wave movement that follows a specific route or potential path only; in *NexGen Systemology*, "*communication processing*" pertaining to a specific flow of energy or information along a channel; *see* also "*feedback loop.*"

Circuit-1 : in *Grade-IV* "communication processing" (introduced in *Metahuman Destinations* as *Route-3*), the flow of energy and information connected to outflow, what *Self* has expressed, projected outwardly or done.

Circuit-2 : in *Grade-IV* "communication processing" (introduced in *Metahuman Destinations* as *Route-3*), the flow of energy and information connected to inflow, what "others" have done to *Self*, what it has received inwardly or had *happen to*.

Circuit-3 : in *Grade-IV* "communication processing" (introduced in *Metahuman Destinations* as *Route-3*), the flow of energy and information connected to cross-flows, what *Self* has witnessed of others (or another) projecting or doing toward others (or another).

Circuit-0 : a more advanced concept introduced to *Grade-IV* "communication processing" (as listed on SOP-2C in *Metahuman Destinations* for "*Pre-A.T*" or "*Route-0*" applications), which targets *'postulates'* and *'considerations'* generated and stored by *Self* for *Self* and the direction, energy or flows representing what *Self* "does" for and/or to *Self*. This circuit is treated further in *Wizard Level* work,

chronologically : concerning or pertaining to "time"; to treat as "units" of "time" ; to sequence a series of events or information with regard to the order it happened or originated (in time).

clockwork : rigidly fixed gear-like systems that operate mechanically and directly upon one another to function; a "clockwork universe theory" is a "closed-system design" popular in Newtonian Physics attributes all actions of energy-matter in space-time as reactions in accordance with a "Divine Decree" or fixed design that functions like a "clock-mechanism" and does not account for the "Observer."

codification : process of collecting, analyzing and then arranging knowledge in a standardized and more accessible systematic form, often by subject, theme or some other designation.

command : in *Metahuman Systemology*, responsibility and ability of Self (I-AM) as operating from its ideal "exterior" *Point-of-View* as Alpha Spirit; to direct communication for control of the *genetic vehicle* and Mind-Body connection that is perfectly duplicated from a source-point to a receipt-point along the ZU-line.

command line : see *"processing command line"* (PCL).

communication : successful transmission of information, data, energy (&tc.) along a message line, with a reception of feedback; an energetic flow of intention to cause an effect (or duplication) at a distance; the personal energy moved or acted upon by will or else 'selective directed attention'; the 'messenger action' used to transmit and receive energy across a medium; also relay of energy, a message or signal—or even locating a personal POV (viewpoint) for the Self—along the *ZU-line*.

communication (circuit) processing : a methodology of Grade-IV Metahuman Systemology that emphasizes analysis of all Mind-System energy flows (information) transmitted and stored along circuits of a channel toward some terminal, thing or concept, particularly: what Self has out-flowed, what Self has in-flowed, and the cross-flows that Self has observed; also *"Route-3"*

compulsion : a failure to be responsible for the dynamics of control—starting, stopping or altering—on a particular channel of communication and/or regarding a particular terminal in existence; an energetic flow with the appearance of being 'stuck' on the action it is already doing or by the control of some automatic mechanism.

concept : a high-frequency thought-wave representing an "idea" which persists because it is not restricted to a unique space-time; an abstract or tangible "idea" formed in the "Mind" or *imagined* as a means of understanding, usually including associated "Mental Images"; a seemingly timeless collective thought-theme (or subject) that entangles together facets of many events or incidents, not just a single significant one.

conceptual processing : a Wizard-Level methodology introduced intermittently throughout materials of Metahuman Systemology that emphasizes fully "getting the sense of" (or "contacting the idea of") a particular condition as prompted by a PCL and on one's own determination; a systematic practice-drill regarding considerations and postulates (Alpha Thought) regarding various reality agreements; a *Route-0* variant employing *Creativeness* and *Imagination* for systematic processing; also *Route-0E* when used for *Ethics Processing*.

condense (condensation) : the transition of vapor to liquid; denoting a change in state to a more substantial or solid condition; leading to a more compact or solid form.

condition : an apparent or existing state; circumstances, situations and variable dynamics affecting the order and function of a system; a series of interconnected requirements, barriers and allowances that must be met; in "contemporary language," bringing a thing toward a specific, desired or intentional new state (such as in "conditioning"), though to minimize confusion about the word "condition" in our literature, *NexGen Systemology* treats "contemporary conditioning" concepts as imprinting, encoding and programming.

conflict : the opposition of two forces of similar magnitude along the same channel or competing for the same terminal; the inability to duplicate another POV; a thought, intention or communication that is met with an opposing counter-thought or counter-intention that generates an energetic cluster.

confront : to come around in front of; to be in the presence of; to stand in front of, or in the face of; to meet "face-to-face" or "face-up-to"; additionally, in *NexGen Systemology*, to fully tolerate or acceptably withstand an encounter with a particular manifestation or encounter.

consciousness : the energetic flow of *Awareness*; the Principle System of *Awareness* that is spiritual in nature, which demonstrates potential interaction with all degrees of the Physical Universe; the *Beingness* component of our existence in *Spirit*; the Principle System of *Awareness* as *Spirit* that directs action in the Mind-System.

consideration : careful analytical reflection of all aspects; deliberation; determining the significance of a "thing" in relation to similarity or dissimilarity to other "things"; evaluation of facts and importance of certain facts; thorough examination of all aspects related to, or important for, making a decision; the analysis of consequences and estimation of significance when making decisions; in *NexGen Systemology*, the postulate or Alpha-Thought that defines the state of beingness for what something "*is.*"

continuity : being a continuous whole; a complete whole or "total round of"; the balance of the equation ["–120" + "120" = "0" &tc.]; an apparent unbroken interconnected coherent whole; also, as applied to Universes in *NexGen Systemology*, the lowest base consideration of space-time or commonly shared level of energy-matter apparent in an existence, or else the lowest degree of solidity or condensation whereby all mass that exists is identifiable or communicable with all other mass that exists; represented as "0" on the *Standard Model* for the Physical Universe (*beta-existence*), a level of existence that is below Human emotion, comparable to the solidity of "rocks" and "walls" and "inert bodies."

control (general) : the ability to start, change or start some action or flow of energy; the capacity to originate, change or stop some mode of human behavior by some implication, physical or psychological means to ensure compliance (voluntarily or involuntarily).

control (systems) : communication relayed from an operative center or organizational cluster, which incites new activity elsewhere in a system (or along the *ZU-line*).

correlate : a relationship between two or more aspects, parts or systems.

correspondence : a direct relationship or correlation; see also "*associative knowledge.*"

Cosmic History : the entire continuous *Spiritual Timeline* of all existence, starting with the *Infinity of Nothingness* and individuation of Self and its Home Universe, running through various

Games Universes and ultimately leading to condensation and so-lidification of this Physical Universe experienced in present-time.

Cosmic Law : the "Law" of Nature (or the Physical Universe); the "Law" governing cosmic ordering; often called "Natural Law" in sciences and philosophies that attempt to codify or systematize it.

cosmology : a systematic philosophy defining origins and structure of an apparent Universe.

Cosmos : archaic term for the "Physical Universe"; semantically implies chaos brought into order; in *NexGen Systemology*, can also include considerations of "Universes" experienced previously as a *beta-existence*.

counter-productive : contrary to the greater or original purpose or intention; in *NexGen Systemology*, anything which brings *Life* away from its sustainable goal or position of *Infinite Existence*.

crash-course : a very intense or steep delivery of education over a very brief time period, usually applied to bring a student "up-to-speed" or "up-to-date" for receiving and understanding newer or cumulatively more advanced material.

creative ability test : see "*CAT.*"

creativeness processing : a *systematic processing* methodology introduced in *Grade-IV Metahuman Systemology* (*Wizard Level-0*) that emphasizes personal use of "*Imagination,*" or else "creative ability" of Self and freeing considerations of the Alpha-Spirit to *Be* or *Create* anything within its Personal Universe, independent of reality agreements with beta-existence; also "*Route-0.*"

Crystal Clear : the second professional publication of Mardukite Systemology, released publicly in December 2019; the second professional text in Grade-III Mardukite Systemology, released as "*Liber-2B*" and reissued in the Grade-III Master Edition "*Systemology Handbook*"; contains fundamental theory of "*Beta-Defragmentation*" and "*Route-2*" systematic processing methodology.

cuneiform : the oldest extant writing system at the inception of modern civilization in Mesopotamia; a system of wedge-shaped script inscribed on clay tablets with a reed pen, allowing advancements in record keeping and communication no longer restricted to more literal graphic representations or pictures.

cuneiform signs : the cuneiform script, as used in ancient Meso-potamia, is not represented in a linear alphabet of "letters," but by a systematic use of basic word "signs" that are combined to form more complex word "signs"—each sign represented a "sound" more than it did a letter, such as "ab," "ad", "ba", "da" &tc.

data-set : the total accumulation of knowledge used to base Reality.

defragmentation : the *reparation* of wholeness; collecting all dispersed parts to reform an original whole; a process of remov-ing *"fragmentation"* in data or knowledge to provide a clear understanding; applying techniques and processes that promote a *holistic* interconnected *alpha* state, favoring observational *Awareness* of continuity in all spiritual and physical systems; in *NexGen Systemology*, a *"Seeker"* achieving an actualized state of basic *"Self-Honest Awareness"* is said to be *beta-defragmented*, whereas *Alpha-defragmentation* is the rehabilitation of the *creat-ive ability*, managing the *Spiritual Timeline* and the POV of *Self* as Alpha-Spirit (I-AM); see also *"Beta-defragmentation."*

degree : a physical or conceptual *unit* (or point) defining the variation present relative to a *scale* above and below it; any stage or extent to which something *is* in relation to other possible posi-tions within a *set* of *"parameters"*; a point within a specific range or spectrum; in *NexGen Systemology*, a *Seeker's* potential energy variations or fluctuations in thought, emotional reaction and physical perception are all treated as *"degrees."*

demographics : segments of the population uniquely identified, whether real or representative; targeting a specific portion of the population, such as for marketing or statistics.

destiny : what is set down, made firm, standard, or stands fixed as a constant end; the absolute *destination* regardless of whatever course is traveled; in *NexGen Systemology*, the *"destiny"* of the *"Human Spirit"* (or *"Alpha Spirit"*) is infinite existence—*"Im-mortality."*

differentiation : an apparent difference between aspects or con-cepts.

discernment : to perceive, distinguish and/or differentiate exper-ience into true knowledge.

dogma : religious doctrines or opinion-based beliefs (data-set) treated socially as fact, especially regarding "divinity" or "God" (the common "Human" interpretation of the "domain" of Infinity) represented by the "Eighth Sphere" on our original Standard Model of Systemology; religiously defined values, taboos and ethical standards emphasized by cultural/religious socialization and mythographic beliefs (even above any observable causal effects, logical sequences or verifiable proofs).

dramatization / dramatize : a vivid display or performance as if rehearsed for a "play" (on stage); a *'circuit'* recording *'imprinted'* in the past and, once restimulated by a facet of the environment, the individual "replays" it as through reacting to it in the present (and identifying that reality as present reality); acts, actions and observable behaviors that demonstrate identification with a particular character type, "phase" or personality program; a motivated sequence-chain, implant series or imprinted cycle of actions—usually irrational or counter-survival—repeated by an individual as it had previously happened to them; a reoccurring or reactively triggered out-flow, communication or action that indicates an individual "occupying" a particular *'Point-of-View'* (*POV*)—typically fixed to a specific (past) identification (identity) that is space-time locatable (meaning a point where significant *Attenergy*—enough to compulsively create and maintain a POV—is "stuck" or "hung up" on the *BackTrack*).

Eastern traditions : the evolution of the *Ancient Mystery School* east of its origins, primarily the Asian continent, or what is archaically referred to as "oriental."

echelon : a level or rung on a ladder; a rank or level of command.

emotional encoding : the readable substance/material (data) of *'imprints'*; associations of sensory experience with an *imprint*; perceptions of our environment that receive an *emotional charge*, which form or reinforce facets of an *imprint*; perceptions recorded and stored as an *imprint* within the "emotional range" of energetic manifestation; the formation of an energetic store or charge on a channel that fixes emotional responses as a mechanistic automation, which is carried on in an individual's *Spiritual Timeline* (or personal continuum of existence).

enact : to make happen; to bring into action; to make part of an act.

encompassing : to form a circle around, surround or envelop around.

end point : the moment when the goal of a process has been achieved and to continue on with it will be detrimental to the gains; the finality of a process when the *Seeker* has achieved their optimum state from the current cycle (whether or not they run through it again at a later date with a different level of *Awareness* or knowledge base doesn't change the fact that it has flattened the standing wave

energy signatures : a distinctive pattern of energetic action.

enforcement : the act of compelling or putting (effort) into force; to compel or impose obedience by force; to impress strongly with applications of stress to demand agreement or validation; the lowest-level of direct control by physical effort or threat of punishment; a low-level method of control in the absence of true communication.

engineering : the *Self-directed* actions and efforts to utilize knowledge (observed causality/science), maths (calculations/quantification) and logic (axioms/formulas) to understand, design or manifest a solid structure, machine, mechanism, engine or system; as *"Reality Engineering"* in *Nex-Gen Systemology*—intentional *Self-directed* adjustment of existing Reality conditions; the application of total *Self-determinism* in *Self-Honesty* to change apparent Reality using fundamentals of *Systemology* and *Cosmic Law.*

entanglement : tangled together; intertwined and enmeshed systems; in *NexGen Systemology*, a reference to the interrelation of all particles as waves at a higher point of connectivity than is apparent, since wave-functions only "collapse" when someone is *Observing*, or doing the measuring, evaluating, &tc.

entropy : the reduction of organized physical systems back into chaos-continuity when their integrity is measured against space over time; reduction toward a zero-point.

epistemology : a school of philosophy focused on the truth of knowledge and knowledge of truth; theories regarding validity and truth inherent in any structure of knowledge and reason; the original "school of philosophy" from which all other "disciplines" were derived; the study of knowing how to know knowledge, reason and truth.

esoteric : hidden; secret; knowledge understood by a select few.

ethics : an intellectual philosophy concerning *rightness* and *wrongness* based on "logic" and "reason" (rationale) combined with observable consequences and tendencies of action or conduct; formal name for a "moral philosophy" (study of moral choices); in ancient times, originally treated *one-to-one* with "Cosmic Law" regarding *causation, order* and *sequence*; an objective (Universal) philosophy of *rightness* and *wrongness*, treated separate from culture-specific (subjective/relative) considerations, such as *morals* and *dogma*; in *NexGen Systemology* (*Grade-IV Metahuman Systemology*), a dynamic philosophy (applying "logic-and-reason") to understand the nature of "reality agreements" concerning *rightness* and *wrongness*, then treating the most optimum conditions of continued existence ("SURVIVAL" in *Beta-existence*; "CREATION" in *Alpha*) for the highest affected "Sphere of Existence" (on the *Standard Model*).

ethics processing : a *systematic processing* methodology introduced for bridging *Grade-IV Metahuman Systemology* (*Wizard Level-0*) with *Grade-V Spiritual Systemology* (*Wizard Level-1*) that emphasizes personal realization of "*Ethics*" and increased ability and responsibility to confront the "rightness" and "wrongness" of past actions (on the Backtrack), including defragmentation of "*Harmful Acts*" (as *Imprinting Incidents*) and any corresponding "*Hold-Backs*" and "*Hold-Outs*" (which reduce *Actualized Awareness* and prompt an individual to *withdraw* their *reach*); also "*Route-3E.*"

evaluate : to determine, assign or fix a set value, amount or meaning.

existence : the *state* or fact of *apparent manifestation*; the resulting combination of the Principles of Manifestation: consciousness, motion and substance; continued *survival*; that which independently exists; the *'Prime Directive'* and sole purpose of all manifestation or Reality; the highest common intended motivation driving any "*Thing*" or *Life*.

existential : pertaining to existence, or some aspect or condition of existence.

exoteric : public knowledge or common understanding; the level of understanding and *Knowing* maintained by the "masses"; how a thing is generally understood "by all" or the opposite of *esoteric*.

experiential data : accumulated reference points we store as memory concerning our "experience" with Reality.

exponent : a person that is a critical example of something.

extant : in existence; existing.

exterior : outside of; on the outside; in *NexGen Systemology*, we mean specifically the POV of *Self* that is *'outside of'* the *Human Condition,* free of the physical and mental trappings of the Physical Universe; a metahuman range of consideration; see also *'Zu-Vision'*.

external : a force coming from outside; information received from outside sources; in *NexGen Systemology*, the objective *'Physical Universe'* existence, or *beta-existence*, that the Physical Body or *genetic vehicle* is essentially *anchored* to for its considerations of locational space-time as a dimension or POV.

facets : an aspect, an apparent phase; one of many faces of something; a cut surface on a gem or crystal; in *NexGen Systemology* —a single perception or aspect of a memory or "*Imprint*"; any one of many ways in which a memory is recorded; perceptions associated with a painful emotional (sensation) experience and "*imprinted*" onto a metaphoric lens through which to view future similar experiences; other secondary terminals that are associated with a particular terminal, painful event or experience of loss, and which may exhibit the same encoded significance as the activating event.

faculties : abilities of the mind (individual) inherent or developed.

fallacy : a deceptive, misleading, erroneous and/or false beliefs; unsound logic; persuasions, invalidation or enforcement of Reality agreements based on authority, sympathy, bandwagon/mob mentality, vanity, ambiguity, suppression of information, and/or presentation of false dichotomies.

fate : what is brought to light or actualized as experience; the actual *course* taken to reach an end, charted end, or final *destination*; in *NexGen Systemology*, the *'fate'* of a *'Human Spirit'* (or *'Alpha Spirit'*) is determined by the choice of course taken to experience *Life.*

flow : movement across (or through) a channel (or conduit); a direction of active energetic motion typically distinguished as either an *in-flow, out-flow* or *cross-flow.*

fragmentation : breaking into parts and scattering the pieces; the *fractioning* of wholeness or the *fracture* of a holistic interconnected *alpha* state, favoring observational *Awareness* of perceived connectivity between parts; *discontinuity*; separation of a totality into parts; in *NexGen Systemology*, a person outside a state of *Self-Honesty* is said to be *fragmented*.

game : a strategic situation where a "player's" power of choice is employed or affected; a parameter or condition defined by purposes, freedoms and barriers (rules).

game theory : a mathematical theory of logic pertaining to strategies of maximizing gains and minimizing loses within prescribed boundaries and freedoms; a field of knowledge widely applied to human problem solving and decision-making; the application of true knowledge and logic to deduce the correct course of action given all variables and interplay of dynamic systems; logical study of decision making where "players" make choices that affect (the interests) of other "players"; an intellectual study of conflict and cooperation.

general systemology ("systematology") : a methodology of analysis and evaluation regarding the systems—their design and function; organizing systems of interrelated information-processing in order to perform a given function or pattern of functions.

genetic-vehicle : a physical *Life*-form; the physical (*beta*) body that is animated/controlled by the (*Alpha*) *Spirit* using a continuous *Lifeline* (ZU); a physical (*beta*) organic receptacle and catalyst for the (*Alpha*) *Self* to operate "causes" and experience "effects" within the *Physical Universe*.

gifted : attributing a special quality or ability; having exceptionally high intelligence or mental faculties.

gnosis : a *Greek* word meaning knowledge, but specifically "true knowledge"; the highest echelon of "true knowledge" accessible (or attained) only by mystical or spiritual faculties whereby actualized realizations are achieved independent of specialized education.

Gnostics : a name meaning "having knowledge" in Greek language (see also *gnosis*); an early sect of Judeo-Christian mysticism from the 1st Century AD emphasizing true knowledge by *Self-Honest* experience of metahuman and spiritual states of beingness, emphasizing defragmentation of "illusion" and over-coming of material "deception"; an esoteric proto-Systemology organization disbanded by the Roman Church as heretical.

gradient : a degree of partitioned ascent or descent along some scale, elevation or incline; "higher" and "lower" values in rela-tion to one another.

GSR-Meters ("galvanic skin response"–"electropsychometer") : a *biofeedback* device used for measuring electrical resistance (in "Ohms") of the skin sur-face; one of many parts used in a polygraph system; a highly sensitive "Ohm-meter" with variable range, set points and ampli-fication used to monitor electrical fluctuations of the skin surface.

help : to assist survival of; aid continuing optimum success.

hold-back : withheld communications (esp. actions) such as *"Hold-Outs"*; intentional (or automatic) withdrawal (as opposed to reach); Self-restraint (which may eventually be enforced or automated); not reaching, acting or expressing, when one should be; an ability that is now restrained (on automatic) due to inabil-ity to withhold it on Self-determinism alone.

hold-outs : in photography, the numerous snapshots/pictures withheld from the final display or professional presentation of the event; withheld communications; in Utilitarian Systemology —energetic withdrawal and communication breaks with a *"ter-minal"* and its *Sphere of Existence* as a result of a *"Harmful-Act"*; unspoken or undiscovered (hidden, covert) actions that an indi-vidual withholds communications of, fearing punishment or endangerment of *Self-preservation* (*First Sphere*); the act of hid-ing (or keeping hidden) the truth of a *"Harmful-Act"*; a refusal to communicate with a *Pilot*; also *"Hold-Back."*

holistic : the examination of interconnected systems as encom-passing something greater than the *sum* of their "parts."

Homo Novus : literally, the "new man"; the "newly elevated man" or "known man" in ancient Rome; the man who "knows (only) through himself"; in NexGen Systemology—the next spir-itual and intellectual evolution of *homo sapiens* (the "modern Human Condition"), which is signified by a demonstration of higher faculties of *Self-Actualization* and clear *Awareness*.

hot button : something that triggers or incites an intense emotional reaction instantaneously; in *NexGen Systemology*—a slang term denoting a highly reactive *channel*, heavily *charged* with a long chain of cumulative *emotional imprinting*, typically (but not necessarily) connected to a significant or "primary" *implant*; a non-technical label, first applied during *Grade-IV Professional Piloting "Flight School"* research sessions of Spring-Summer 2020, to indicate specific circuits, channels or terminals that cause a *Seeker* to immediately react with intense emotional responses, whether in general, directed to the *Pilot*, or even at effectiveness of processing.

Human Condition : a standard default state of Human experience that is generally accepted to be the extent of its potential identity (*beingness*)—currently treated as *Homo Sapiens Sapiens,* but which is scheduled for replacement by *Homo Novus*.

humanistic psychology : a field of academic psychology approaching a holistic emphasis on *Self-Actualization* as an individual's most basic motivation; early key figures from the 20th century include: Carl Rogers, Abraham Maslow, L. Ron Hubbard, William Walker Atkinson, Deepak Chopra and Timothy Leary (to name a few).

identification : the association of *identity* to a thing; a label or fixed data-set associated to what a thing is; association "equals" a thing, the "equals" being key; an equality of all things in a group, for example, an "apple" identified with all other "apples"; the reduction of "I-AM"-*Self* from a *Spiritual Beingness* to an "identity" of some form.

identity : the collection of energy and matter—including memory—across a *"Spiritual Timeline"* that we consider as "I" of *Self*, but the "I" is an individual and not an identification with anything other than *Self* as *Alpha-Spirit*.

imagination : the ability to create *mental imagery* in one's Personal Universe at will and change or alter it as desired; the ability to create, change and dissolve mental images on command or as an act of will; to create a mental image or have associated imagery displayed (or "conjured") in the mind that may or may not be treated as real (or memory recall) and may or may not accurately duplicate objective reality; to employ *Creative Abilities* of the Spirit that are independent of reality agreements with beta-existence.

Imaginomicon : the fourth professional publication of Mardukite

Systemology, released publicly in mid- 2021; the second professional text in Grade-IV Metahuman Systemology, released as *"Liber-3D"*; contains fundamental theory of *"Spiritual Ability"* and *"Route-0"* systematic processing methodology.

immersion : plunged or sunk into; wholly surrounded by.

implant : to graft or surgically insert; to establish firmly by setting into; to instill or install a direct command or consideration in consciousness (Mind-System, &tc.); a mechanical device inserted beneath the surface/skin; in *Metahuman Systemology*, an "energetic mechanism" (linked to an Alpha-Spirit) composing a circuit-network and systematic array of energetic receptors underlying and filter-screening communication channels between the Mind-System and *Self*; an energetic construct installed upon entry of a Universe; similar to a platen or matrix or circuit-board, where each part records a specific type or quality of *emotionally encoded imprints* and other "heavily charged" *Mental Images* that are "impressed" by future encounters; a basic platform on which certain *imprints* and *Mental Images* are encoded (keyed-in) and stored (often beneath the surface of "knowing" or *Awareness* for that individual, although an implanted "command" toward certain inclinations or behavioral tendencies may be visibly observable.

imprint : to strongly impress, stamp, mark (or outline) onto a softer 'impressible' substance; to mark with pressure onto a surface; in *NexGen Systemology*, the term is used to indicate permanent Reality impressions marked by frequencies, energies or interactions experienced during periods of emotional distress, pain, unconsciousness, loss, enforcement, or something antagonistic to physical (personal) survival, all of which are are stored with other reactive response-mechanisms at lower-levels of *Awareness* as opposed to the active memory database and proactive processing center of the Mind; an experiential "memory-set" that may later resurface—be triggered or stimulated artificially— as Reality, of which similar responses will be engaged automatically; holographic-like imagery "stamped" onto consciousness as composed of energetic *facets* tied to the "snap-shot" of an experience.

imprinting incident : the first or original event instance communicated and *emotionally encoded* onto an individual's *"Spiritual Timeline"* (recorded memory from all lifetimes), which formed a permanent impression that is later used to mechanistically treat future contact on that channel; the first or original occurrence of some particular *facet* or mental image related to a certain type of *encoded response*, such as pain and discomfort, losses and victimization, and even the acts that we have taken against others along the Spiritual Timeline of our existence that caused them to also be *Imprinted*.

inadvertent : an unintended (knowingly) result caused by low-Awareness actions; applying effort (enacting change) outside Self-Honesty, leading to negligent oversights with harmful outcomes.

incarnation : a present, living or concrete form of some thing, idea or beingness; an individual lifetime or life-cycle from birth/creation to death/destruction independent of other lifetimes or cycles.

inception : the beginning, start, origin or outset.

individual : a person, lifeform, human entity or creature; a *Seeker* or potential *Seeker* is often referred to as an "individual" within Mardukite Zuism and Systemology materials.

inhibited : withheld, held-back, discouraged or repressed from some state.

"in phase" : see *"phase alignment."*

insistence : repeated use of a communicated energy into a form that demands acknowledgment, is more difficult to avoid or ignore.

intention : the directed application of Will; to intend (have "in Mind") or signify (give "significance" to) for or toward a particular purpose; in *NexGen Systemology* (from the *Standard Model*) —the spiritual activity at WILL (5.0) directed by an *Alpha Spirit* (7.0); the application of WILL as "Cause" from a higher order of Alpha Thought and consideration (6.0), which then may continue to relay communications as an "effect" in the universe.

inter-dimensional : systems that are interconnected or correlated between the Physical Universe and the Spiritual Universe—or between "dimension states" observably identified as "physical," "emotional," "psychological" and "spiritual." The only point of true interconnectivity that we can systematically determine is called *"Life"* or the POV of *Self.*

interior : inside of; on the inside; in *NexGen Systemology*, we mean specifically the POV of *Self* that is fixed to the *'internal' Human Condition,* including the *Reactive Control Center* (RCC) and Mind-System or *Master Control Center* (MCC); within *beta-existence*.

intermediate : a distinct point between two points; actions between two points.

internal : a force coming from inside; information received from inside sources; in *NexGen Systemology*, the objective *'Physical Universe'* experience of *beta-existence* that is associated with the Physical Body or *genetic vehicle* and its POV regarding sensation and perception; from inside the body; within the body.

interrogation : obtaining specific information through responses to questions, such as in 'systematic processing' and other forms of two-way communication.

invalidate : decrease the level or degree or *agreement* as Reality.

invest : spend on; give or devote something in exchange for a beneficial result; to endow with.

knowledge : clear personal processing of informed understanding; information (data) that is actualized as effectively workable understanding; a demonstrable understanding on which we may 'set' our *Awareness*—or literally a "know-ledge."

KI : an ancient cuneiform sign designating the *'physical zone'*; the *Physical Universe*—comprised of physical matter and physical energy in action across space and observed as time; a direction of motion toward material *Continuity*, away from or subordinate to the Spiritual (*'AN'*); the physical condition of existence providing for our *beta* state of *Awareness* experienced (and interacted with) as an individual *Lifeform* from our primary Alpha state of Identity or *I-AM-Self* in the *Spiritual Universe* (*'AN'*).

kinetic : pertaining to the energy of physical motion and movement.

law : a formal codified outline (or list) of *ethical* standards regarding social participation and acceptable behavior, like a "*code*," except that it *is* enforced by civic consequences (or even "*Cosmic Law*") when not adhered to, usually with punishment coming either by the group (exclusively) or by involvement with an "outside party" or societal (legal) authority; a predictable sequence of naturally occurring events that will consistently repeat under the right conditions (such as *"Cosmic Law"* or *"Natural Law"*).

level : a physical or conceptual *tier* (or plane) relative to a *scale* above and below it; a significant *gradient* observable as a *foundation* (or surface) built upon and subsequent to other levels of a totality or whole; a *set* of *"parameters"* with respect to other such *sets* along a *continuum*; in *NexGen Systemology*, a *Seeker's* understanding, *Awareness* as *Self* and the formal grades of material/instruction are all treated as *"levels."*

Liber-One : First published in October 2019 as *"The Tablets of Destiny: Using Ancient Wisdom to Unlock Human Potential"* by Joshua Free; republished in the complete *Grade-III* anthology, *"The Systemology Handbook"*; revised in August 2022 as *"The Tablets of Destiny (Revelation): How Long-Lost Anunnaki Wisdom Can Change the Fate of Humanity."*

Liber-Two : First published in October 2020 as *"Metahuman Destinations: Piloting the Course to Homo Novus"* by Joshua Free; an anthology of the *Grade-IV* "Professional Piloting Course," containing revised materials from *Liber-2C*, *Liber-2D* and (most of) *Liber-3C*; republished in the complete *Grade-IV* anthology, *"The Metahuman Systemology Handbook."*

Liber-Three : see *"Liber-3E."*

Liber-2B : First published in December 2019 as *"Crystal Clear: The Self-Actualization Manual & Guide to Total Awareness"* by Joshua Free; republished in the complete *Grade-III* anthology, *"The Systemology Handbook"*; revised in April 2022 as *"Crystal Clear (Handbook for Seekers): Achieve Self-Actualization and Spiritual Ascension in This Lifetime."*

Liber-2C : First published in April 2020 as *"Communication and Control of Energy & Power: The Magic of Will & Intention (Volume One)"* by Joshua Free; revision republished as an integral part of the *Grade-IV* "Professional Piloting Course," in October 2020 within *"Metahuman Destinations"* (*Liber-Two*); republished in the complete *Grade-IV* anthology, *"The Metahuman Systemology Handbook."*

Liber-2D : First published in June 2020 as *"Command of the Mind-Body Connection: The Magic of Will & Intention" (Volume Two)"* by Joshua Free; revision republished as an integral part of the *Grade-IV* "Professional Piloting Course," in October 2020 within *"Metahuman Destinations"* (*Liber-Two*); republished in the complete *Grade-IV* anthology, *"The Metahuman Systemology Handbook."*

Liber-3C : First published in July 2020 as *"Now You Know: The Truth About Universes & How You Got Stuck in One"* by Joshua Free; a discourse in the *Grade-IV* Metahuman Systemology series; a revision of one part republished in October 2020 within the *"Professional Piloting Course"* manual, *"Metahuman Destinations"* (*Liber-Two*), a revision of the remaining part republished in June 2021 within the *"Imaginomicon"* (*Liber-3D*); republished in the complete *Grade-IV* anthology, *"The Metahuman Systemology Handbook."*

Liber-3D : First published in June 2021 as *"Imaginomicon: The Gateway to Higher Universes (A Grimoire for the Human Spirit)"* by Joshua Free; a manual completing the *Grade-IV* (Metahuman Systemology) professional series with a treatment of "Wizard Level-0"; revised in June 2022 as *"Imaginomicon (Revised Edition): Approaching Gateways to Higher Universes (A New Grimoire for the Human Spirit)"*; republished in the complete *Grade-IV* anthology, *"The Metahuman Systemology Handbook."*

Liber-3E (Liber-Three) : First published in April 2022 as *"The Way of the Wizard: Utilitarian Systemology (A New Metahuman Ethic)"* by Joshua Free; a professional manual bridging *Grade-IV* (Metahuman Systemology, *Wizard Level-0*) with *Grade-V* (Spiritual Systemology, *Wizard Level-1*); republished in the complete *Grade-IV* anthology, *"The Metahuman Systemology Handbook."*

logic : philosophical science of correct *reasoning*.

logistics : pertaining to the movement or transportation between locations.

manifestation : something brought into existence.

Marduk : founder of Babylonia; patron Anunnaki "god" of Babylon.

Mardukite Zuism : a Mesopotamian-themed (Babylonian-oriented) religious philosophy and tradition applying the spiritual technology based on *Arcane Tablets* in combination with "Tech" from *NexGen Systemology*; first developed in the New Age underground by Joshua Free in 2008 and realized publicly in 2009 with the formal establishment of the *Mardukite Chamberlains.* The text *"Tablets of Destiny"* is a cross-over from Mardukite Zuism (and Mesopotamian Neopaganism) toward higher spiritual applications of Systemology.

"Master Grades" : literary materials by Joshua Free (written between 1995 and 2019) revised and compiled for the "Mardukite Academy of Systemology" instructional grades—"Route of Magick & Mysticism" (*Grade I, Part A*), "Route of Druidism & Dragon Legacy" (*Grade I, Part D*), "Route of Mesopotamian Mysteries" (Grade II) and "Route of Mardukite Systemology" or "Pathway to Self-Honesty" (*Grade III*).

mental image : a subjectively experienced "picture" created and imagined into being by the Alpha-Spirit (or at lower levels, one of its automated mechanisms) that includes all perceptible *facets* of totally immersive scene, which may be forms originated by an individual, or a "facsimile-copy" ("snap-shot") of something seen or encountered; a duplication of wave-forms in one's Personal Universe as a "picture" that mirror an "external" Universe experience, such as an *Imprint*.

Mesopotamia : land between Tigris and Euphrates River; modern-day Iraq; the primary setting for ancient *Sumerian* and *Babylonian* traditions thousands of years ago, including activities and records of the *Anunnaki*.

metahumanism : an applied philosophy of *transhumanism* with an emphasis on "spiritual technologies" as opposed to "external" ones; a new state or evolution of the *Human Condition* achievable on planet Earth, rooted in *Self-Honesty*, whereby individuals are operating *exterior* to considerations that are fixed exclusively to the *genetic vehicle* (Human Body) and independent of the *emotional encoding* and *associative programming* typical of the present standard-issue *Human Condition*.

Metahuman Destinations : the third professional publication of Mardukite Systemology, released publicly in October 2020; the first professional text in Grade-IV Metahuman Systemology, released as *"Liber-Two"* and containing materials from *Liber-2C, Liber-2D* and *Liber-3C*; contains fundamental theory of *"Professional Piloting"* and *"Route-3"* systematic processing methodology; revised for the Mardukite Academy as a two-volume set in September 2022.

meter : a device used to measure; see *GSR-Meter.*

methodology : a complete system of applications, methods, principles and rules to compose a *'systematic'* paradigm as a "whole"—esp. a field of philosophy or science.

misappropriated : put into use incorrectly; to apply ineffectively or as unintended by design or definition.

morals : widely held culturally conditioned (socially learned) ethical standards of conduct used to "judge" *rightness* from *wrongness* of an individual's character, personality or actions (which may or may not be intellectually and emotionally influenced by "local" religious customs, taboos and *dogma*; basic social reality agreements determining "proper conduct" and "right actions" (behavior) based on civic *laws*, social *codes* and religious *doctrines* of a particular society or group and its own cultural experiences of *Reality*.

motor functions : internal mechanisms that allow a body to move.

Nabu : the *Anunnaki* "god of wisdom, writing and knowledge" for Babylonian (Mardukite) Tradition.

neophyte : a beginning initiate or novice to a particular sect or methodology; novitiate or entry-level grade of training, study and practice of an esoteric order or mystical lodge (fellowship).

neurotransmitter : a chemical substance released at a physiological level (of the genetic vehicle) that bridges communication of energetic transmission between the *Mind-Body* systems, using the "nervous system" of the physical body; biochemical amino acids and peptides (neuropeptides), hormones, &tc.

NexGen Systemology : a modern tradition of applied religious philosophy and spiritual technology based on *Arcane Tablets* in combination with *"general systemology"* and *"games theory"* developed in the New Age underground by Joshua Free in 2011 as an advanced futurist extension of the *"Mardukite Chamberlains"*; also referred to as *"Mardukite Systemology,"* *"Metahuman Systemology"* and *"Spiritual Systemology."*

objective : concerning the "external world" and attempts to observe Reality independent of personal "subjective" factors.

one-to-one : see *"A-for-A."*

optimum : the most favorable or ideal conditions for the best result; the greatest degree of result under specific conditions.

organic : as related to a physically living organism or carbon-based life form; energy-matter condensed into form as a focus or POV of Spiritual Life Energy (*ZU*) as it pertains to beta-existence of *this* Physical Universe (*KI*).

oscillation-alternation : a particular type of (or fluctuation) between two relative states, conditions or degrees; a wave-action between two degrees, such as is described in the action of the *pendulum effect*; a flux or wave-like energy in motion, across space, calculable as time; in systematic processing, alternation is the shift between two direction flows on a circuit channel, such as *inflow* and *outflow*, or between two types of processing, such as *objective* and *subjective*; alternation of a POV creates "space."

paradigm : an all-encompassing *standard* by which to view the world and *communicate* Reality; a standard model of reality-systems used by the Mind to filter, organize and interpret experience of Reality.

parameters : a defined range of possible variables within a model, spectrum or continuum; the extent of communicable reach capable within a system or across a distance; the defined or imposed limitations placed on a system or the functions within a system; the extent to which a Life or "thing" can *be*, *do* or *know* along any channel within the confines of a specific system or spectrum of existence.

participation : being part of the action; affecting the result.

patterns (probability patterns) : observation of cycles and tendencies to predict a causal relationship or determine the actual condition or flow of dynamic energy using a holistic systemology to understand Life, Reality and Existence as opposed to isolating or excluding perceived parts as being mutually separate from other perceived parts.

PCL : see *"processing command line."*

perception : internalized processing of data received by the *senses*; to become *Aware of* via the senses.

personality (program) : the total composite picture an individual "identifies" themselves with; the accumulated sum of material and mental mass by which an individual experiences as their timeline; a "beta-personality" is mainly attached to the identity of a particular physical body and the total sum of its own genetic memory in combination with the data stores and pictures maintained by the Alpha Spirit; a "true personality" is the Alpha Spirit as Self completely defragmented of all erroneous limitations and barriers to consideration, belief, manifestation and intention.

perturbation : the deviation from a natural state, fixed motion, or orbit system caused by another external system; disturbing or disquieting the serenity of an existent state; inciting observable apparent action using indirect or outside actions or 'forces'; the introduction of a new element or facet that disturbs equilibrium of a standard system; the "butterfly effect"; in *NexGen Systemology*, *'perturbation'* is a necessary condition for the *ZU-line* to function as a *Standard Model* of actual *'monistic continuity'*— which is a *Lifeforce* singularity expressed along a spectrum with potential interactions at each degree from any source; the influence of a degree in one state by activities of another state that seem independent, but which are actually connected directly at some higher degree, even if not apparently observed.

phase (identification) : in *NexGen Systemology,* a pattern of personality or identity that is assumed as the POV from *Self*; personal identification with artificial "personality packages"; an individual assuming or taking characteristics of another individual (often unknowingly as a response-mechanisms); also *"phase alignment."*

phase alignment or *"in phase"* : to be in synch or mutually synchronized, in step or aligned properly with something else in order to increase the total strength value; in *NexGen Systemology*, alignment or adjustment of *Awareness* with a particular identity, space or time; perfect *defragmentation* would mean being "in phase" as *Self* fully conscious and Aware as an Alpha-Spirit *in* present *space* and *time*, free of synthetic personalities.

physics : regarding data obtained by a material science of observable motions, forces and bodies, including their apparent interaction, in the Physical Universe (specific to this *beta-existence*).

pilot : a professional steersman responsible for healthy functional operation of a ship toward a specific destination; in *NexGen Systemology*, an intensive trained individual qualified to specially apply *Systemology Processing* to assist other *Seekers* on the *Pathway.*

ping : a short, high pitched ring, chime or noise that alerts to the presence of something; in computer systems, a query sent on a network or line to another terminal in order to determine if there is a connection to it; in *NexGen Systemology*, the sudden somatic twinge or pain or discomfort that is felt as a sensation in the body when a particular terminal (lifeform, object, concept) is 'brought to mind' or contacted on a personal communication channel-circuit; the accompanying sensations and mental images that are experienced as an automatic-response to the presence of some channel or terminal.

player (game theory) : an individual that is making decisions in a game and/or is affected by decisions others are making in the game, especially if those other-determined decisions now affect the possible choices.

point-of-view (POV) : a point to view from; an opinion or attitude as expressed from a specific identity-phase; a specific standpoint or vantage-point; a definitive manner of consideration specific to an individual phase or identity; a place or position affording a specific view or vantage; circumstances and programming of an individual that is conducive to a particular response, consideration or belief-set (paradigm); a position (consideration) or place (location) that provides a specific view or perspective (subjective) on experience (of the objective).

postulate : to put forward as truth; to suggest or assume an existence *to be*; to state or affirm the existence of particular conditions; to provide a basis of reasoning and belief; a basic theory accepted as fact; in *NexGen Systemology*, "Alpha-Thought"—the top-most decisions or considerations made by the Alpha-Spirit regarding the "*is-ness*" (what things "are") about energy-matter and space-time.

potentiality : the total "sum" (collective amount) of "latent" (dormant—present but not apparent) capable or possible realizations; used to describe a state or condition of what has not yet manifested, but which can be influenced and predicted based on observed patterns and, if referring to beta-existence, Cosmic Law.

POV : see "*point-of-view*" and/or "*POV Processing.*"

POV processing : a methodology of *Grade-IV Metahuman Systemology* emphasizing systematic processing toward realizations that improve a Seeker's willingness to manage a present POV and associated *phases*, their ability to transfer POVs freely, increased tolerance to experiences (or encounters) with any other viewpoint, and finally, an actualized realization that a POV is not one-to-one with *Beingness* of *Self*; an extension of *creativeness processing* and "Wizard Level" training that systematically handles *Awareness* of "points" and "spots" in space, from which an Alpha-Spirit may place its own viewpoint of a dimension or Universe—also a prerequisite to upper-route practices such as *"Zu-Vision"* and *"Backtrack."*

precedent : a matter which precedes or goes before another in importance.

premise : a basis or statement of fact from which conclusions are drawn.

presence : the quality of some thing (energy/matter) being "present" in space-time; personal orientation of *Self* as an *Awareness* (*POV*) located in present space-time (environment) and communicating with extant energy-matter.

prevalent : of wide extent; an extensive or largely accepted aspect or current state.

probability : the causal likelihood for something to result, "effect" or manifest in and as a certain way, manner or degree, based on "observed evaluation" of programming and tendencies that follow Cosmic Law.

"process-out" or **"flatten a wave"** : to reduce *emotional encoding* of an *imprint* to zero; to dissolve a *wave-form* or *thought-formed* "solid" such as a *"belief"*; to completely run a *process* to its end, thereby *flattening* any previously *"collapsed-waves"* or *fragmentation* that is obstructing the *clear channel* of *Self-Awareness*; also referred to as "processing-out"; to discharge all previously held emotionally encoded imprinting or erroneous programming and beliefs that otherwise fix the free flow (wave) to a particular pattern, solid or concrete *"is"* form.

processing, systematic : the inner-workings or "through-put" result of systems; in *NexGen Systemology*, a methodology of applied spiritual technology used toward personal Self-Actualization; methods of selective directed attention, communicated language and associative imagery that targets an increase in personal control of the human condition.

processing command line (PCL) or **command line** : a directed input; a specific command using highly selective language for *Systemology Processing*; a predetermined directive statement (cause) intended to focus concentrated attention (effect).

projecting awareness : sending out (motion) or radiating *"consciousness"* from *Self* ("I") to another POV.

Proto-Indo-European (PIE) : in Linguistic-Semantic Sciences, a hypothetical single-source Eurasian root language (c.4500 B.C.) demonstrating common origins of many "word-roots" found in European languages.

psychokinesis (PK) / telekinesis : influencing a (physical) system without (physical) interaction; *psychokinesis* from the Greek for 'soul' and 'movement', and *telekinesis* from the Greek for 'at a distance' and 'movement'.

rationality / reasoning (game theory) : the extent to which a player seeks to play (make decisions, &tc.) in order to maximize the gains (or else survival) achievable within any given game conditions; the ability and willingness of an individual to reach toward conditions that promote the highest level of survival and existence and make the best choices and moves to see the desired goal manifest.

reality : see *"agreement."*

realization : the clear perception of an understanding; a consideration or understanding on what is "actual"; to make "real" or give "reality" to so as to grant a property of "beingness" or "being as it is"; the state or instance of coming to an *Awareness*; in *NexGen Systemology*, "gnosis" or true knowledge achieved during *systematic processing*; achievement of a new (or "higher") cognition, true knowledge or perception of Self; a consideration of reality or assignment of meaning.

recursive : repeating by looping back onto itself to form continuity; *ex.* the "Infinity" symbol is recursive.

relative : an apparent point, state or condition treated as distinct from others.

religion : a concise spiritual *paradigm*, set of beliefs and practices regarding "Divinity," "Infinite Beingness"—or else, "God"—as representative symbol of the *Eighth Sphere of Existence* for *Beta-Existence* (or else "Infinity").

responsibility : the *ability* to *respond*; the extent of mobilizing *power* and *understanding* an individual maintains as *Awareness* to enact *change*; the proactive ability to *Self-direct* and make decisions independent of an outside authority.

Route-0 : a specific methodology from *SOP-2C* denoting "*Creativeness Processing*," as described in the text "*Imaginomicon*" (*Liber-3D*).

Route-0E : a specific methodology (expanding on *Route-0* from *Liber-3D*) denoting "*Conceptual Processing*" applied to *Ethics Beta-Defragmentation*, as described in the text "*Way of the Wizard*" (*Liber-Three* or *Liber-3E*).

Route-1 : a specific methodology from *SOP-2C* denoting "*Resurfacing Processing*," as described in the text "*Tablets of Destiny*" (*Liber-One*) as "RR-SP" (and reissued in "*The Systemology Handbook*").

Route-2 : a specific methodology from *SOP-2C* denoting "*Analytical-Recall Processing*," as described in the text "*Crystal Clear*" (*Liber-2B*) as "AR-SP" (and reissued in "*The Systemology Handbook*").

Route-3 : a specific methodology from *SOP-2C* denoting "*Communication-Circuit Processing*," as described in the text "*Metahuman Destinations*" (*Liber-Two*); also the basis for *SOP-2C* routine.

Route-3E : a specific methodology (expanding on *Route-3* from *SOP-2C*) denoting "*Ethics Processing*," as described in the text "*The Way of the Wizard*" (*Liber-Three* or *Liber-3E*); also related to "Standard Procedure R-3E."

science : a systematized *paradigm* of Knowingness—from the Latin '*scire*', meaning "know"; an empirical and objective understanding of data collected by observation, calculation and logical deduction—and which may usually be used to predict phenomenon or occurrences in the Physical Universe ("*Beta-Existence*").

Seeker : an individual on the *Pathway to Self-Honesty*; a practitioner of *Mardukite Systemology* or *NexGen Systemology Processing* that is working toward *Spiritual Ascension*.

Self-actualization : bringing the full potential of the Human spirit into Reality; expressing full capabilities and creativeness of the *Alpha-Spirit*.

Self-determinism : the freedom to act, clear of external control or influence; the personal control of Will to direct intention.

Self-honesty : the basic or original *alpha* state of *being* and *knowing*; clear and present total *Awareness* of-and-as *Self*, in its most basic and true proactive expression of itself as *Spirit* or *I-AM*—free of artificial attachments, perceptive filters and other emotionally-reactive or mentally-conditioned programming imposed on the human condition by the systematized physical world; the ability to experience existence without judgment.

semantics : the *meaning* carried in *language* as the *truth* of a "thing" represented, *A-for-A*; the *effect* of language on *thought* activity in the Mind and physical behavior; language as *symbols* used to represent a concept, "thing" or "solid."

sensation : an external stimulus received by internal sense organs (receptors/sensors); sense impressions.

simulacrum : an tangible likeness, image, facsimile or superficial representation that is similar to or resembles someone or something else; in *NexGen Systemology*, any *genetic vehicle* or physical body is considered a reflective "simulacrum" of, and used as a "vessel-shell" by, the *Alpha-Spirit* or *Self* (I-AM), which otherwise maintains no true finite locatable form in *beta-existence*.

sine-wave : the *frequency* and amplitude of a quantified (calculable) *vibration* represented on a graph (graphically) as smooth repetitive *oscillation* of a *waveform*; a *waveform* graphed for demonstration—otherwise represented in *NexGen Systemology* logic equations as 'Wf,' or in mathematics as the *'function of x'* (fx); graphically representing arcs (*parameters*) of a circular *continuity* on a *continuum*; in the *Standard Model of NexGen Systemology*, the actual 'wave vibration' graphically displayed on an otherwise static *ZU-line* (of Infinity) is a *'sine-wave'*.

somatic : specifically pertaining to the physical body, its sensations and response actions or behaviors as separate from a "Mind-System"; also *"pings."*

space : a viewpoint or *Point-of-View* (POV) extended from any point out toward a dimension or dimensions; the consideration of a point or spot as an *anchor* or *corner* in addition to others, which collectively define parameters of a dimensional plane; the field of energy/matter mass created as a result of communication and control in action and measured as time (wave-length), such as "distance" between points (or peaks on a wave).

spectrum : a broad range or array as a continuous series or sequence; defined parts along a singular continuum; in physics, a
gradient arrangement of visible colored bands diffracted in order
of their respective wavelengths, such as when passing *White
Light* through a *prism*.

Spheres of Existence (dynamic systems) : a series of *eight* con-
centric circles, rings or spheres (each larger than the former) that
is overlaid onto the Standard Model of Beta-Existence to demonstrate the dynamic systems of existence extending out from the
POV of Self (often as a "body") at the *First Sphere*; these are
given in the basic eightfold systems as: *Self, Home/Family,
Groups, Humanity, Life on Earth, Physical Universe, Spiritual
Universe* and *Infinity-Divinity.*

spiritual timeline : a continuous stream of moment-to-moment
Mental Images (or a record of experiences) that defines the
"past" of a spiritual being (or *Alpha-Spirit*) and which includes
impressions (*imprints, &tc.*) form all life-incarnations and significant spiritual events the being has encountered; in NexGen
Systemology, also "*backtrack.*"

standard issue : equally dispensed to all without consideration.

Standard Model, The (systemology) : in *NexGen Systemology*
—our existential and cosmological *standard model* or cabbalistic
model; a "*monistic continuity model*" demonstrating *total system*
interconnectivity "above" and "below" observation of any apparent *parameters*; the original presentation of the *ZU-line*,
represented as a singular vertical (y-axis) waveform in space
across dimensional levels or Universes (*Spheres of Existence*)
without charting any specific movement across a dimensional
time-graph x-axis; The Standard Model of Systemology represents the basic workable synthesis of common denominators in
models explored throughout Grade-I and Grade-II material.

static : characterized by a fixed or stationary condition; having
no apparent change, movement or fluctuation.

successively : what comes after; forward into the future.

succumb : to give way, or give in to, a relatively stronger superi-
or force.

Sumerian : ancient civilization of *Sumer,* founded in Mesopotamia c. 5000 B.C.

superfluous : excessive; unnecessary; needless.

symbol : a concentrated mass with associated meaning or representative significance.

sympathy : a sensation, feeling or emotion—of anger, fear, sorrow and/or pity—that is a *personal reaction* to the misfortune and failure of another being.

syntax : from the Greek, "to arrange together"; the semantic meaning that words convey when combined together; the manner in which words are arranged together to provide an understandable meaning, such as following the structure for a sentence.

system : from the Greek, "to set together"; to set or arrange things or data together so as to form an orderly understanding of a "whole"; also a *'method'* or *'methodology'* as an orderly standard of use or application of such data arranged together.

systematization : to arrange into systems; to systematize or make systematic.

Systemology : see *"NexGen Systemology."*

Systemology Procedure 1-8-0 : advanced spiritual technology within our Systemology, which applies a methodology of systematic practice for experiencing: (1) Self-Awareness, (8) Nothingness and (0) Beingness, introduced for "Crystal Clear" but expanded on for *"Imaginomicon"*; *'one-eight-zero'* is included in, but not the same as application *'one-eighty'*—or else the *Beta-Defrag-Intensive* called *"SOP-180"* or *"Systemology-180."*

systems theory : see *"general systematology"*

Tablets of Destiny : the first professional publication of Mardukite Systemology, released publicly in October 2019; the first professional text in Grade-III Mardukite Systemology, released as *"Liber-One"* and reissued in the Grade-III Master Edition *"Systemology Handbook"*; contains fundamental theory of the *"Standard Model"* and *"Route-1"* systematic processing methodology; revised for the Mardukite Academy as *"The Tablets of Destiny Revelation"* in Summer 2022.

telekinesis : see *"psychokinesis."*

terminal (node) : a point, end or mass on a line; a point or connection for closing an electric circuit, such as a post on a battery terminating at each end of its own systematic function; any end point or 'termination' on a line; a point of connectivity with other points; in systems, any point which may be treated as a contact point of interaction; anything that may be distinguished as an 'is' and is therefore a 'termination point' of a system or along a flow-line which may interact with other related systems it shares a line with; a point of interaction with other points.

thought-experiment : from the German, *Gedankenexperiment*; logical *considerations* or mental models used to concisely visualize consequences (cause-effect sequences) within the context of an imaginary or hypothetical scenario; using faculties of the Mind's Eye to *Imagine* things accurately with *considerations* that *have not* already been consciously experienced in *beta-existence*.

thought-form : apparent *manifestation* or existential *realization* of *Thought-waves* as "solids" even when only apparent in Reality-agreements of the Observer; the treatment of *Thought-waves* as permanent *imprints* obscuring *Self-Honest Clarity* of *Awareness* when reinforced by emotional experience as actualized "thought-formed solids" ("*beliefs*") in the Mind; energetic patterns that "surround" the individual.

thought-habit : reoccurring modes of thought or repeated "self-talk"; essentially "self-hypnosis" resulting in a certain state.

thought-wave or **wave-form** : a proactive *Self-directed action* or reactive-response *action* of *consciousness*; the *process* of *thinking* as demonstrated in *wave-form*; the *activity* of *Awareness* within the range of *thought vibrations/frequencies* on the existential *Life-continuum* or *ZU-line*.

threshold : a doorway, gate or entrance point; the degree to which something is to produce an effect within a certain state or condition; the point in which a condition changes from one to the next.

tier : a series of rows or levels, one stacked immediately before or atop another.

time : observation of cycles in action; motion of a particle, energy or wave across space; intervals of action related to other intervals of action as observed in Awareness; a measurable wavelength or frequency in comparison to a static state; the consideration of variations in space.

timeline : plotting out history in a linear (line) model to indicate instances (experiences) or demonstrate changes in state (space) as measured over time; a singular conception of continuation of observed time as marked by event-intervals and changes in energy and matter across space.

transhumanism : a social science and applied philosophy concerning the next evolved state of the *"Human Condition,"*; progress in two potential directions, either "spiritual" technologies advancing *Self* as an "Alpha-Spirit," or the direction of "external"-"physical" technologies that modify or eliminate characteristics of the *Body*; a theme describing contemporary application of material sciences emphasizing only "physical" and "genetic" parts of the *Human* experience, such as brain activity, cell-life extension and space travel; *NexGen Systemology* recently began distinguishing its emphasis on "spiritual technology" as *"metahumanism."*

traumatic encoding : information received when the sensory faculties of an organism are "shocked" into learning it as an "emotionally" encoded *Imprint*; a duplicated facsimile-copy or *Mental Image* of severe misfortune, violent threats, pain and coercion, which is then categorized, stored and reactively retrieved based exclusively on its emotional *facets*.

treat / treatment : an act, manner or method of handling or dealing with someone, something or some type of situation; to apply a specific process, procedure or mode of action toward some person, thing or subject; use of a specific substance, regimen or procedure to make an existing condition less severe; also, a written presentation that handles a subject in a specific manner.

turbulence : a quality or state of distortion or disturbance that creates irregularity of a flow or pattern; the quality or state of aberration on a line (such as ragged edges) or the emotional "turbulent feelings" attached to a particular flow or terminal node; a violent, haphazard or disharmonious commotion (such as in the ebb of gusts and lulls of wind action).

unconscious : a state when *Awareness* as *Self* is removed totally from the equation of *Life* experience, though it continues to be recorded in lower-level response mechanisms (fixed to a simulacrum or genetic vehicle) for later retrieval.

understanding : a clear 'A-for-A' duplication of a communication as 'knowledge', which may be comprehended and retained with its significance assigned in relation to other 'knowledge' treated as a 'significant understanding'; the "grade" or "level" that a knowledge base is collected and the manner in which the data is organized and evaluated.

validation : reinforcement of agreements or considerations as "real."

vantage : a point, place or position that offers an ideal viewpoint (POV).

via : literally, "by way of"; from the Latin, meaning "way."

vibration : effects of motion or wave-frequency as applied to any system.

viewpoint : see *"point-of-view" (POV).*

wave-form : see *"sine-wave."*

Western Civilization : modern contemporary culture, ideals, values and technology, particularly of Europe and North America as distinguished by growing urbanization, industrialization, and inspired by a history of rebellion to strong religious and political indoctrination.

will *or* **WILL** (5.0) : in *NexGen Systemology* (from the *Standard Model*), the Alpha-ability at "5.0" of a Spiritual Being (*Alpha Spirit*) at "7.0" to apply *intention* as "Cause" from consideration or Alpha-Thought at "6.0" that is superior to "beta-thoughts" that only manifest as reactive "effects" below "4.0" and *interior* to the *Human Condition*.

willingness : the state of conscious Self-determined ability and interest (directed attention) to *Be, Do* or *Have*; a Self-determined consideration to reach, face up to (*confront*) or manage some "mass" or energy; the extent to which an individual considers themselves able to participate, act or communicate along some line, to put attention or intention on the line, or to produce (create) an effect.

ziggurat : religious temples of ancient Mesopotamia; stepped-pyramids and towers used for spiritual and religious purposes by Sumerians and Babylonians, many of which are presented as seven tiers, levels or terraces representing "Seven Gates" (or "7 Veils") of existence, separating material continuity of the Earth Plane from "Infinity" ("8").

ZU : the ancient Sumerian cuneiform sign for the archaic verb —*"to know," "knowingness"* or *"awareness"*; in *Mardukite Zuism and Systemology*, the active energy/matter of the "Spiritual Universe" (AN) experienced as a *Lifeforce* or *consciousness* that imbues living forms extant in the "Physical Universe" (KI); "*Spiritual Life Energy*"; energy demonstrated by the WILL of an actualized *Alpha-Spirit* in the "Spiritual Universe" (AN), which impinges its *Awareness* into the Physical Universe (KI), animating/controlling *Life* for its experience of *beta-existence* along an individual Alpha-Spirit's personal *Identity-continuum*, called a *ZU-line*.

***Zu*-Line** : a theoretical construct in *Mardukite Zuism and Systemology* demonstrating *Spiritual Life Energy* (*ZU*) as a personal individual "continuum" of Awareness interacting with all Spheres of Existence on the Standard Model of Systemology; a spectrum of potential variations and interactions of a monistic continuum or singular *Spiritual Life Energy (ZU)* demonstrated on the Standard Model; an energetic channel of potential POV and "locations" of Beingness, demonstrated in early Systemology materials as an individual Alpha-Spirit's personal *Identity-continuum*, potentially connecting *Awareness (ZU)* of *Self* with "*Infinity*" simultaneous with all points considered in existence; a symbolic demonstration of the "*Life-line*" on which *Awareness (ZU)* extends from the direction of the "Spiritual Universe" (AN) in its true original *alpha state* through an entire possible range of activity resulting in its *beta state* and control of a *genetic-entity* occupying the *Physical Universe (KI)*.

***Zu*-Vision** : the true and basic (*Alpha*) Point-of-View (perspective, POV) maintained by *Self* as *Alpha-Spirit* outside boundaries or considerations of the *Human Condition* "Mind-Systems" and *exterior* to beta-existence reality agreements with the Physical Universe; a POV of Self *as* "a unit of Spiritual Awareness" that exists independent of a "body" and entrapment in a *Human Condition*; "spirit vision" in its truest sense.

ACKNOWLEDGEMENTS

Addie S., for supplying many hours of editing services and other research assistance at the office for 'Projekt-011'; Arianna, for promotional support and enthusiasm over the project; A.T. 'Red Bear', who was there for me when it all began; Chad C., for providing the seed-money to launch Systemology over a decade ago; D. and P. L., for being tolerant of the work (usually), even without always understanding; David Z., for Self-honestly "play-testing" our systematic processing for the Systemology Society these many years; Deryk S.M.S., for sharing in the conspiracy; Douglas M., for supporting these pursuits into the 'higher metaphysics'; Goria L., for legal advice on proceeding with this project; Heather A.K., for reinforcing material science and biology; Ikis V.I., for continued support of the projects; James T., for sensory deprivation experiments and encouraging ongoing development; Jon L., for consistently checking up on the progress; Ken O., for being a true "Pilot" and mapping out a flight-route toward higher research potentials; Kodi B., for years of high-level friendship, support and office assistance; Kyra K.A.S., for years of graphic assistance and supportive research; Leeloo M., for additional editing assistance and keeping tabs on the research library (most of the time); Nicholas de Vere, for breaking down barriers between fantasy and reality; Reed P., for overseeing the integrity of Mardukite Zuism maintained in all Systemology reports; Renee Z.G.C., for many discussions on Zu-Vision; Rowen G., for adding decades of "old school" occult experience to our pool; Timothy Leary, for encouraging humanity to 'Think For Yourself' and 'Question Authority' while teaching the next generations 'how to operate your brain'; Tracy R. Twyman, for personally welcoming me into the underground almost two decades ago; Uncle Ron, for dedicating half of a lifetime toward uncovering the ultimate vehicle for the "New Age" before it was ruined; and William W.A., for pioneering the 'Cause' and trailblazing the very "New Thought" catalyst we have been riding strong since the inception of Systemology. And finally, the planet Mercury, for so conveniently being in retrograde during the entire month of September 2022, while I set up 'Liber-011' for publication.

AVAILABLE FROM THE **JOSHUA FREE** PUBLISHING IMPRINT

SYSTEMOLOGY
The Pathway to Self-Honesty

A Basic Introduction to Mardukite Systemology

THE WAY INTO THE FUTURE

A Handbook for the New Human

a collection of writings by Joshua Free selected by James Thomas

available in Paperback and Hardcover

Here are the basic answers to what has held Humanity back from achieving its ultimate goals and unlocking the true power of the Spirit and highest state of Knowing and Being.

"*The Way Into The Future*" illuminates the *Pathway* leading to Planet Earth's true "metahuman" destiny. With *excerpts from "Tablets of Destiny," "Crystal Clear," "Systemology—Original Thesis"* and *"The Power of Zu."* You can help shine clear light on anyone's pathway!

Carefully selected by Mardukite Publications Officer, James Thomas, this critical *collection of eighteen articles, lecture transcripts and reference chapters* by Joshua Free is sure to be not only a treasured part of your personal library, but also the perfect introduction for all friends, family and loved ones.

(*Basic Grade-III Introductory Pocket Anthology*)

WOULD YOU LIKE TO KNOW MORE ???

Take your first steps on the

SYSTEMOLOGY

Pathway to Self-Honesty

with the book that started it all!

*Rediscover the original system of perfecting the
Human Condition on a Pathway that leads to Infinity.
Here is a way!—a map to chart spiritual potential and
redefine the future of what it means to be human.*

*A landmark public debut of Grade-III Systemology
and foundation stone for reaching higher
and taking back control of your*

DESTINY

(Mardukite Systemology Grade-III Research Volume, Liber-One)

AVAILABLE FROM THE **JOSHUA FREE** PUBLISHING IMPRINT

SYSTEMOLOGY
The Pathway to Self-Honesty
ORIGINAL UNDERGROUND INTRODUCTIONS
REVISED AND REISSUED IN HARDCOVER

SYSTEMOLOGY
The Original Thesis of Mardukite New Thuoght
by Joshua Free
(*Mardukite Systemology Liber-S-1X*)

The very first underground discourses released to the "New Thought" division of the Mardukite Research Organization privately over a decade ago and providing the inspiration for rapid futurist spiritual technology called "Mardukite Systemology."

THE POWER OF ZU
Applying Mardukite Zuism & Systemology to Everyday Life
by Joshua Free
Foreword by Reed Penn
(*Mardukite Systemology Liber-S-1Z*)

A unique introductory course on Mardukite Zuism & Systemology, including transcripts from a 3-day lecture series given by Joshua Free in December 2019 to launch the Mardukite Academy of Systemology & Founding Church of Mardukite Zuism just in time for the 2020's.

AVAILABLE FROM THE **JOSHUA FREE** PUBLISHING IMPRINT

SYSTEMOLOGY

The Pathway to Self-Honesty

CRYSTAL CLEAR
Handbook for Seekers

*Achieving
Self-Actualization
& Spiritual Ascension
in This Lifetime*

by Joshua Free

*Mardukite Systemology
Liber-2B*

*available in both as
premiere hardcover or
revised collector's edition*

Take control of your destiny and chart the first steps
toward your own spiritual evolution.
Realize new potentials of the Human Condition with
a Self-guiding handbook for Self-Processing
toward Self-Actualization in Self-Honesty using actual
techniques and training provided for the coveted
"Mardukite Self-Defragmentation Course Program"
—once only available directly and privately from the
underground International Systemology Society.

Discover the amazing power behind the
applied spiritual technology
used for counseling and advisement in
the Mardukite Zuism tradition.

** Mardukite Academy Revised Second Edition **

AVAILABLE FROM THE **JOSHUA FREE** PUBLISHING IMPRINT

SYST𝗘MOLOGY

The Pathway to Self-Honesty

SYSTEMOLOGY HANDBOOK

*The ultimate operator's manual to the Human Condition
and unlocking the true power of the Spirit.*

** *"Modern Mardukite Zuism"* **
** *"The Tablets of Destiny"* **
** *"Crystal Clear"* **
** *"The Power of ZU"* **
** *"Systemology—Original Thesis"* **
** *Human, More Than Human* **
** *Defragmentation* **
** *Patterns & Cycles* **
** *Transhuman Generations* **

(Complete Grade-III Master Edition Anthology)

AVAILABLE FROM THE **JOSHUA FREE** PUBLISHING IMPRINT

MARDUKITE
MASTER COURSE
The Key to Gates of Higher Understanding

Now you can experience the Legendary "Master Course" from anywhere in the Universe, exactly as given in person by Joshua Free to the "Mardukite Academy of Systemology" in September 2020.

800+ pages of materials collected in this volume provide Seekers with full transcripts to all *48 Academy Lectures* of the legendary "*Mardukite Master Course*" combined with all course outlines, supplements and critical handouts from the original "*Instructor's Manual*"—making this the most complete definitive single-source delivery of New Age understanding and spiritual technology.

Referencing 25 years of research, development and publishing, including "*Necronomicon: The Complete Anunnaki Legacy,*" "*The Great Magickal Arcanum,*" "*The Systemology Handbook*" and "*Merlyn's Complete Book of Druidism.*"

AVAILABLE FROM THE **JOSHUA FREE** PUBLISHING IMPRINT

SYS☥EMOLOGY
The Gateways to Infinity

IMAGINOMICON
Accessing the Gateway to Higher Universes
A New Grimoire for the Human Spirit
by Joshua Free

Mardukite Systemology Grade-IV Metahumanism, Wizard Level-0, Liber-3D

available in both as premiere hardcover or revised collector's edition

The Way Out. Hidden for 6,000 Years.
But now we've found the Key.
A grimore to summon and invoke, command and control,
the most powerful spirit to ever exist.
Your Self.

Access beyond physical existence.
Fly free across all Gateways.
Go back to where it all began and reclaim that
personal universe which the *Spirit* once called "*Home*."

Break free from the Matrix;
control the Mind and command the Body
from outside those systems
— because *You* were never "human" —
fully realize what it means to be a *spiritual being*,
then rise up through the Gateways to Higher Universes
and *BE*.

AVAILABLE FROM THE **JOSHUA FREE** PUBLISHING IMPRINT

SYSTEMOLOGY
The Gateways to Infinity

THE WAY OF THE WIZARD

Utilitarian Systemology

A New Metahuman Ethic

by Joshua Free

Mardukite Systemology Liber-3E

available exclusively in hardcover

Your ticket off of a Prison Planet...
...and a Pathway leading to Spiritual Ascension!

Accumulated involvement in dangerous situations, states of confusion, unjust destruction and being at the effect end of faulty—or—blatantly false information, all lend to fragmented purposes that may very well be painted to appear "for our own good." Instead they are non-survival or counter-survival oriented, leading us away from routes to achieve "greater heights"—higher, more ideal, states of knowingness and beingness—including the Magic Universe immediately preceding this one.

Here then is a bridge from Grade-IV to Grade-V, the next great frontier of the *Pathway* crossed by participants in the "Freedom From" workshops led by Joshua Free in 2021.

The Original Mardukite Master Course Lecture Volumes!
Experience the Legendary Course From Anywhere
in the Universe—Available in Four Volumes!

MAGICK & MYSTICISM
The Academy Lectures – Vol. I

DRUIDS, ELVES & DRAGONS
The Academy Lectures – Vol. II

MESOPOTAMIAN TRADITION
The Academy Lectures – Vol. III

Based on the lectures by Joshua Free

Transcripts of the Mardukite Master Course Academy Lectures
given at the Mardukite Academy in September 2020.

This is part of a four-part series, each volume providing a serious Seeker with transcripts to 12 of the 48 Academy Lectures previously published in the mega-anthology *"Complete Mardukite Master Course."*

Each volume is designed to match the correlating Master Edition textbook, such as *"Great Magickal Arcanum," "Merlyn's Complete Book of Druidism," "Necronomicon: The Complete Anunnaki Legacy"* and *"Systemology Handbook."*

AVAILABLE FROM THE **JOSHUA FREE** PUBLISHING IMPRINT

The Ultimate Necronomicon of the 21st Century!
Hardcover! Nearly 1000 Pages!

NECRONOMICON:
THE COMPLETE ANUNNAKI LEGACY
(*Complete Grade-II Master Edition Anthology*)
collected works by Joshua Free

And don't miss the newly released portable abridgment
of the original "Anunnaki Bible" scriptural edition...

ANUNNAKI BIBLE

THE CUNEIFORM SCRIPTURES
NEW STANDARD ZUIST EDITION

Premiere Founders Edition for
Church of Mardukite Zuism

edited by Joshua Free

Premiere Edition Hardcover
and
Pocket Paperback Available

AVAILABLE FROM THE **JOSHUA FREE** PUBLISHING IMPRINT

THE UNDERGROUND OCCULT CLASSICS

*Collector's Edition Hardcover now available
for this 21st Anniversary Commemoration!*

SORCERER'S HANDBOOK
A GUIDE TO PRACTICAL MAGICK
by Joshua Free writing as "Merlyn Stone"

*And don't miss the never before published sequel from the 1990's
originally released privately as "The 1998 Book of Shadows."
A long-lost classic of 20th century wicca-witchcraft is alive again!*

THE WITCH'S HANDBOOK
A COMPLETE GRIMOIRE OF WITCHCRAFT
Premiere Edition Hardcover

*by Joshua Free
writing as Merlyn Stone*

*edited and introduced by
Rowen Gardner*

JOSHUA FREE

19
95

20 20

PUBLISHED BY THE **JOSHUA FREE** IMPRINT REPRESENTING
The Founding Church of Mardukite Zuism
& Mardukite Academy of Systemology

mardukite.com

www.ingramcontent.com/pod-product-compliance
Lightning Source LLC
Chambersburg PA
CBHW030401130626
46549CB00004B/1590